The Crystal Set, the BBC and Ali:

PEACE, WORLD WAR II, AND THE AFTERMATH

Marie Lanham

TWO MOUNTAINS PUBLISHING, 2014

Published by *Two Mountains Publishing*

ISBN 978-1500453992

Typeset in *Old Style* with *Britannic* display at
SpicaBookDesign

Printed with www.createspace.com

*Dedicated to the memory of all those victims
of World War II whom I met in Europe, particularly
Holocaust Survivors Renée and Herta Chomed of
Salzburg and Geneva.*

Thanks to Mark Kunen and Eileen Fudge for their interest and assistance.

Table of Contents

Skylarking

W hen the meteorite fell on northwestern Saskatchewan in November, 2008, within a short distance of the two family homesteads, I reeled with amazement and delight as the TV cameras covering the event focused on an icy patch of prairie. What a fantastic event from an imaginative point of view, I thought, if not astronomically singular! That I, as a descendant of these pioneers, should catch the item on the morning newscast was a choice bit of luck.

As it was the centennial of the arrival of the two families from England in 1908, I burst out into howls of derision, "Oh, the folly of the enterprise, to force the women and children from the comfort of English life to the wilderness. Had the men no sense of responsibility?" Then the paintings came to mind. By this time I was laughing uproariously, adding "Wow, that meteor celebrates Uncle Will's paintings as never before!"

As the whole crazy set of images of my amazing ancestors flooded my mind, my imagination took flight into a moment of delectable, *tongue in cheek* amusement. I sensed the presence of an extra-terrestrial being, about to salute the memory of the long-suffering female members of this pioneer family as well as all the other unlikely immigrants since colonization began. Hovering in the night sky, in outer space, appeared the image of then Governor-General *Michaele* Jean. Enraptured, pleased and smiling as usual, she announced in her compassionate throaty voice, "Congratulations, despite all adversity, you did it, you pioneered, you colonized the west!"

Of course, all joking aside, life in the New World thrilled some, drove others into the depths of despair. Just as no two garlic bulbs are alike as to the size of the cloves, or sections, you may be poised, knife in hand over the frying-pan, choosing the most perfect, fully rounded ones, discarding any that are shrivelled, useless, finally turning out a memorable dish. As in life, some parts of the whole are quite perfect, quite delectable, others best forgotten.

Although Gunter Grass, Nobel laureate in literature, talks of his own youth in terms of 'peeling the onion,' it follows that as in my cooking, I have tried to bring out only the key events and thoughts running through this story. As with shrivelled cloves of garlic, I have cast aside the more common concerns of early Canadians as being too repetitive in the twenty-first century. Their stories are already well documented. I have, therefore, simply chosen to sketch in the main issues affecting the women in my family, concentrating on the greater challenge of survival to European women and girls in Hitler's Europe. I have carried each group, both family and war victims, as being of paramount importance in my heart and in my mind throughout my life.

Quite naturally, with such a world in which to pick one's way, I could not rest until I had one day set down their stories in print. Yet, I always wondered "where would I begin?" Unlike in times of peace and prosperity, those were the days when one encountered life as an uncertain affair, both in Canada and in the chaos of the early post-war period in Europe. It was nothing like the ordered life envisioned on reading T.S. Eliot's famous lines, his life being marked with a sequence of tinkling coffee spoons and cups. "Anything but!" I said to myself imagining life in high places.

At thirteen years of age, my heart was burdened with the misfortunes of my immigrant family. Outright heartbreak set in three years later, in June 1942, when my father died of a sudden heart attack during the Sunday noon BBC news broadcast of the war. Up until this time, much to my parents' distress, we had not yet begun to repulse Hitler's advances, especially in North Africa. It came a few months later.

A staunch Englishman, Dad had taught me all I knew about the perils of war and the women and children caught up in it. Together, as a family, we had seen the newsreels at the local movie theatre and the photographs, as well as listened to the nightmarish reports in 1938 at the local movie theatre and seen the photographs, as well as listened to the horrific reports of the doomed Jewish parents at the train station putting their little ones on the *Kindertransport*, in Vienna for the safety of Britain. By then, we also knew that the adults would die shortly in the gas chambers set up by Nazi Germany to annihilate its more than six million victims.

In my fanciful imagination it seemed only natural that I should become a reporter like Dad earlier in his life. Much water would run under the bridge before an opportunity allowed me to get a glimpse of the early aftermath of the war, the suffering, the people and the friends along the route.

Fortunately, my own first impressions of the world were happy ones, far from such scenes of war. At four years old, as I clearly recall, my favourite great uncle Will looked down at me from a towering height and said, "Hello, Ginger," with a broad grin. I knew he would become my special friend. Not only did I like the aroma from his pipe, clenched between his teeth, but also the two gold teeth gleaming with each smile. Although not rare among the older generation, such amazing dental work was new to me. Surely, some secret magical charm hid behind a face radiating such pleasure.

Removing his pipe, he stooped to drop chocolate mints into my hands and pockets, while thrilling me with the appealing vapours of turpentine and linseed oil clinging to his clothes. Dad said, "This is your Uncle Will. Say 'thank you,' to him." Pressing on, my great uncle asked, "Have you seen any of the fairy rings in the woods around here yet?" Another thrilling prospect. He had taught his four children the lore of old England, that *demi-paradise* still so close to his heart. Now it was my turn. "Fairy rings," he explained carefully, "are the very green circles of grass where they dance and skip through the woods ...." Wagging his finger, he repeated, "Now, be sure to look for them in the grass, on the way home, won't you?" He had been harking back to his own childhood in England and as Mother said, to the tales he had told his own children. "But will I see the leprechauns, the pixies and the sprites as well?" I asked, anxious for an exciting variety of the bewitching creatures whose names and differentiations I had already learned from Dad. "Of course you will;" he insisted, puffing on his pipe, "just keep an eye open for their dark green circles, in the grass; you can't miss them." I wasn't sure I could really trust him. England also had what they called "woodland bluebells." How could anything be so perfect? It seemed that his country had everything in this world. Adults were magical! How could they grow so large? Where did they come from? My head was in a whirl. Life was really wonderful.

Sometime in my teens I began to hear about Will's youth, his year at the famous Parisian art school called *l'Academie Julien*. Arriving in Paris in 1890 to enroll, he was fortunate to be there at a time when pivotal change shook academicians and the whole art establishment to its foundations. Impressionism and modern art were born. By 1902, Pablo Picasso himself had arrived on the scene, at first creating traditional art as practiced by his father in Spain. At the same time, the museums of primitive art in Paris, formerly the hallowed preserve of scholars, were thrown open to the public, immediately attracting Picasso and other prominent young artists. Shock waves raced through the art world as it witnessed each new canvas.

"Not for me" echoed Will and others, referring to *les avant guard* artists. "No, *la nouvelle vague*, the new wave, is a passing craze, it won't last! I will continue to paint nature as I see it and love it," he proclaimed. "Give me Corot, the Frenchman. Turner, England's genius. Titian, the incredible Venetian. Those are my models." And stick to them he did with satisfying results without ever once having indicated that he was aware of modern art in France or the presence of the Impressionist school of painting in his midst in Paris. Apparently he kept his eyes fixed almost exclusively on traditional landscape painting, missing much of the excitement, and ferment of the whole world of modern art. Blissfully unaware, it seems that he was totally preoccupied by the great adventure of adapting instead to the new world in pursuit of fortune as well as artistic freedom. By the time the plan to emigrate took form, the well-being and the future of the family in the whole scheme, while acknowledged, had obviously become of secondary concern. After all, women were not legally declared to be persons for another two decades. Women were *chattels*.

It was almost as if he had said to himself, at some point of his deliberations on the next phase of his career, *have art credentials, will travel,* and then consulted a shipping agent. Although his closest descendants considered the whole mad migration to Canada as a purely practical move, citing land, money, family responsibility as key considerations, I take the view that art was the driving force in his life. Looking at his several accomplishments, it seems clear to me that immigration and ranching were simply a means to an end. In an era when western Canada was so widely advertised in Britain it became irresistible to many stout-hearted men. I imagine that notably good-natured, he never lost that generous smile or the contented puff at his pipe despite facing huge adjustments to the wilderness.

If the great western skies which he had originally envisioned as being so important to him in Canada subsequently failed to inspire him to paint in the manner of Turner or Titian, all was not lost. He eventually turned his gaze northward from the prairies. There he found the great expanse of lakes, forests, rock outcroppings and waterfalls, still then largely undiscovered and unknown to most people. They became the subject matter of his later works. When a summer art school was established by the University of Saskatchewan at Emma Lake, just north of Saskatoon in 1936, he took charge of it. The enterprise flourished for many successful seasons. He lived to enjoy the dream of the rugged northland as the focus of his new paintings and, as he suggested, perhaps the future development of the country. My own father, a minor English artist and close associate of uncle Will, was among those to encourage the university to set up the school.

Among Will's colleagues in eastern Canada was Dr. Arthur Lismer of the Group of Seven, one of Will's old school friends from England. Lismer, later in the 1930's visited us in Saskatchewan, suggested that Will join the Group in Ontario. Will, however was firmly rooted in the west and enjoying recognition as a Canadian artist.

Remote from the world of art and more down to earth, or so it might seem at first glance, were my grandfather Nelson's urgent business problems. Nelson was married to Rose, my grandmother, sister of my great uncle Will. She too would be deeply involved. The news of the bankruptcy had ripped through the offices of the Sheffield headquarters of the firm early in January 1907. One had to face it now. If this were more than a rumour, the company and the entire family could be in deep trouble. Taking two steps at a time up the stairs, Nelson anxiously rushed to his brother's quarters.

"Is it true, Colin, is it true? Tell me, did one of the ships go down en route to Cape Town?" At the same time, it flashed across his mind, "How will I tell Rose?"

Colin stood up when the door opened and looked the picture of distress. As if painfully, he said, "Yes, the entire cargo of boots. All hands lost. It was the left foot boots."

Pairs of boots were split up at the company's warehouses to avoid theft by the stevedores unpacking the cargo. Depending on one's own involvement, one might wish to laugh or cry. For our grandfather Nelson and his brother Colin, for the whole family headed by their father, Josiah, and for all the employees, it came as a profound shock. It was the *writing on the wall,* although not yet the final *coup de grace* in a long chain of adversities. It was, rather the *writing on the waves,* those turbulent waves which would eventually take the two families across the North Atlantic forever.

"Why on earth did we ever decide to expand overseas, anyway?" raged Nelson, a normally mild-mannered person with greenish-blue eyes, who was usually calm despite his ginger colored hair associated in those days with hot tempers.

"Greed, pure greed," Colin muttered disgustedly, wondering how he or any of them would tell their wives. "To think that we had all begun to talk of holidays at the Cape, or Capetown, to see Edgar and the new branch of the business out there," his voice trailed off in incredulity.

"Yes, holidays in sunny Cape Town. What a hope," added Nelson, full of anger. "Edgar seemed to be doing so well. Father did not keep up with the styles. Times are changing. He's lost his grip on reality, if you ask me!"

Soberly, Colin reminded him. "Actually things have been going downhill for some time. Dreams are cheap!"

Nelson, Colin, and all the men involved in the firm besides their father were well aware that Britain was in the grips of a severe economic recession. As nations go, so go families. It had been obvious for some time that the firm was *slipping into the red*. The idea of actual bankruptcy becoming an eventual reality had been just too much to assimilate. Having known only the good life, they had tried to persuade themselves that the *show must go on*.

As it happened, theirs was just one of a great many typical Victorian bankruptcies, such as Charles Dickens had written of earlier in the century. It has been said that the high cost of repulsing Napoleon at Waterloo in 1815 seriously impaired the British treasury over the long term, resulting in such commercial disasters. It was to cause the family the usual privations, including the overwhelming Victorian sense of shame at having *lost face*. This was the most unforgivable of situations, with complete loss of belongings, homes, and personal treasures. All must go before the block. Bankruptcy was a condition from which there could be no possible redemption. Friends scattered to the winds.

While the two brothers discussed their worries, Nelson's wife Rose sat in the drawing-room of their home listening to her artist brother Will who had just dropped in to give her his own latest news.

"Jane and I are thinking of going out to Canada, just for a few years," he announced airily as he sat down across from his sister.

"Have some tea," Rose offered, as she passed it to him, hoping vaguely to dissuade him in what was perhaps just his latest implausible reverie.

"The good news is that there is still some land left for settlers," he continued as he accepted a piece of pound cake. Flashing his brown-eyed, gold-toothed smile he added, "in case we decide to remain there."

Now in a state of shock, Rose thought it best to stay silent for a moment. For comfort she helped herself to a tart.

Thus encouraged, Will continued. "I really need the chance to paint the wonderful western skies way out there on the prairies."

Accepting another cup of tea and considerably encouraged by the lack of admonition from Rose he went on, "They say that the horizons are vast, that the country is quite incredibly beautiful. Why, you never know," he chuckled, in a somewhat self-deprecating tone of voice, "I may even come back to England as famous as J.M.W. Turner himself."

"Well, you have been dreaming a brave future, Will, which costs nothing, of course," Rose teased, and she began to laugh at the idea of such a transformation in her brother's life.

"What an idea, you with four children, an established art career and a thriving photography business. Really! What has Jane to say about it?"

Rose was shocked to think that he could lose his reason so far as to even entertain so bizarre an idea. Still wreathed in smiles, Will ignored her and insisted "The government is encouraging artists to go to Canada to paint the wilderness. You see, the idea is that their creations could be used as promotional posters to encourage further immigration across the west. It's the mood of the times, Rose. See if I am not right. Times are so hard now for many people here in England, you know," he commented, thinking that she probably did not read the papers.

It has to be admitted, Rose thought as she poured second cups for both of them, Will has succeeded in everything he has ever undertaken. She was thinking of his years of study in England and Paris, his established professional status, not to mention his lucrative photography business.

Will had also inherited all the benefits of their father's will, the four daughters receiving a token gift of only fifty pounds each. After all, Englishwomen, mere *chattels,* were not yet classified as persons on official documents. Although Rose had once dreamed wildly of studying music and drama, her widowed father had very quickly reminded her, "Rose, you'll marry Nelson and have a family." To him, she had been 'just Rose,' an obedient daughter in a motherless household.

Neither rebellion nor a sense of entitlement to a future had occurred to her. In general, middle-class girls did not dare to assert themselves in the eighteen-eighties. Her father took her to operas, concerts, and plays, allowing her to become the music teacher for the entire extended family. It went no further. Between him and Nelson's father, Josiah, business partners of long standing, the long-established understanding was that the two young people, Rose and Nelson, friends since childhood, should marry thus uniting the business interests of the two families in the traditional manner.

With tea-time well concluded, Will got up from the tea-table, strolling into the hall towards his coat and hat. He summed up his remarks light-heartedly. With a wide smile he explained, "After all, I can always send home for more money if the going is a little rough at first."

"And are you not the lucky one," Rose said quietly, but true to form, restrained herself tactfully from further comment and bid her brother the usual warm, light-hearted farewell, each promising the other to meet again shortly.

Yes, Will has all of father's fortune. We girls each have fifty pounds. Nothing more to be said, thought Rose without rancour as she closed the door behind him.

With that she tried to put such a ridiculous plan for the future out of her mind, feeling thankful that she and the two children would never have to accompany Nelson across the ocean. They would not become immigrants, mere *hostages to fortune*, as the saying was. Nelson's mother had become her second mother after the death of her own. No, she could never think of life apart from them; they were at the centre of her life. Besides, her own eleven year-old daughter Mary was now inseparable from her cousins, aunts and uncles who spoiled her. She never forgot those Christmas celebrations around the enormous Christmas tree alight with the blaze of wax candles.

Nelson's family home meant so much to her too as she thought of it now. A rambling house with verandas all along the back of it, opening onto a large garden complete with tennis courts and dotted with flowers, it was the most welcoming of places she knew outside of her own family home. On visits with her father, Richard, she could always find a partner for a game, because "Nel" had so many eager siblings, aunts, uncles and cousins ready to participate. Now, even her children, Mary and John looked forward to going there. For them, croquet was fun too. Of course, as they began to grow up, Nelson and his brothers had become more interested in soccer.

As with most English people, gardening and pets were a passion. Both their gardens, Nel's, here at Granby House, and at her home, so humbly called Rose Cottage, despite its imposing yet delightful style were a riot of colour. She thought of it all now. Will's remarks had made her think, "How I love my surroundings, my home, our extended family, our countryside and the glades of woodland bluebells! The Lake Country, scene of our luxurious honeymoon, complete with coach and four. Wonderful! We'll take the children there for a holiday too! And the annual sailing holidays on the Norfolk Broads is coming up soon." Certainly we will never have to leave. England is our heart's desire, forever!"

Preparing for Nelson's arrival home for the evening meal, she looked forward to relating Will's preposterous ideas. As a reminder to Susan to serve one of Nelson's favourite accompaniments to cold roast beef, she put out a small oblong dish and special fork on the counter. He liked to eat finely sliced white onion and cucumber rings well sprinkled with vinegar.

Just then it came to her that Will might indeed have wanderlust in his veins. Down the ages the men of the family had felt the lure of foreign places. Even at the present time their cousin John, originally a sea captain, was part of a firm of English shipping agents in Kobé, Japan. The very locket she was wearing had been sent to her from there. Her first known ancestors had left northern England in a sailing ship for the Quaker colony in Philadelphia in the late 1600's. They were among the dissenters in the vicious conflict between Catholic and Protestant zealots, a legacy of the reign of Charles I.

As Rose laughingly began to recount the afternoon's discussion to Nelson during dinner, she was suddenly aware that he was not responding but cast his eyes downward. "What's the matter, Nel?" she asked in alarm. Staring at the tablecloth, with his head in his hands and his dinner untouched, Rose could see that he was in deep distress. With difficulty the whole sorry tale of the business failure began to emerge. While Nelson raged with anger, Rose remained calm, controlling her emotions. Despite the fateful blow, she finally stood up, straightened her shoulders, insisting that, "Our family will survive. We will find an opening somewhere. We must not leave England. Never, ever, Nel! You must promise me! You must!" Those blue eyes convinced and comforted him. She was right, they would find a way, he kept saying to himself, over and over again as they left the table in a state of shock.

Tragically though, no one in the family was able to work out a new future together. Tough economic times in the manufacturing sector coupled with loss of the army boot contract after the sinking of the two ships had sealed their fate. It being 1907, rather than later in the century after World War I, women had not yet been included in the work force. There were two daughters, a number of sons, Josiah's wife, Martha, and all the daughters-in-law. Today, such a number of people with common cause might have combined their skills, pooled their resources, and survived modestly. However, as yet, *ladies* did not work.

So minimal were the duties of the sons that even Nelson, a senior member in his father's firm had learned very little to serve the present need. Preposterously he began to dream of a farming-ranching future in Canada with Will, his brother-in-law. That which had until so recently seemed absurdly unrealistic now became the ideal. After all, he had hoped in his youth to become a veterinarian, much to the disapproval of his father. His mother had said he would become a gambler as in those days vets worked at the racetracks. Perhaps, qualified or not, if he joined forces with Will, he could somehow still get to work with animals.

Was this new ambition what today we call a midlife crisis, brought on by an ill-conceived response to shock and grief? The immigration propaganda posters depicted western wheat fields as *prairie gold.* "Definitely I'll go for it," he said to himself "and one day return to England proud of my efforts. It is time to prove myself!" One look at Rose and the children made him swear to himself to do the impossible. Urban, inexperienced at farming, middle-aged, bankrupt, and accustomed to a comfortable life, Nel was an unlikely immigrant grasping at a straw.

A totally different individual, Will had never been known to admit to anything but a charmed view of life. Innately he was convinced that should farming fail he would prove to be an able rancher. At a special event at Buckingham Palace he had been chosen to be part of Queen Victoria's horse guard. He knew horses. Full of confidence, he thought out loud, "I'll become a Canadian homesteader," as he mixed his oil paints happily and puffed away. At work on his canvas, he seems to have been, as usual, quite oblivious of the feelings of his young family on the matter.

The two families sailed from Liverpool early in 1908, with much weeping on the part of friends and family gathered at the deck to bid farewell. Although Will was not at all akin to Gauguin, the French artist who left his family behind for Tahiti, he was nevertheless with every watery mile at sea drawing both families closer and closer to extreme privation for the sake of his towering ambition. For Will, the expedition was all in the interests of "great skies." Yet one wonders about it still. If J.M.W. Turner could do all his paintings in Europe, why couldn't Will have done likewise and prevented the suffering of all concerned?

After many tiresome days on the stormy north Atlantic, they entered the Gulf of the St. Lawrence River. The ship plowed its way along the great waterway en route to Montreal and the cross-country train.

Rose was captivated by the scenery. Dotted as it was with French Canadian *habitant farms*, scores of silvery church spires between cliffs, rocks and forests, the shoreline delighted her as they ploughed along past Rivière du Loup, Matane, and Trois Rivières.

"It's a dream, a marvel!" she exclaimed.

Will joined her enthusiastically, intent on attracting the attention of his own four children, then absorbed in a game.

Nelson and Jane, their partners, sat there, however, quite unaffected by landscape, soberly weighing their situations from a purely practical point of view. Cities were what interested them, not miles of forests, tiny settlements and the cultivated seigneurial strips of the Kamouraska countryside. When all was said and done, cities were where one could expect to make a living.

Nelson had just been talking with another businessman on the train, who, like himself, claimed to know the country well. "Go no further than Ontario," he advised, shaking his finger emphatically. As the coach rattled on uncomfortably under his feet, Nelson could see the rest of his life could become as uncertain as he felt at that moment. Having assumed legal obligations to the new province of Saskatchewan, he had no options. Lloydminster, named for an Anglican bishop involved in its settlement, was little more than a whistle-stop through the three-year-old jurisdiction. Established in 1905, it might well have been called *Arrowheads* after the number left scattered by the native hunters.

18

"You'll never make it in the west," the stranger warned, "unless you go right through to Vancouver, but you could fit right into the retail trade here in Ontario," he repeated several times.

Eleven year old Mary counted church spires while her young brother and his cousin fidgeted with their tin soldiers. Worrying about them as *hostages to fortune,* Nelson watched all six children of the two families. "How will they react to getting off the train in the middle of the 'wild west?" he wondered. He had a sinking feeling that all those government promises of fine living conditions and advantages for the young might not actually materialize after all in this vast, raw country.

Will's petite, brunette wife Jane frowned and lowered her dark eyes in worrying about their three girls and a boy, and the fact that she had seen nothing yet which could remind her of England in any way, even though Canada was part of the Empire. She had counted on it. As she said then and often repeated with emphasis as those eyes took on an even darker, haunted-look. "I'll go back with the first tramp who'll take me!" Women did not yet expect to travel alone or be treated according to their wishes.

Rose shuddered to think her sister-in-law would speak in such a way. It did not seem at all respectable. Certainly not her style. Rose was prepared to take things as they came, keeping her own counsel as she had always done, comforting everyone in distress, including Jane's children, led to tears by their mother's anger. Knowing that she at least would never fail to comfort them for years to come, they cried their hearts out on Rose's delicate little shoulders.

One day a few months after their arrival at the Lloydminister, Saskatchewan station, and now established in side-by-side homesteads together on 'Pike's Peak,' Rose sauntered about enjoying the novelty of prairie birds, the red-wing blackbirds, the bobolinks and the sound of the meadow-larks from the edge of the adjacent slough. The name for their new location reflected their unanimous longing for one of their holiday spots in the Lake Country of England. She was waiting to see a sign on the horizon of Nelson, Will and the hired man returning from a haying trip across the fields.

"Ah, yes, look, there they are," she called out to her children, Mary and Jack, playing nearby in the tall grass. To Mary, now twelve, she said, "Don't they look wonderful! It's a marvel, it's a picture!" They stood and watched as the heavily loaded hay-rick came closer into view. Rose went on laughing, lightly and prettily as always, "Yes, a marvel, just like a 'lark' of some sort, a holiday. No bowler hats and dark suits, just farm overalls, red neckerchiefs and straw hats. My word, what a sight!"

Mary now stood in front of her, sulking darkly and looking thinner than ever.

"I don't like it here," she said. "You know that, Mother. I want to go home to England to see Dorrie and all my friends. I miss my friends. I love my school. I won't ever go to school here!" By now she was in a rage and stamping her feet. Suddenly Rose was jolted back to reality by this oft repeated declaration from the now crying child. After trying repeatedly to placate her, she went indoors, too moved to continue.

"Out of the mouths of babes," she muttered to herself with a shudder. Half an hour ago, gazing off into the horizon, she had been in a reverie, thinking how beautiful, how fresh it all was, a caprice, a lark. But then, Rose, like her brother Will, always found beauty in nature and rejoiced at it. Suddenly she wept also, acknowledging to herself that it could be forever, not just the settlers' dream, the dream of staying a few years to make enough money to return to England. "But forever," she began to burst out loud, "Perhaps we will never get back, never in our whole lives. Impossible! Terrible! Terrible!"

Pulling her lace-trimmed handkerchief from the pocket of her blue dress to dab her eyes, she recalled it as a parting gift from Aunt Polly. A moment of comfort washed over her. Then she went resolutely out into the sunshine to welcome the men to the waiting lunch table, pretending to be as buoyant herself as the morning's exercise had rendered them. She made it seem as if this new life were actually just a "lark," reinforcing the moment by serving the ever-popular native Saskatoon berry pie, delicious, blue-purple, and almond-flavoured at the end of the meal. That evening they would sample the dandelion wine for which in time she gained a certain renown.

Could Will and Nelson have packed a bottle of it for the regular forty-eight hour trip by ox-cart to Lloydminster to replenish food supplies? Most of us would imagine that apart from basic rations, such endurance would require a strong drink. This was no easy trip. Survival depended on transporting food in extremes of cold and heat, using animals prone to stop at random unless forcefully motivated by lighting a fire under them.

One can envision the state of mind of the two wives awaiting their overdue arrival on a frigid, late winter afternoon. With the sun beginning to set, the coyotes howled in the distance. Could it be that the hard-working Swedish settlers in the area were paid to keep the heaters full of wood? Certainly neither Rose nor Jane were capable. What would happen in the case of unexpected blizzard conditions or a child in need of medical help? Neither cars nor telephones were yet a part of life.

Perhaps it was just as well that they had not heard of the earlier pioneers, like the Moodie sisters, had never read their stories, *Roughing it in the Bush* and *The Backwoods of Canada*, by Susanna and her sister Catherine Parr Traill, respectively, who recorded family life in early nineteenth century rural Ontario, before the land was cleared. Nor did my immigrant family know that according to common consensus much of the best land in the country had been taken by the time they arrived in 1908.

By 1911, Will and Nelson had worked their homesteads for the required three-year period settlers were given to show a viable enterprise to the government. Their three consecutive crop failures due to frost proved the land to be too far north for grain production. Consequently, Nelson was disqualified as a homesteader, whereas Will, with access to his father's money in England, put cattle on the land, in order to keep it and become a rancher. This, like everything he undertook, became a highly successful venture.

Far from being free to return to England, Rose and Nelson moved only a few miles away to the village of Lashburn. Ironically he named it *Eden*. It had a poplar bluff, a station, an elevator and little else. Their obligations as settlers would continue for twenty-two years. Nelson operated whatever regional transport was needed, both horse drawn and later motorized, to get the children of the area to school safely. The once prosperous British businessman found himself faced with bumpy terrain, dusty trails, ice, snow, extreme thunderstorms and muddy ruts. "Lucky Tom," he often said ruefully to Rose. Tom, his younger brother, an agriculture school graduate in Britain, had a successful ranching career awaiting him before emigrating. Their father had at last understood the severity of their situation and managed to provide financial support for training his youngest son.

However, considering the problem with getting children to school safely at great distances in those early years, some form of transport was essential. Without it, the parents endured a constant worry until the children returned unscathed on horseback. Due to the fact that most settlers, as unmarried men, refused to pay a school tax, several years passed before a basic one-room schoolhouse was opened in the area. Neither Mary or John, nor their cousins had been to school since leaving England. When the issue was finally settled, it proved to be a disaster for Mary in particular, already prejudiced against Canada. She and her brother were constantly mocked and bullied as *greenhorns*.

"Look at them," the locals jeered. "Just look at *the green hanging around their ears*. Look at their clothes!" This was a reference to their hand-me-downs from England and their English accents.

"I won't go, I won't go!" Mary raged as she stamped her feet in anger and humiliation. School was something to fight against especially before Nelson arranged for transport. Facing the fear of the twelve-mile daily ride on horseback in all weather had been enough to bear without the added constant threat of attack from so-called *turkey gobblers*. These were the menacing wild turkeys, those large, ghoulish and phantom-like creatures, perched in the branches of the poplar bluffs dotting the prairies. Threatening to swoop down upon the children, they frightened the horses into rearing up, very nearly throwing them under the thrashing hooves.

Haunted by the fear of these long rides home on frigid afternoons in a biting wind, she had to face an impending thunderstorm, the cry of the coyotes, or the occasional brush with settlers overcome by isolation. One such individual, who sometimes stopped them, would announce "I'm the Duke of Bedford and this 'ere is my neighbour, the Duke of Norfolk, so you'd best be off with ya, eh!" Mary, who was always badly unnerved and repulsed by the abnormal, was now becoming an embittered loner, destined to remain in that same mold to the end of her life.

Being far from home in England, she began to see herself as a leaf blown hither and yon by the endless soughing and moaning of the wind across this vast wilderness. Most conversations in both households expressed endless homesickness and longing for mail from England. A sense of humour about any of it was difficult to cultivate.

Prior to the outbreak of World War I in 1914, events of the new century in Europe had begun to reverberate across Canada. Disturbed at the thought of the mother country being in danger, the family in England became a lively subject of concern at the dinner table. At seventeen, Mary was growing into a young person who questioned such *inhumanity of man to man* and the affairs of the world at that time. Taking aim at her mother's snug code of Victorian ideas, belief and behavior, she found them to be absurd and hypocritical.

Choosing instead to embrace Nelson's concealed agnosticism, his Darwinian views, that *it's a disinterested universe*, she began to evolve into a modern young woman. Thrilled by Nelson's concerns over social justice and the industrial progress applauded by Victorians, she renounced her mother's Church of England views, determined to escape this narrow mentality and the settlers' life. Soon to work in overcrowded wards of World War I veterans, she was convinced that as she had heard it said, *the veneer of civilization is only skin deep*. Subsequently, she began to insist vehemently, "If there were a God, he would prevent war."

Much later I learned all this at the dinner table, stunned, but fascinated As a ten-year-old, such talk was not what I heard at school or in church activities. However, I knew enough not to comment, that I must be seen and not heard. Dad would help me out with a smile and a humorous remark on another subject. He was letting me know that I should not think about such things. Silence was the best policy. Consequently, pretending to ignore my mother's ideas on the subject, I remained a thoroughly concerned and confused child of the 1930's.

It had all begun when she escaped the wilderness to join the war effort in 1915. Entering the three-year registered nurses' training program at the Winnipeg General Hospital at eighteen, she was soon pressed into service in the overcrowded wards of casualties at the Deer Lodge Military Hospital. Some veterans were too grossly injured to rise from their beds ever again or be seen by the public. By this time she had begun to react with added disdain to the human condition, adapting Tennyson's refrain, *nature, red in tooth and claw* to her list of heated observations.

At ten years old I knew these phrases by memory. At the dinner table they flowed as freely as salt and pepper during her discussion of the world news with Dad. Mother being an extraordinarily good cook, the adult conversation was easier to tolerate than if, like many others, we had faced the often scarce rations of the 1930's. Perhaps as a way of easing the tension after the dessert was served, my father would burst into song. With a wide range of carefree tunes from England, he tactfully enabled us to take the world in stride.

In having escaped the dreary village of Eden to engage in the war effort and its early aftermath, Mary had actually opened a "Pandora's Box" of misfortune. The years of deprivation in Europe, 1914 to 1918, had bred successive, deadly waves of diphtheria and scarlet fever, leaving her in critical condition from them both. Then the world-wide spread of the Spanish Flu, which alone killed some twenty millions in its wake, left her at death's door. Anxiety overtook the family back in Eden, knowing that she was all alone in a hospital bed in a strange city.

Needless to say, these near-death exposures to three notorious killers, for which there were as yet no vaccines, would leave Mary frail and marked by the beginnings of the permanent physical and emotional impairments of her later years. Suffering the same fate was Joe, the young Englishman whom in due course she would marry. Discharging himself from a badly overcrowded Toronto hospital for victims of Spanish flu, rather than sitting in a huge ward full of dying men led to complications. This sorry adventure as a new immigrant was later attributed to the worsening of his congenital heart disease. The infection from the

Spanish flu had spread into his heart muscle. In this sense, he was typical of the many victims who would continue to suffer from the effects of the war in years to come and eventually succumb to them.

As the conviction that *the show must go on* is always an imperative in the minds of normally ambitious young people, each of these two individuals picked themselves up from their respective disasters, sure of a bright future in the heady, optimistic post-war mood of the early 1920's. Before Joe were a few more enjoyable years of journalism across the country with the Canadian Press. For her part, Mary, now a graduate nurse, eagerly took on a career of arduous public health service in rural Manitoba.

At the same time, gratified to embrace an intoxicating new post-war period of freedom from the old Victorian restraints she had despised, she applauded modernity, rejecting the hypocrisy and backwardness of the nineteenth century. Women now had the vote, granted in 1918, in part due to their war effort. Unfortunately though, until 1929 they remained *chattels*, rather than persons in other respects. Equality for Canadian women was to come much later when they became definable as 'persons' by decree of the Privy Council in England on October 18, 1929. The term *chattel* which had applied to women as property was finally removed from legal documents.

Adopting a new freedom of dress as well as outlook, the long tresses or coils pinned to the head and the fussy ankle length clothing disappeared. *Bobbed* hair was all the rage. Parting with her long, luxurious auburn hair, she now wore the new, close-fitting brimless and flirtatious *cloche* hat, designed for short hair. Typical of the youth of the frenzied post-war era, she danced the *Charleston*, then a popular passion, in the fashionable, tight, short *hobble* skirt, sometimes sporting burnt orange culottes, the new pant-skirt that marked a certain sense of feminine equality.

Women began to smoke, enjoying the elegance of the long stylish cigarette holder, the kind then being turned out as souvenirs of the discovery of the burial chamber of Egypt's young King Tut.' This was part of the craze which followed the opening, in 1922, of King Tut-ankh-amen's tomb, circa 1325 B.C.

A year later, Ataturk, the Turkish leader, hit the news as a hero who had brought his country into the modern world, the secular world in which women were free to adopt western attitudes and dress for the first time. Naturally captivated with such progressive politics and exoticism, Mary was as yet ignorant at that time of the political excesses attributed to Ataturk in other domains.

Back home in Eden, unaware of the new age, Rose had always insisted that they survive the immigrant experience with as much grace and equanimity as possible. If the role of peacemaker came easily to her, the idea of the need for stability and justice in daily life may have begun at school in England. As an eager young thespian she had played the role of Portia in Shakespeare's *The Merchant of Venice*. As she read those great lines on justice tempered by mercy in the

29

trial against Shylock, she had become Portia, the female judge, the negotiator, wearing a long red velvet robe and cap. Some of Shylock's lines in his own defense may have resonated, stayed in her mind, particularly when he says that despite being a Jewish money-lender he is, after all, only human. He is

> 'fed by the same food, hurt by the same weapons, subject to the same disease, heal'd by the same means warm'd and cool'd by the same winter and summer... If you prick us, do we not bleed?'

Over the years Rose may well have said these lines over to herself as she faced the harsh reality of being denied the rightful portion of her father's will. It must have been painful, especially when, in 1933, now also successful as a Canadian painter, her brother Will went alone on a world tour at the very depth of the Great Depression. Had he practiced the golden rule, read Portia's lines on justice and mercy, and shared the proceeds of the will with Rose, as in his life-time his father would have insisted, she and Nelson need never have left England.

Also in 1933 Nelson's twenty-five year contract as a settler came to an end. Retiring at the age of sixty-five, to a modest apartment beside the ocean in Vancouver, Rose and Nelson felt almost young again. They walked miles along the ocean front and through Stanley Park, enjoying the lush temperate climate and vegetation of the west coast. Exulting in their new freedom to enjoy urban life, even meeting old friends from England who had settled there also, they probably felt that they had *made it* at last. It was almost like home. Rose called it a marvel, that word which she had always loved to use.

And it was home, not just a lark this time, with only Will's "great skies" and the starkness of the wilderness around her. Enough of "sky-larks" and the dreadful conditions they had endured all those years! Like a war veteran, she never talked about it. Refusing to admit to bitterness, she looked to the enjoyment of each day. Nevertheless, in sober, reflective moments, the depth of her prolonged suffering showed itself clearly enough in her lined-face and her painfully thin, fragile-looking figure. For her part, Will's wife Jane, totally immobilized by arthritis, and carried about on a stretcher-type device seemed almost literally turned to stone by the immigrant experience.

Similarly, thousands of others, remittance men and women among them, who had not understood the difficulties of farming and had registered as immigrants had now at long last made their way to the west coast. It was a final reprieve from bondage. They came because it reminded them of England and offered an English climate. Time had severed their connections "at home" for England was now a different homeland than the one they had known.

That was perhaps the cruelest punishment of all, for having allowed themselves to believe the immigration propaganda. They had long since stopped talking of going home. That wound had finally been left to heal quietly in so far as it were possible. To risk the challenge of having *lost face* again, that was too much to think of now. They loved Vancouver. It was enough. It was a marvel, itself.

Many years later, in 1965, my grandfather, Nelson, slowly dying in his ninety-sixth year, his sense of humour still intact, quipped gleefully as the confirmed non-believer he was, "The Lord won't punish me; after all, he let me off the train at Lloydminster!" He had made sure that Grandma was not present at that moment. We all knew, nevertheless that neither his Victorian sense of shame ever left him, nor his profound regret over the effect of his admittedly appallingly poor judgement.

Sitting in his high-backed upholstered chair seemingly wrapped in thought, he would smile, gently rub the backs of his freckled hands then take another puff from his fragrant old pipe, and a sip of tea before taking up his favourite paper. For years he had sat there and pored over books and papers while keeping an ear open for all political radio programs. Intent on social justice, he came by his passion honestly, firm and proud in the belief that he was a descendant of Wat Tyler himself, his own namesake, an ancient Briton who was beheaded in the revolt of the common people against the Crown in 1381.

Neither of my grandparents ever talked to us about the physical work necessary to survive pioneer life. Since they had not been brought up "to work," such activity had had no appeal to them, and therefore they believed it would bore other people to hear of it. As such labour was not considered to be a subject of polite conversation among Victorians, we know very little about how they mastered it. We can only assume that they had somehow managed to pay others for hard physical work. While Mary became bitter, neither of her parents expressed such an attitude, or seemed to harbour one, despite the glaringly obvious incentive in regard to the will. Perhaps they were secretly proud of surviving the impossible, and rightly so.

Finally, enduring widowhood, shortly before her death at age one hundred and three, and sorely missing Nelson, I saw my grandmother Rose's anger rise for the first and only time in my life. Chatting with her I asked "Was your father, our great-grandpa Richard, alive at the time of the bankruptcy of Grandpa's Nelson's family business?" Suddenly she drew herself up out of her armchair, ramrod straight, frowning and tapping the floor sharply, deliberately, with her cane. "No," she said, "Father died in 1903. If he had been alive in 1908 we would never have left England, of course not!" Grandma thought I knew the story.

Lotus Land and After

Pulling out of Winnipeg by train, enroute to her rural public health assignment one day in the winter of 1923, Mary, now a Registered Nurse, realized that she faced long cold hours, especially from the train-stop to the farm in question. As usual, a farmer waiting with his team of horses would pick her up and take her to the patient. For starters, she had so to speak, to brave it, to *run the gauntlet*, past the growling farm dogs. Given the fact that modern medicines did not yet exist, it could take a week to complete treatment. It was a career commitment more suitable to a strong young person rather than one of delicate stature, a survivor of the Spanish flu and those two other barely survived deadly scourges of the era.

Looking for a seat, she found the last double space in the coach and chose the window view, hoping no one would take the other. The woman across from her smiled and remarked, "Awfully crowded coach, isn't it? Just look at those drifts out there, one wonders how they can clear the tracks." Trying in vain to stuff her medical supplies away, Mary replied, "Yes, I can see that it won't be an easy trip." Someone chimed in, "I wonder if we are heading into a blizzard?"

"Quite likely," another suggested, "Sun dogs were reported high in the sky. It always means bad weather in these parts, you know."

Passengers were still flooding the aisles, trying to find seats in one coach or another, when a tall, deep blue-eyed young man, grey fedora in one hand, his suitcase in the other, obviously intent on finding a place to sit, leaned in from the aisle. He enquired, "May I share this seat with you?"

Thanks to a little help from the stranger, Mary managed to stuff her medical bag into the overhead storage area. She had noticed that he had a gentlemanly overseas English accent. In turn, Joe saw in her a slim brown-eyed girl with auburn hair cut short in this new post-war style called a "bob." He guessed that she was somewhat younger than himself, all of thirty-three. As they watched the growing intensity of the unrelenting blasts of the hard granular snow of a prairie blizzard gather momentum during the ensuing hour, she learned that Joe was from Norwich, England. "Oh, yes," he said, "Norwich is a delightful old city in East Anglia, that's the east coast; we call it "the garden of England, nothing like this, you know!"

Working as a Canadian Press reporter, he was now located in Vancouver and was saying, "I like it very much out there, of course," when suddenly the train screeched, rattled, lurched and derailed. Strangely, they were able to reach the exit without more than a bruise or two, their coach being relatively unscathed. While some of the passengers were trapped inside the other coaches and could be heard moaning and crying out for help, others tossed into the snow were helpless, freezing fast among the toppled coaches.

Desperate to help as the day wore on, Mary and Joe floundered about in the drifts, distributing blankets from the sleeping cars, trying to assist their helpless fellow-passengers. With the all-pervading and intensifying cold of sundown the situation became even more grim, more menacing. Yet they were an effective working combination, given that he as well as Mary had dealt extensively with severely injured World War I victims. Turned down for military service in England on grounds of poor health due to abnormality of the heart, Joe had spent those years in war work. Although he had been the recipient of a box of white feathers, in London, that mark of disgrace to any man not yet in uniform in 1914, he was the most patriotic and staunch Englishman. He was a typical "John Bull" and a loyal subject of the Empire.

Before they were finally taken to the nearest village to thaw out, recuperate, and wait for the next train, Joe made sure to ask for the address of this hard-working young woman. He would like to correspond with her. It had been a dramatic, memorable meeting, perhaps even a symbolic foretaste of the life they would lead together, meeting the challenges to come. Through the decade of the Great Depression and the impact of

World War II, two more train trips, and another storm would shape their lives.

The following year they were married and living in Vancouver's West End, near Stanley Park and English Bay beach. "Great to find a place so near the water, isn't it!" he enthused. "I can hardly believe it," she replied. Strolling around 'Lotus Land' in their spare time, it was more and more tempting to imagine the home and family that would be theirs one day. "Yes, if all goes well," she would often remind him when he envisioned a rosey future. "You poor girl," he said, "you've had a bad time until now; you seem to lack all faith in the future."

In 1929, the Stock Market crashed, plunging them and thousands of others across the continent and around the world into the catastrophe of the Great Depression. With their lives disrupted overnight, every turn of the train wheels reversing their dreams, they fled the breadlines in Vancouver back through the Rocky Mountains by train. Disembarking halfway across the country at Eden, they left me there with my grandparents so they could find work. Possibly it had been realized that mother would be accepted in her home town hospital. Somehow they both scratched out a subsistence living for a couple of years.

I recall the day that, as a pre-schooler, I found myself with my mother instead of Grandma in what she explained was a hotel room. Noticing a window with a dark green blind pulled down over the glass, I peeked outside. Lifting the shade an inch or so, I looked out at an amazing sight. There was a bright red brick building in front of me. Rural dwellings around Eden were small one-storey wood frame structures of drab appearance, huddled together here and there between the occasional poplar bluff dotting the vast open plains. There was no beautiful bright red colour anywhere.

Close to this building was a street full of shops, called Central Avenue, running for several blocks toward the river in one direction and leading upwards in the other to the homes on the east and west hill. Terminating just past the imposing yellow brick courthouse and its formal grounds, dominating the brow of the hill, this was the well-designed centre of our town.

The Court House, Prince Albert, overlooking the town below and th forest-lake country.

No ordinary place, Prince Albert is situated just north of the prairie, heavily treed with conifers as well as deciduous growth. It is a centre of administration, boasting several architecturally agreeable buildings, fine homes and an impressive park. Known as "The Gateway to the North" it is at the edge of the woods and lakes leading to Emma Lake and Waskesiu Lake in the Prince Albert National Park and all points beyond. Indeed, standing on the court-house steps one sees beyond the town below, the great blue-green forests forming a massive background on all sides.

When Dad put on the grey fedora hat and smart suit coat and strode square-shouldered, down the street toward Central Avenue, I knew that he was going to his office in the town hall. Set in the centre of a small park adjacent to the building was an elaborate three-tiered, old bronzed fountain of great attraction to me as the water cascaded over it. On special occasions we went there after supper to hear the band concert being performed by players resplendent in fancy red and gold-trimmed uniforms filling the ornate Victorian era bandshell.

As the crowd thickened, they took to the pavement surrounding the grassy square, circulating around it in carefree summer garb, enjoying ten-cent ice-cream cones and the sociable atmosphere, free to all comers. On the corner of the intersection of Central Avenue and a side street stood a young policeman. Very tall and slim, he beamed down on all *small fry* like myself. I gazed eagerly up to him, certain that he was the very model of a London *Bobby* Dad had shown me in his British newspaper. With his smart, white summer cap, shiny brass buttons gleaming on his dark uniform, arms extended, white gloved hands waving people on, should they clog the intersection or the sidewalk, the scene was more exciting than the tinny-sounding concert. It made me feel as if I were actually in London itself. I knew from my father that I would go there one day.

The move to Prince Albert had brought yet another excitement to my life. Like my father, I left home at regular intervals. I rode off in a van to Aunt Glad's kindergarten in a rambling old building up on the hill, called St. George's Anglican College. This was a comfortable residential neighbourhood beyond the grand and stately courthouse marking the early layout of the town into 'the flat' and 'the hill.'

Both the Anglicans and the Roman Catholic Church had earlier established their presence and marked it with several pleasant and well laid out properties. Large verandahs bounded by stately columns in grounds fenced with attractive stone walls provided an ideal, almost classical setting for long-robed priests on leave from African missions to take the air. By contrast, St. George's wood structure was homelier, yet had large sunny rooms, verandahs, and extensive fenced in gardens.

Mother, like most women, was unemployed. There was the fact that married registered nurses must decline work in the face of the economic plight of their unmarried counterparts as well as the prevailing tradition that "ladies don't work." This Victorian distinction between one class and another vanished into thin air after World War II, ushering in a new age in which all women chose for themselves. In the meantime, in the 1930's, as advertised in every copy of the monthly American magazine, 'Good Housekeeping,' the popular and highly esteemed image of a married woman was already that of a revered homemaker Afford it or not, every household aimed to have a copy. It showed the modern way to live and the purchases required to fill the dream of being a good homemaker, American style, from appliances to pots and pans, as well as a constant stream of new ingredients and recipes being developed.

Homemaker or not, Mother had her own ideas as to how to cope with her particular situation. That is perhaps why I clearly recall her pronouncement that she would keep me at home until I was seven years old. I had learned to read, write and add while at kindergarten. "Now is the time," she proclaimed emphatically to Dad "to enjoy my preschooler while I can." It seems that this was quite in accordance with an English attitude to schooling and proved to be a pleasant interlude.

Learning to read, write, count, dance, socialize, at kindergarten and trying out traditional domestic handiwork skills with Mother made for an exciting life. After the quiet existence with my grandparents, there were now so many amazing and friendly adults in my life that I began to love this place called Prince Albert.

Beyond this snug domestic haven, protected from some of the worst experiences of the Depression years, were all the veterans of World War I, struggling with miniscule pensions and outright incapacitation from their injuries or latent effects of the 1919 Spanish Flu.

While having escaped becoming part of the more than twenty million world-wide who had succumbed to it at the time, the veterans still suffered from the side effects which were nevertheless encroaching upon them, killing them gradually. Among these multitudes, Dad could not escape its claws. Insistent and disabling chest pain had driven him to a medical specialist in Winnipeg. There he learned that he had a life expectancy of about three months! The infection had spread to the heart muscle. The verdict had been delivered, calmly, professionally and cruelly. It stared him in the face.

As people said afterwards, "If only he hadn't known!" Enduring the overnight vigil of loneliness, cold and dejection on the train, he seems to have adopted the attitude pronounced by the Welsh poet Dylan Thomas some years later, "Do not go gently into that good night." As much as the hurried rhythm of the train wheels seemed to shriek, "death, death, death," as they skimmed along in the unfriendly dark, the old boy scout thought more about his family than himself. He had lost both parents in his own childhood. It would be impossible to think of leaving the scene without first of all having the comfort of a little family life.

He would make sure that we observed "the Golden Rule." This was the basic need for mankind above and beyond any branch of organized religion. He wanted to make us understand his values, to convince us that there was no place in life for racism or class distinction. Nor were poor speech, careless handwriting, or poor posture tolerable. He had been brought up with the typical Victorian schoolboy fare, reading the tales of Rudyard Kipling and the Empire, the values of *fair play,* bravery, and the courage to endure hardship.

A little later on came the works of Charles Dickens and the hardworking reformers concerned with the plight of the ordinary people. A major influence in my father's development in this context had been through Lord and Lady Baden-Powell, world founders and leaders of the Boy Scouts and Girl Guide movement with whom he worked in London, long after his membership as a boy in the original troop.

It was through this experience that he had been sent to Canada to assist with the needs of veterans. Based in Montreal, he went on to study at McGill University, still working with veterans across the country in the summer months. For many years afterwards, they were reported to have asked for his whereabouts and to tell stories about the fine *glee clubs* and other popular musical entertainment of the era he had organized and led in those days long before the advent of radio and TV provided cheer. Now, barring the diagnosis, he was, I am convinced, ready to return to journalism at the first indication of a normal economic life across the country. In the meantime, he would naturally explore and exploit all other possibilities.

As for mother's state of mind, the person I knew then seemed in retrospect to vanish overnight on receiving the shocking news of the diagnosis. Insofar as I knew her, the friendly familiarity of mother and child seemed to have congealed into stony silence. Refusing to smile except in Dad's presence cast a veil of shadowy confusion between us. Before long I began to fear her and longed for comfort from my father. It seemed that only he could induce smiles and pleasant remarks from her. I dared not ask him what had happened. In my innocence of any knowledge of the diagnosis, I imagined some mysterious guilt on my part. For her, the happiness she had known in Lotus Land, in Vancouver, had entirely dissipated.

For mother as for most women in 1930, it would have been most difficult to have had a positive outlook on life. In the Great Depression years, as wives of employed men were not allowed to return to the nursing profession or other work, Mother would have begun to suffer those constant excruciating headaches and to lie awake at night probably anticipating a frightened, penniless widowhood.

Naturally, single women were the most needy and the most desperate, some of them being rumoured to be near starvation, with or without the municipal "relief" allotment. Examples of despair and degradation brought on by extreme poverty were not at all unknown. Whispered about in shocked tones, they were kept well out of reach of the ears of children.

However, quite suddenly my own burden of sadness and confusion stemming from my parents' situation evaporated into thin air. The cloud of depression hanging over the household had lifted. Now that I had started school, I had to learn something useful in the summer holidays. At that time it was perfectly normal to sew by hand and by machine. One day I saw Mother seated at the sewing machine hemming large white squares. She sat me down to learn how to embroider a decorative stitch around one of the squares. From this I learned that there would soon be a new baby in the family.

On the birth of my sister, Dad took me to see her and Mother, inadvertently turning the event into a fantastic evening extravaganza for me. As we walked the short distance to the hospital under the starry mid-October evening sky, he pointed out the *Big Dipper*, the *Little Dipper* and all the other heavenly bodies I was to learn to identify. It was even more thrilling than coming home from a Christmas party one night the year before, when they had showed me the pattern of individual snowflakes falling on my sleeve cuffs. "No two of them are the same; each one has a different pattern, more beautiful than the last," Mother said, as I jumped up and down with excitement at this amazing revelation.

The tiny pink bundle I had peeked at on that starry night with Dad held promise, I knew, yet it did not quite match the stars and hadn't quite learned to smile. Yet I imagined it to be some sort of wizardry from the firmament itself as we walked home from the hospital. Earlier, when I had asked Mother where Dad and all the wonderful big men I knew came from, she had replied "a small seed." I liked her explanation, equating it all with miracles, garden seeds, growing things and now with stars.

There seemed to be a fresh gaiety around the house now that we were an audience of six around the table for Dad's after dinner songs. Alice, a young cousin spent the year with us while attending the local business college. The funds her parents had donated for her board and room enabled us to pay a young aboriginal girl as helper. While Lizzy seemed to find this all very much to her liking, cousin Alice did not feel at home. From her continual pouting one would gather that our songs and high spirits were inappropriate. Perhaps her parents, completely overcome by the Great Depression, like thousands of others, had left Alice with nothing better than a strict and downcast attitude.

Taking us for lunatics who sang at the table, she frowned and nervously tapped her cup with a spoon as if to say, "Stop it." For Dad, good humour and songs were only as normal as hospitality. For the baby watching from her carriage beside the table, he would throw in a trick or two with his fingers to make her laugh. Thanks to the sunset and the deepened evening shadows, the image of a rabbit's ears flashed momentarily on the wall.

At any rate, the more spectacular the glow of sunset in the dining room window, along with the excellence of Mother's tarts, the more songs filled the air. With a wide range of music, from operatic snatches to children's favourites, we heard "Row, row, row your boat gently down the stream," "Old Man River," "Frere Jacques," "Just a song at twilight when the lamps and low, and the flickering shadows softly come and go," and countless others. As far as I was concerned, Dad was our version of the then operatic stars Lawrence Tippet or Paul Robeson rolled into one, long before our late-lamented Pavarotti.

Although it was probably very difficult in 1933 to find the money for Christmas gifts, Dad's gift to Mother served a double purpose, as it also thrilled me. "The Good Companions," written by J.B. Priestley, the widely admired British author of the day, had just won the Book of the Month award for 1933. An innocent tale of young actors touring the north of England, enroute to London, in search of both success and love, he inscribed it, "To Mary, the best of all good companions." An attempt perhaps at a moment of light-hearted diversion from the nightmare of their own realities, it may have had some resonance with his own carefree youth if not with Mother's always restricted existence.

Surprised as I was to be allowed to read it, I was also thrilled with this imagined avowal of his affection, something I craved and hoped I would someday merit. To be called a "best of all good companions" seemed a great honour and had a hint of something mysterious which the grownups called "romance." I hoped that Mother would once again be truly happy and smile like everyone else. Yet earlier when I had dared to ask her why she had stopped smiling, she suddenly turned away from me rather than refer to the terrifying ill-health of my father.

Indeed, there was nothing in her understanding of parenting which allowed for a natural show of affections. Hugging and kissing were considered inappropriate at the time, perhaps due to the severe code of English discipline necessary to control children. A child could easily feel confused and unloved among female English relatives. As to their responses to each other, I could only try to learn to read between the lines. Happily, anyone could understand Aunt Glad. She was unique, always unfailingly affectionate with all of us in her bluff, amused English way as if to announce with a chuckle, "All's well with the world, cheer up!" Just like Dad, she was in my view, another really good sport.

Christmas 1933 will have been remembered by many thousands of financially distressed parents and children as one they would like to forget. If a tree could be found free of charge, as well as a few yards of tinsel rope to drape it, and a box of colored glass balls, there was still the question of gifts for the children. Fortunately, our tree had all of these as well as a string of the new multi-coloured electric lights twinkling through the branches.

This commercial innovation would supplant the use of real candles and the obvious fire hazard. Apart from games and books, gifts were largely handmade by relatives and friends and treasured for many years. One afternoon, just before Christmas, we heard sounds at the door. Dad and I went to discover the cause and found a small box of children's toys, chipped and broken on the door step. "Oh," said Dad, "it's a mistake," as he strode out to the street to return it to the municipal "relief wagon" which was being pulled up and down the snowy streets by a team of horses for those less fortunate than ourselves, professionals among them.

That and every other Christmas Dad was with us was made to glow with family celebration and to offer a warm atmosphere for visitors, to be remembered for a lifetime, although I recall that Christmas, 1933, my eighth, as very special, due to the presence of the baby trying to wave at the coloured lights. Already I sensed that our life was extremely difficult for the adults who were trying to do their best for us despite these "hard times" they talked of and worked so incessantly to beat.

One can only surmise that until New Year's Day our parents would make a desperate pretense in front of each other to regard the diagnosis of imminent death as an error and the birth of a healthy child as a gift. Yet brave as they were, they knew their true situation and probably drew each breath with apprehension. Watching them drink a tiny dram of whisky together on New Year's day, I stood unhappily before them. Somehow I knew that *liquor* was a part of festivity among grown-ups; yet they were tense, rather than joyful. I wanted to ask, "What's wrong?" Quite possibly Dad was suffering pain. Doctors of that era were known to prescribe whisky for cardiac patients, or perhaps the occasion brought back memories of good times in Lotus Land, now painful to recall due to illness.

A little earlier in time, perhaps in 1930, Dad came home with something that would improve our lives. Sliding it onto the table with a smile and unwrapping it, he said, "Well, I finally managed to get a crystal set." We crowded around him. Although still a child at this juncture, I knew that all across Canada, we were expecting another miracle to follow. It was called "the radio."

Being the same height as the table, I observed at close range the knobs of a small metal box before me. As he turned them, a loud, crackling sound, as if from outer space, burst into the room, intermittently at first, then intelligibly, startling Mother and me. We cried out in surprise. I could see that they were both very excited over the acquisition. Despite the cost, it was regarded as a necessity, and a prelude to the radio Dad purchased shortly afterwards as soon as it became available. Our 'Philco' standard table model radio, cheap at any price, thrilled us as it brought the entire world into our living room.

Encased in the fashionable, brown walnut-finish of the era, the domed wooden box stood about twenty inches high and was slightly less in width. Almost alike in depth, it had to have the interior space at the back to contain the replaceable 'tubes' on which it was said to operate and without which, despite the electric cord, it could not perform. Made to look imposing, in keeping with its importance, a gilt plaque emblazoned with the name 'Philco' decorated the front, near the apex of the dome, just above the speakers.

For the first time in history, via *short-wave,* news was relayed from thousands of miles away by the BBC, while great musical performances from the Metropolitan Opera, as well as from Ottawa, Montreal and Toronto caused repeated amazement amongst us. The occasional deep rumbling noises, or the suddenly sepulchral tones of the announcer, could seem fancifully to emanate directly from the tossing on the sea-bed of the trans-Atlantic cable into those delicate 'tubes' inside the walnut box beside us.

As a pre-schooler who hated to be put to bed at seven and shut out of this dazzling new world of adults, I tried to eavesdrop from a crack in the door. Otherwise, I had no chance to listen in again until lunchtime the next day. Then Mother would ask Dad in a differential tone of voice, "And so what's new under the sun today?" as if he were still a working journalist.

About that time we first heard the shocking report of the use of mustard gas in the Chinese–Japanese conflict. There was also the horror of the kidnapping and murder of the infant son of the celebrated pilot Charles Lindbergh in 1932. Although the murderer was being hunted half a continent away, I hid under the dining room table and in the hedge for fear of imagined gangsters in our midst. At the same time a neighbour's child died suddenly after a short illness.

Knowing nothing about beginnings or endings of life at this stage of my existence, I could not believe that my playmate was gone. Persuading Dad to bend down to my level under the gate-legged table, I put the problem to him. Considering his situation, the patient explanation that life is finite must have been painful to him, despite his kind smile. Nevertheless, I recall being assured of many years of blue sky ahead. When he left me still cowering, yet comforted under the table, I began to try to imagine the bright, sunny skies with the fluffy small, cumulous clouds of Saskatchewan, stretching so far ahead that it defied my imagination to even follow the enormity of the vision he had left with me. As he intended, I forgot all about it.

Quite suddenly, in the mid-thirties, when I was ten, the conversation at mealtimes turned to Europe and the growing possibility of war. Hitler's name and ambition was part of every broadcast. The steady rise of the Nazi party was openly visible on the streets of Germany from 1933. Despite being prohibited from joining in at the table, unless addressed directly, I was thrilled with these discussions of current events, emanating from the radio and the pictures in the newspapers and magazines. It was the world itself before our eyes.

Rumours of War and War

O ne of the first sensations of the world crumbing around us in Hitler's wake, came on January 20, 1936 with the announcement of the death of King George V. The sound of the "death knell" chimes seemed to reverberate slowly and darkly across the Atlantic, as was then so often the case, followed by a short silence. Finally we heard the formal BBC announcement, "The King is dead."

News of the death of the old monarch startled me as I descended the staircase. In those days our loyalty, our roots, our world was entirely synonymous with the King of England and the British Empire. Canada paled in comparison. Apparently equally moved, Mother had been stopped in her tracks in the hallway by the news as she looked up at me. We would tell Dad the minute he arrived from the office. At home in England his own Boy Scout troop had paraded in front of the king at a Royal jamboree. "Without our king, who will stop Hitler?" I wondered childishly. Would the Prince of Wales become King Edward the Eighth? People were not sure about him as the future monarch.

With Fascism on the rise not only in Germany but also in Italy under Mussolini, we soon learned of the Italian campaign in Abyssinia. Our world was full of horror as for the first time ever, during the Spanish civil war in 1937 the newsreels showed bombers bearing down mercilessly on helpless civilians. Then one day that year our cousins suddenly arrived from Kobe, Japan. We found them standing on our front lawn. Their British shipping interests had been confiscated. Expelled on twenty-four hours notice, and in shock, they were enroute to Ottawa. They had stumbled over bodies, trying to get to the port, to find a ship, and to escape. Japan would become part of the 'Axis' group of combatants with Nazism and Fascism against the Allied forces.

On Sunday morning, September the third, 1939, huddled around the radio as usual, we waited for the latest report on the encroaching war clouds. This time, however, we had been alerted to listen for a specific message. Tense with dread, we heard the BBC announcer say that Prime Minister Neville Chamberlain was about to speak. There was to be no "Peace in our time." In his preceding and much ridiculed campaign, he had promised to negotiate with Hitler.

His voice noticeably unsteady as it came crackling over the trans-Atlantic cable to us, quietly he told the world of his regret in having to announce that "We are now at war with Nazi Germany." A moment later Dad and I heard the paper-boy drop the Sunday edition of the newspaper on the doorstep. Looking down

at it, we saw the dreaded headlines, "Extra, Extra –
War Declared!" across the top of the page.

Mother probably held her breath, fearing that
Dad might collapse and die on the spot. Instead, he
dressed and went down to the armoury to see if there
was anything he could do. As always, the Empire and
its old Boy Scouts from England would heed the call.

Before long, a patriotic event took place on
Central Avenue, the main artery of the town. Men of
all allied nationalities marched solemnly, shoulder to
shoulder, past the town hall and on down to the river
bank and back. Beside my father, his Czechoslovakian
friend probably mourned his ancestral country, already
lost to the invaders, and thought of family left to face
brutality.

The day it happened, Mother had burst into the
room to announce flatly, as if it were inevitable, as it
was, that, "Today, the skies are black with the planes
of the Luftwaffe!" The same thing was happening over
the low countries of Holland, Belgium, Denmark and
Luxembourg. No one who heard the radio reports, saw
those newsreels, or looked at the full-page photos in the
British publication, the Picture Post, will ever forget
the horror of those skies. Everyone asked, "What is to
become of those millions of innocent people trapped in
the bombing and takeover of those countries?" Hitler
had promised a *thousand year Reich*, to replace the
twenty-year hiatus between World Wars I and II. As
might was right, the Nazi party would settle the issue
for all time. For the last twenty years they had suffered

the humiliation of the vanquished, the starvation, the impoverishment, at the hands of the Allies. Now, they would be made to understand the superiority of the Aryan race once and for all time.

We had known that the war was inevitable, having watched the build up of the Nazi regime in the newsreels since Hitler became Chancellor of Germany in 1933. With the military goose-stepping, the speeches, the enormous rallies of Hitler Youth and the public under the intensely dramatic massed waving of flags and swastikas, it seemed that the entire German nation was marching to the Hitler salute. As intended, it was a terrifying spectacle.

Already in 1935 Jewish citizenship and the normal rights accompanying it had been revoked. With the assassination of a German embassy official in Paris by a seventeen year-old Polish youth, Hitler had his cue to start his *pogrom* with the long anticipated move toward the elimination of all Jews, first in Germany and Austria.

His Nazi Party, the NSDAP, or National Socialist Workers' Party, had blamed the Jews, a mere .76% of the population for the hyper-inflation of the 1920s and the Great Depression. Now they moved to seize Jewish property and businesses, especially to appropriate the funds required to wage war and to exterminate the entire Jewish population of western Europe. By the mid-1930's the concentration camps were already in use.

Hitler ordered a next step in the *pogrom*, for the nights of November 8 and 9, 1938. Jewish homes all across the country were ransacked for goods, while at the same time two hundred synagogues were destroyed and more than two thousand Jews were killed. Cemeteries were desecrated and seven thousand Jewish shops reduced to rubble. The massive breaking and smashing of the windows of synagogues, homes and businesses earned the event the name of Kristallnacht.

The vivid memory of the BBC radio report and the newsreel of that barbarous black night can never fade. The sight and sounds of the violent shattering of glass across Berlin and the fanatical eagerness with which the Nazis threw Jewish books, scrolls, etc., on an enormous crackling fire were monstrous, savage, and uncivilized. It burned into the mind forever. Other school girls, in Europe, Jewish rather than gentile, like myself, safe here in Canada, had seen and heard it too.

All Jews and their businesses were marked with the Star of David. Though doomed to extinction, some were led to believe that they were to be "relocated." In the end, as we know, more than six million perished in the unspeakable brutal inhumanity of the concentration camps and gas chambers by the end of the war in 1945. Those with financial resources, youth, health and the courage to do so had relocated to the United States and other countries during the 1930's. Failure to flee due to family responsibilities was, of course, another story.

On June 14, 1940 the Nazis marched into Paris. Immediately we were confronted on the newsreels and in photographs by the unforgettable images, as clear now as then, of Parisians frantic to flee the city, surging forward, completely clogging the narrow roads to the countryside. A long, pathetic stream of doomed humanity, they pulled or pushed their children and belongings with them. Searching for a hideaway in the bushes, they were the instant prey at close range, of extremely diligent, low-flying aircraft intent on strafing them. The Maginot Line, the French defence system had been criticized as inadequate by Britain, then completely disabled by German forces. Now the people of France must face the consequences. The *Occupation* was underway.

In London people were living and dying, month after month in *the tube*, the tunnels of the London underground subway system, as bombs and fire rained down on them. East London became a bombed out shell with large numbers of people perishing in flames. The bombs ripped through the warehouses and workers' homes along the Thames in the haste to destroy the docks. In solidarity with the plucky, long-suffering *East enders*, the Royal Family refused to leave London, despite the fact that Buckingham Palace was struck.

When on December 6, 1941, Japan bombed Pearl Harbor, destroying the American fleet, President Franklin D. Roosevelt agreed that the United States must abandon its traditional isolationist policy and join the fight, as long requested by British Prime Minister Winston Churchill. Despite the number of Allied Forces deployed against them, the Nazis were still in the ascendant position. Now, as American air power took to the sky, here, at last, with time, we could hope to see a reversal of fortune.

With every one of Churchill's outstanding eloquent, moving orations crackling, growling its way across the Atlantic cable, one was spurred on to try to believe in an eventual Allied victory, without the whole of Britain and Europe being obliterated for all time. From morning to night the constant flood of war news via the BBC overseas shortwave service, gave us the sense that we were among millions tuned in world wide. Some listened furtively, some starving, fearing for their lives, knowing that discovery of a radio transmitting a BC news report could mean prison or death.

One day Mother drew my attention to a photograph in the *Picture Post* magazine of enemy ski troops streaking along the Scandinavian woods, exactly like our own forests. It was difficult to believe they were not in our own forests a few miles north of town. It looked like an error on the part of the printer. "Why not us next?" she wondered, reading my thoughts. "Or an attack by the Japanese forces on Vancouver, right down in English Bay where our grandparents live, old and helpless? They are responsible for shelling Pearl Harbour to smithereens last year, don't forget, and are partners in Hitler's 'Axis' hordes against our Allied forces."

On many occasions her fears of impending widowhood were magnified to even more alarming levels of unease when she thought of trying, alone, to protect her children and her parents, should Canada itself eventually face invasion. She was probably thinking of

'Mrs. Miniver,' the then popular war movie starring Greer Garson and Walter Pigeon. Cast as two British parents, they were caught up in the story of the real life emergency evacuation of three hundred thousand troops of the Allied Commando Offensive, dying on the beach at Dunkirk in 1940. It illustrated the possibility of imminent invasion and a face-to-face confrontation with the enemy. Mr. Miniver is enroute to the evacuation scene in his small pleasure craft at the same time as all his east coast neighbours have been called out.

Operating from the French Channel Islands, the Germans try to cut off their return sea route to England. The RAF confronts the enemy while the rescue attempt proceeds. Meanwhile, Mr. Miniver's wife strolls in her garden only to find an armed German soldier hiding in the shrubbery. Far from seeking shelter or surrender, as she first assumes, he is aggressive, armed and totally indoctrinated with Nazi propaganda. Nevertheless, Mrs. Miniver "keeps her cool." Finally the enemy is captured without violence as help arrives.

In the Canada of the nineteen forties, the average person was not likely to be aware of whatever measures might be in place for the security of our northern regions. Arctic Canada represented the unknown to most of us at the time, except for the names of the communities of Churchill, Manitoba and Aklavik, now known as Nunavut, North West Territories, which might as well be on Mars, for all we ever knew of them. We assumed that all resources and thoughts were directed to the security of Britain.

On this basis I tend to understand Mother's concern for our own place on the losing side in early 1942, the ever-widening theatre of war casting deep shadows about us all. However, by the later part of the year, Hitler's troops were deflected away from their losing struggle for North Africa as the Battle of Stalingrad lay ahead. The Allies began to see progress of their own as they fought their way northward through Italy.

After the war, Mother faced ridicule by her family in England as to her reported fears on the subject. Residing in the south, only twenty miles across the channel from Europe, they had faced the fact in 1939 that Hitler had announced his intention to invade the country. Britain had not yet had a chance to prepare for an attack. Our relatives had been quick to point out that a cyanide pill kept in a pocket was the answer in the event of a forced surrender.

After the Battle of Britain the *Fuhrer* changed his mind, and Brits intensified the race to fortify the island against all impending onslaught. The Luftwaffe had attempted to overcome coastal fortifications and the Royal Air Force installations and aircraft factories, losing well over twice as many planes during the decisive months of August through September 1940, as the battle raged. This early success was attributed in part to the development of radar and Churchill's renowned decoding station at Blechley Park, known as the National Code Centre. The Luftwaffe then began the bombing of inland Britain.

I began to imagine that I would one day cross the Atlantic myself. As Dad was a reporter, why not his daughter? Besides I was growing up with good marks for writing essays and passing French tests. Finally, there was Italy. No small influence in my desire to record what would be the aftermath of the war, after university, was a recent film in which a stylish young reporter, Robert Taylor, leans glamorously over the side of an ocean liner, enroute to cover the war. As a designation for such important assignments, the term "foreign correspondent" seemed to replace reporter.

What could be more suitable as a future career for those of us endlessly asking ourselves and others "What will be left of Europe after the war?" "How will they have survived starvation?" One heard these questions constantly as we saw the great cities of Germany in ruins from our bombing raids and our own ruins in London and elsewhere. "What will be left of Europe? What could be done to restore normal life?" People shook their heads in disbelief at the pictures and the casualty lists. It would be an urgent problem, "How will it be dealt with this time? Certainly not as in 1919, the last time it happened," everyone repeated. "Don't forget that the peace treaty was the disaster that led us into World War II!"

Carrying on

As severe food rationing had become an urgent problem in Britain, everyone with family overseas endeavored to provide regular food shipments. Among the most popular provisions was Canadian ham. Packaging regulations issued by Canada Post were sometimes difficult, given the perishable nature of the product, especially if not sealed in a can.

Vivid memories recall the struggle to secure unwieldy packages with mandatory layers of cloth over paper, stitched together and securely labeled according to stringent regulations. In an era yet to develop plastic for the purpose, available packaging generally consisted of brown paper, string and rolls of heavy, gummed brown paper, perhaps the forerunner of today's gummed plastic tape, to secure a heavy package. It seems likely that some of it sank in the Battle of the Atlantic.

Yet there were also the poverty-stricken people of our own town in need of help to exist on the meager municipal allowance of the lingering Depression era economy. The opening up of post-war prosperity was yet to come. Up a steep flight of stairs to the closet-sized domain of Miss Emily Harman, we found the diminutive and frail looking old lady about to begin her carefully laid out evening meal.

Once a hat designer in London, she was now the local seamstress who solved Mother's most difficult sewing problems. Those were the days when even an old coat was not discarded, but "turned," literally, to get additional wear out of it by reversing the fabric. The inside became the outside.

On this particular occasion on which Dad had brought her a gift of butter and a half pound of bacon, he was astonished by what he saw on her table. Enquiring about it, he said, "Miss Harman, why do you eat your eggs black with pepper?" Just five feet tall, or less, with an ashen complexion, and wisps of white hair pulled back in a knot, she looked up at us, explaining in a small, raspy voice, "Well, you see, I get the rotten ones free. I try to help with my nephew's schooling whenever I can." From then on we made sure that she had fresh eggs.

Our next stop was to pay the handyman for the repair of a storm window. When we interrupted the evening meal in a bare kitchen a half a dozen, pale, thin, and dispirited looking children sat around a large table with their parents. On each plate was a slice of limp white bread and a knife. With no odours from a possible first course just cleared away, no glasses of milk or a pitcher of it on the table, the prospect was startling enough to be recalled today. Adorning the centre of the table, however, was one item, a large can of the very inexpensive, thin strawberry jam sold by E.D. Smith. "Was that the whole meal or just a very simple dessert?" we wondered uneasily as we departed. We hoped that white bread and jam was not the entire supper menu for anyone. One heard that many people went to bed hungry.

Dad would no doubt try to take them something special later, or if he had an extra bill in his pocket he may have slipped it in with the cash he pulled out of his pocket to pay for the repair. Perhaps the only reason that everyone was able to buy the jam was that according to the newspaper of the day, most of the fruit and berry harvest of British Columbia was actually discarded due to the poor state of the economy. Who could afford to pay for fresh fruit transported across the country? For those who could pay a few cents for them, the stewed apples, pears and peaches on our table had been dried and bagged prior to shipping, providing lasting enjoyment in pies and puddings throughout the winter.

In order to be able to offer sustenance to others in need, many women, including Mother, made a point of having a soup-bone simmering on the back of the stove. It was of prime importance to the young men who "rode the rails" or, to be exact, the tops of the freight cars. Looking for temporary work such as planting or harvesting, at one stop or another across the country, they would need a meal and often appeared at the back door to ask for breakfast. Everyone understood the seriousness of the situation and kept a bowl of hot cooked cereal ready to pass through the door. Although they were usually quiet, sober young men with downcast faces, I noticed that Mother's hand might sometimes shake as she offered it. With no faithful dog standing by, and Dad having departed for work, she could only hope that the stranger would not force his way into the house.

For me as a small child, it seemed to be an interesting event to see one of these young adventurers, able to sit on the top of a train without falling off. The only comment I ever heard about their behaviour was the humourous tale that clean socks disappeared from clothes lines, the soiled ones left behind in gratitude. The possibility of hungry *hobos,* or intruders as they were called, was quite another question, causing adults to frown, but say nothing in front of children.

One day, when I was ten, a friend came over to invite me to go for a truck ride in the country with her father and big brother. Try as Mother did to dissuade me, I finally won the argument, then quickly regretted it. Hurtling around the countryside on bumpy, dusty roads, searching out the farmers owing money for her father's welding repairs we discovered that payment was in carcasses rather than cash. Here was an unexpected lesson on the barter system. Hot, smelly and mosquito-ridden, we returned to town after much masculine shouting and tossing of cattle parts into the truck, only to roar off in search of the next unhappy farmer.

Compared to the present era, there was as yet little protective clothing suitable for winter wear in temperatures habitually dropping to forty degree below zero Fahrenheit and on occasion to fifty degrees. Large, rough coats of buffalo hide were seen here and there enveloping the more elderly, rotund male members of the population. Dyed rabbit enjoyed a short season of popularity among women but offered little warmth, whereas a stiff and unattractive form of dyed, sheered sheepskin called *mouton,* both bulky and unattractive, was known to be warm, if expensive. Most people wore heavy woolen coats lined with *shammy,* or correctly, the French word, *chamois,* pronounced s*hamwah* literally the hide of sheep, goats or deer.

Parka hoods, woolen caps, toques, earmuffs, even hand-muffs were a necessity. To have a fur collar was the ultimate luxury one might dream of, whereas a fur hat represented the wealth of a visiting politician from the east or some such person of official standing. Oddly enough, even these were usually designed to freeze the ears, standing high on the head well above the ears, like a military-style cap or one typically worn in hot climates by the Indian Prime Minister Nehru and British officers serving in that country.

Although the Ukrainian rural population still wore the sensible warm winter head gear of their homeland, covering the head from forehead to the back of the neck and including earflaps, urban men usually chose frost-bitten ears, rather than submit to reason. To cross cultural lines in haberdashery or anything else was as yet unthinkable. That was yet to come.

Sturdy country boots were worn only in rural areas. In the small urban centres, the male inhabitants preferred to freeze their feet in rubber-soled, cloth and buckled *overshoes.* The women's model, in the interests of fashion, laced up the front and was trimmed around the top with fake fur, its ankle hugging "velvetized" cloth sides giving the false impression of warmth as well as luxury and style.

Worst of all, for the many men unable to pay for overshoes, were the *rubbers* which kept out moisture, protecting only to the level of the first inch of the leather uppers, but not the cold. With the price of a "re-sole" being out of the question in many households suffering severe deprivation, for the rest of the year one's shoes might well have to be stuffed with cardboard. All shoes being made entirely of leather, the utility and comfort of today's permanent sole was unknown. A constant worry, the problem occurred as frequently as the pressing need for dentistry, especially in families with growing children.

Basic clothing needs were sometimes met by sewing empty flour sacks together to obtain the required yardage necessary for a garment. Lengths of coarse unbleached cotton could be turned into drapery, sheets and bed-spreads. With a packet of fabric dye and a formidable amount of patience, energy and firewood, the colour of one's choice could be added to these articles. In order to get an even distribution of the colour tone, one had to have an additional supply of wood to keep the water near the boiling point. Mother's favourite apricot-coloured drapes began with constant stirring of dye and cotton in a tub of very hot water on top of our wood stove.

The need for soft, stretchy knitted garments from England, no longer affordable or available, was met by expediency. One could wind the lengths of string from the parcels handed to us every day, over the meat, cheese or other shopping counters, into balls for knitting. This was the era before the development of the synthetic fabric industry. I recall being told by other girls that being obliged to use of lengths of grocer's string for economy meant learning to splice the ends together to avoid the sight of hundreds of knots in the finished article. "How could you muster the patience?" I asked? Fortunately, I never had to try. Everyone learned to knit or crochet their own outerwear, skirts included, from balls of string or wool, depending on the season and the budget.

Although I rarely saw anyone knit or crochet in public in Canada, it was common enough immediately after war's end in a post-war Europe still suffering economic deprivation. In Canada, to keep the needles flying at top speed in the 1930s, we combined this work with reading, listening, conversing and socializing. At thirteen I completed a short-sleeved woolen pullover in seven days, just in time for a special event. As it took a little longer to make a vest in a large size for my father, I worked in the dark with the stealthy use of a flashlight. Mother had insisted on lights out. "Bedtime!" Making cardigans required both more work and cash outlay; therefore one triumphed on finding thicker "yarn," and larger needles at a bargain price, to get through the worst of the winter weather without illness from the cold.

However, for those with cash to spare, the mail order catalogue of T. Eaton Company in Toronto was the answer to almost every need from clothing to household needs or tools. Eagerly awaited twice a year, its arrival in spring and fall editions offered exciting reading to a ten-year old bent on checking it out and to the thousands of homes served by it across the country. More than an inch thick or so it seemed, it was ablaze with small red stars denoting items at special reduced prices. Timothy Eaton had something for everyone. Speedy, efficient and ready to refund or exchange for other sizes or colours, the service operated on the amazing rule that "the customer is always. right."

Playwright Rock Carriere, in the National Film Board production of an animated film called "The Sweater," or "The Hockey Sweater" in 1980 produced an outstandingly droll, yet subtle comedy, perhaps looking back to his own childhood in Quebec. The mother of a small boy had ordered the red hockey sweater worn by his Quebec team, the Montreal Canadiens, yet receives instead the blue pullover of the Toronto Maple Leaf and forces it upon her small, humiliated son. One gathers from the intonation in the voice of the mother that timidity towards the strange Anglo world of Toronto prevents her from requesting that "Mr. Eaton" send the correct order, the red sweater of the Québec team, required by her now tearful boy.

The priest gets the last word, punitive in nature, reflecting life before the "Quiet Revolution" or the decline of the authority of the Catholic clergy in Quebec. The boy prays for a huge cloud of moths to destroy the Maple Leaf sweater. His mother would get the red one. He would no longer be ridiculed by his teammates. However, as far as I know, we enjoyed perfect service from Eaton's for all the times we needed the retailer to get through the years of the Great Depression. I am reasonably confident that in real life the Timothy Eaton Company satisfied every customer it ever had.

While Woolworth's "five and ten cent store" stocked many of our other needs such as the fabric dyes, the cotton, the knitting wool, the needles and most household items, survival demanded still more ingenuity, not only in obtaining warm winter clothes as protection against the eventuality of the mercury sinking to fifty degrees, but in "beating the heat." The seductively pleasant days of June usually turned into a blistering July and August, at times registering one hundred degrees Fahrenheit.

When, in consternation, someone remarked, "You know, today I could have fried an egg on the pavement downtown," he may have longed for a cool drink, yet lacked money to buy it. Perhaps at home he would look in the icebox for cool lemonade or some other thirst-quenching drink. Without the services of the 'iceman' to deliver a block of ice for the icebox on his daily rounds, a kitchen would need a trap-door in the floor with a cool shelf under it. This was the way to chill the freshly baked lemon pie for dinner as well as cool drinks.

For those outside the urban areas, the deep, cool well replaced refrigeration as a place to lower bottled food, such as jellied meats, or desserts in a bucket on a cord to chill and congeal. After a burning day in the fields, reward was at hand as the sun set and the family gathered around the table.

Acutely aware of Dad's fragile state of health and knowing that such people are even more vulnerable in high heat than in normal temperatures, Mother kept up a constant supply of fresh lemonade on the verandah to provide tempting hydration. She spiked the drinks with the popular fizzy mineral salts called Andrews Little Liver Salts and then carried out a tray with tall glasses around the pitcher. Always a treat in those days, bottled drinks were regarded as rare, expensive, unhealthy and unregulated.

At the dinner table we could further cool ourselves with her delicacies. Gleaming on a newly starched white damask cloth were the enticements of the popular menus of the decade, such as tomato aspic, jellied meats, salads and desserts including compote. On Sundays Bavarian cream, crème brulée or English custard tarts and pies were served. Most of these dishes owed their decorative shapes to the use of gelatin and metal or glass moulds. Irresistible as they looked, they were also satisfyingly chilled, allowing peak flavour to hit the palate. No one at our table ever complained, "It's too hot to eat today!" As usual, Mother did it all with amazing panache long before modern refrigeration was available.

This is not to say that she was in any way party to the notion that a woman's place was solely in the home. Given her background as a registered nurse, intent on service to humanity, she had hoped in her graduation year to begin to save enough money for advanced training. Her dream had been to qualify as a staff member under the celebrated Dr. Wilfred Grenfell on his hospital ship serving the deprived Newfoundland outposts. Then she met Dad.

Should I venture to snoop my way through the kitchen before dinner to ask, "What are you making today, Mother?" I would be sure to go away disappointed. Always disclamatory, her reply would be "Wait and see pudding" or, wryly, "The chicken's not yet plucked," the latter being a reference to *Punch*, the English magazine. I recall the cartoon in question, so amusing to her, with the caricature of a distraught housewife running around the farmyard in search of dinner for the guests already arriving at the front gate.

In the 1930's the purchase of prepared chicken parts was unheard of. Considered a luxury and rare find, a "plucked" or de-feathered bird required evisceration. It was then *singed* with burning newspaper to remove any stray feathered bits of skin before being roasted or cut into pieces. Tough old hens were available at low cost to be boiled and grumbled about for the sake of economy.

In the face of her perpetual refusal to agree to teach me to cook and to insist with her admonishment that "Any fool can learn to cook," I was taken by surprise one day when she began to talk about it. Quite out of character, she explained that her culinary efforts were all for Dad, "because," she said softly, "he has had such a hard time, you know, with so much chest pain, and the disappointment over being too ill to return to his reporting career, even if the Depression ended tomorrow."

73

It was her first cautious hint that I was old enough as a pre-teen to know that Dad was in serious trouble, and so were we. Squelched by poverty for so much of her life, she had found something she could do to make each day a little more bearable for him in the face of the insistent chest pain. In the middle of the Depression years, while old-fashioned doctors still foolishly recommended sea travel as a cure for heart disease, she had instead been practical in outlook. With Dad's remarkably courageous morale, he deserved every kind of thoughtful gesture available. Despite her lack of passion for it, she had learned to be an especially good cook.

And so this was it. Learning that Dad could never recover and return to his career as a journalist, in a sense I now understood her troubles. Why she disappeared behind a veil of melancholy whenever we were alone became more plausible. Earlier I had gathered up my childish courage daring to ask meekly, "Why don't you smile like the other mothers?" Probably overcome by the shock and distress assailing her from such a pointed question, she had silently looked away from me. Yet she had now, with her moment of confidence, given me an answer, not the whole story, but enough of it for the time being.

It has often been remarked that the common plight of the Great Depression did not in general cause people to come together socially. In many cases hurt pride was endured in silence, alone, behind closed doors, in order not to *lose face*. To let anyone else see the increasing shabbiness of the interior of one's home or look too closely at one's appearance was to be avoided at all costs. As a woman who had enjoyed choosing good design, certain colours and fabrics in that chic era of the 1920's, it was especially difficult with each new season to endure her own drab personage, so different from her own image of herself.

Exasperated by all this one day, when we four were dressed to leave the house together, she remarked vehemently, "Just look at us!" I suppose that at that moment she felt that she had lost the battle to "keep up appearances." Whereas she would normally have refrained from comment rather than upset Dad, she had somehow blurted it out only to feel sorry about it later. As with the remarks about cooking, the truth was out.

Evasion and subterfuge, the effort to keep smiling and to maintain the status quo despite the general family misfortune is bound to give way at some point. Kept in the dark about it all, as an innocent child, I was forced to spy on this poor woman. I would try to catch her unaware, so in need of cheer, so desolate as she seemed, to learn her thoughts and to be helpful to her would surely make her feel better.

Out of the corner of my eye one day while reading, I could see her running her long tapered fingers over her old 1920's style *chic* kid purse, a gift from Dad, stroking the stylish, *cloisonné* inspired lapis lazuli and gold toned enameled clasp, quietly murmuring a word or two to herself. Nostalgia and grief darkened her painfully thin countenance. She had forgotten my presence in the room, succumbing to the moment ever so briefly. According to the old photos they had shown me, the equally chic cloche hat she still wore in winter and the purse had been part of her ensemble in Lotus Land, in Vancouver in the days preceding the Crash, that momentous world event which together with Dad's fateful diagnosis, stripped her of youth and hope.

Just as surreptitiously, I had watched her examine a china cup. I keep it in memory of her. It may have been in the family for a very long time, yet it had never been mentioned. As she held it up to the light from the dining-room window, the same secretive, tragic expression suffused her face in dark thoughts. Like the 1920's purse, this exquisite handiwork was another valued art object. From a set sent by the family in England as a wedding present, the delicately shaped cup was hand-painted in rich and traditional deep blue tones by Royal Crown Derby in the elegant Mikado pattern. The gift must have thrilled her.

Possibly expressing the same degree of anguish she had felt on leaving the set behind in Lotus Land, she slowly returned it to the shelf and closed the door of the cabinet. With the high cost of shipping or packaging things of value in those days, it was one of the first sacrifices they had faced. Such objects, though trivial in themselves compared to other deeper issues, yet rich in meaning to her, could never be replaced. Now consumed by the vicissitudes of life, like millions of others, she was a thin, frail shadow of her former self, as revealed in the photos of the previous decade.

Such observations had begun to imprint themselves permanently on my mind. At ten years of age, I had not yet lived long enough to know that deep significance as well as consolation could be found in the arts. Perhaps as never before, art comforted her. With artists in all four branches of the family, it is not surprising that we all appreciate it. Obviously, she was fortunate that Dad was a man well versed and inspired by the arts, enabling him to keep up the will to survive adversity. Later in life art meant everything to her.

Although for adults the drought and deprivation of the prairies to the south of us was another depressing fact of daily living, we children knew nothing about it, the grasshopper plague, or the erosion of the top-soil blown off the fields and lost forever. The common sight of abandoned farms were fortunately beyond our experience.

A couple of years later, while driving along a narrow gravel road to our aunt's cottage at the lake she said, "Quick, roll up the window!" There was a sudden downpour, a "green rain" of grasshoppers. Perhaps blown north of their area a hailstorm of locusts landed on the windshield and roof of her new two-seater Henry Ford coupe. Several of them were already down my neck and leaping about, others pouncing on our hair and clothing.

In a moment or two an abandoned farm came into view. Derelict and weather-beaten as if unpainted, the house and its outbuildings were leaning, and crumbling into the earth, just as the dust storms had left them, half-submerged in dust and decay. "The poor family," I groaned in shock, "Whatever happened to them? Where did they go?" A teacher in the south of the province, my aunt knew too many sad stories to want to elaborate on disaster, an everyday event she knew intimately.

Like the dust storms, the mosquitoes and even in some places the army worms, the grasshoppers had to be endured, indoors and out, despite all futile attempts to elude them. If not through an open door, their route was through the spaces between the door and the frame, the window and the sill. Every green shoot sticking up through the parched, cracked soil was stripped and devoured by the voracious army of locusts. For many desperate people who lost their crops to this marauder, there was no way to keep bread on the table.

For us, and for them, survival was the difference between life south or north of the treeline. We lived close to the land, the lakes, the boreal forest and the rocky outcroppings of the Canadian Shield. It was also a matter, in most cases, of the difference between rural drought-ridden desperation of the south and relative urban well-being, such as ours to the north, albeit on a style unacceptable to the affluent life-style of the twenty-first century.

Surprisingly, then three years of age in 1936, my sister Janet had something to say about life. "Mom, give it to the 'pore'," came the urgent request from the sleigh. Amazed, Mother and I stopped in our tracks in the snow. The infant was still learning to speak coherently, yet amusingly, in a clear voice, she had delivered the wisdom of the ages. We had been discussing who would inherit a piece of clothing to be given to the most needy amongst us. Startled by her retort, we burst into laughter. "What! Does the wee one not know that we are also poor?"

Later, at six years of age she had awakened to find a cheap pair of tan-coloured ribbed cotton stockings, a standard necessary item at the time. Standing up, she bounced on the bed crying out, "How refreshing!" over and over again, as she proudly waved them like a flag. That was life in 1939. One could almost think she had been born knowing that "things are scarce." Over the years, articles based on medical studies of the fetus have appeared suggesting the possibility of absorption of information from outside the womb. While laughable in this context, the idea has seemed more plausible in studies of young musical prodigies born to mothers who were singers or who played an instrument.

Ultimately, after so many difficult years during the Depression, came the most important aspect of security necessary for wellbeing when "Tommy" Douglas, a prairie resident and politician brought health care to us in the 1950's. As chosen by the Canadian public in recent years, our "father of Medicare" is the most popular Canadian of all time. Dad was one of the many in the 1930's intent on the need for a universal system of health care and for a social security net. Naturally, although he would not live to know of Douglas's left-leaning aspirations, the ongoing problem weighed heavily upon his mind.

Town Life

At the Strand Theatre, newest of the two "movie houses," as the cinema was called in those days, we sat on red plush seats under a star-studded midnight blue ceiling. Embellished with ornate imitation Italian balconies on the walls on each side, this romantic decoration delighted us. A pampered lot, for a fee of ten cents per child we were treated to a steady stream of the latest Hollywood and British films. As youngsters we spent much of the time sitting on the edge of our seats in astonished excitement, watching films selected for us, Robin Hood, the Three Musketeers, the Scarlet Pimpernel, the Disney films and Shirley Temple.

However, the second and older site, the Orpheum, was the venue for my first "movie," an outing at night with my parents. As one of the first "talkies" to replace the silent films of the nineteen-twenties, 'Showboat' was a new experience. To me, then, as a preschooler, it was, of course, a breath-taking extravaganza of frivolity and wonderment.

To my parents it was also a reflection of the racial question south of the border. Written by Oscar Hammerstein, it highlighted his concern for American blacks still subject to the brutality of the slave mentality and the Klu Klux Clan. His 'Ole Man River, sung by Paul Robeson in the deep rich tones of his magnificent voice was unforgettable by anyone fortunate enough to hear it or who cared for their plight. It marked his place in the struggle for freedom of black Americans. He and the great contralto, Marian Anderson, whose name is synonymous with *Negro spirituals*, also continued to enthrall my parents for the courageous part they played in the struggle against segregation. First ignored in America and then accepted as an opera singer in Europe, she finally became the first black woman to sing at the Metropolitan Opera in New York.

When it was a time for ice-cream treats, the decorative, wrought iron sets of small round tables and chairs in the ice-cream parlour windows beckoned to small children. Through the impressively gleaming rows of glass jars of assorted candies and cookies on the high counter, the Greek merchants beamed down upon us. On special occasions, Dad took me there for an ice-cream served to us in their excitingly elaborate quarters.

In my early teens, I was often sent to the tobacconist's shop to pick up the British papers for Dad or to buy a special Sunday treat for the family, usually a "brick" of Neapolitan ice cream. Striped chocolate, strawberry and vanilla, it was wrapped in waxed paper and a light cardboard box. The trick was to get home before it melted, insulated boxes being as yet unknown. Or I might have been paid for my after-school job at "the five and ten cent" store, bought my own cone, only to have Bert, the tobacconist's rotund assistant gaily string off a fanciful list of at least a dozen new flavours, such as *tutti fruiti*, then treat me to a double size.

The place was old, smelled of oiled wooden and sawdust floors, tobacco, newsprint and 'confectionary.' It was a veritable cornucopia of all our weekend treats, cookies, candies, tobacco, newspapers, magazines and miscellaneous items. Mr. McConnell, the dour, old Scots proprietor kept our predominantly English town in touch with "the old country." Not the least among these were the English papers, the *Picture Post* and the ever popular *Punch*, keeping us abreast of important war news.

How did the proprietor manage to get delivery of it all, on a regular basis at a time before air service, with the enemy blockading the convoys across the North Atlantic, taking the lives of some of our own youths in the process? It was a great service to us. Many of Mr. McConnell's former young customers were now fighting for their lives or killed in action. Indeed I was already aware of the absence on the streets of many of the young sons newly graduated from high school. Signs on door fronts proudly listed two or sometimes three sons known to us all, now serving overseas in one of the three armed services.

There were, of course, immigrants from Europe scattered through the area. Whereas in typical English immigrant fashion, the older generation lived within their own circle often bounded by the influence in their lives of their own Anglican parish, we youngsters would have been thrilled to meet some of the newcomers. There were youngsters of our own age of whom we were curious and vaguely aware at the skating rink or some other chance meeting.

Olga, with her dark eyes, flashing smiles and thick dark braids wrapped around her head, attracted us with her brilliance at school and her wonderfully patterned and highly coloured clothes. Although she once agreed with the three of us to show the interior of her stunning silver-domed Ukrainian Orthodox church near the river bank, we never actually carried out the plans.

I suppose that it was due to the fact that vestiges of ingrained, insular Victorian behaviour had been transmitted to our own sensibilities and we tended to circulate among our own kind. By war's end people had moved on into the much more open society we enjoy today.

Another exciting stranger, the attractively diminutive Mrs. Burton sailed past us on the street in all her East Indian splendour of veils, coloured chiffon scarves and darkly outlined eyes. Too short of money to be enrolled in her dancing lessons, we did not expect to meet her. "Had there been a homesteader by the name of Burton? Where had he found her? Perhaps when stationed in India with the British Army? Would she ever go back? We never learned, but she stirred up much more interest than some of the mysterious local "belles," parading around in very high heels, coloured wigs, showy make-up, and excessive jewelry.

Reportedly a witch, Maggie Jones never crossed my path although she was said to haunt my favourite tobogganing hill. Another person called "Mr. Popoff," sold hot popcorn on the bridge leading out of town. Why did he stand there for hours in the cold, waiting for a car to pass? Where did he come from and where did he live? Perhaps he was a Greek, neighbour of a countryman a mile or so away attempting to grow figs in a severely cold climate.

As a pre-schooler, and on a visit to a Greek farm with Dad and our own neighbour, Mr. John Diefenbaker, then known only as a lawyer, I accidentally set off a fight between this stern man and the white lice on the fig tree beside me. When they crawled over the top of my thick reddish curls, the eminent gentleman noticed their presence. Bashing my head about angrily in no uncertain terms with the sides of his thin, bony hands he sent them flying. Dad, who had been talking to the Greek fig grower, had no idea of my chastisement.

It would seem that the childless Mr. Diefenbaker did not particularly enjoy my presence. The friendly Greek fig grower was called 'Will,' just like my own Uncle Will. Be it the desire to create art or to grow figs, people come to Canada for all sorts of reasons, incongruous as it may seem to others to choose climatically inhospitable parts of the country.

Warned by timid children to keep clear of the weather-beaten white house with the drawn curtains next to the Presbyterian church, we feared that it was haunted and lived in by old Chinese men. In actual fact, these lonely men were the café owners, looking out on that street, probably longing to see their own families come up the walk and wishing they could make new friends in our community. Due to the "whites only" policy of the Canadian government of the day, wives and children were forbidden entry into the country as immigrants.

Picking up derogatory names for immigrants, undisciplined street kids labeled the Chinese as *Chinks*, the Poles and others as *Polaks* and *Bohunks* and the Italians as *Dagos*. Among the Brits, the scent of garlic alone was enough to rule out association with newcomers from the Ukraine and Poland as foreigners. There were, of course, great numbers of Ukrainians, Poles and even Russians Doukhabors settled on the land, as well as Scandinavians, Icelanders, Italians, French, and Jews.

Due to the insularity of our own background, with the exception of the last two groups, we knew nothing of any others living in town. Colour, language and class differences were still rigidly upheld before the war. The occasional sight of a black person passing through town led to wonderment, especially if the skin were a beautiful *café au lait,* considered an exotic marvel. It was not until after World War II that the public began to reject racism. Oscar Hammerstein had made it clear in one of his songs, with the repetitive line, beginning with *You've got to be carefully taught* ... meaning that hatred is not an inborn human trait.

Concerning derogatory nick-names, pre-war Germans in our midst got away with the term derived from a comic strip, called the Katzenjammer Kids. These *jolly Germans* as they were called, loved their sauerkraut. It was a healthy dish, but we disdained it as being un-English and therefore ridiculous, in favour of plain, limp English boiled cabbage. Very different names for the Germans began to fly around among the street kids when Hitler suddenly called them all back to Germany. As Aryans, members of the superior race, they were to fight for the Fuhrer. I always wondered whether many Germans answered the call and what became of the boisterous family down the street after they moved away.

On a national level, one of the worst examples of intolerance was the refusal of the Canadian authorities, under the leadership of Prime Minister McKenzie King to allow Jewish refugees fleeing Hitler's Germany to land in Halifax in 1939, knowing full well the alternative of certain death in internment. These concentration camps were known to be in operation as early as the mid-thirties. Shortly after Hitler's accession to power as Chancellor of Germany in 1933, he announced his program, promising a "thousand year Reich." By 1935 he had withdrawn Jewish citizenship, property rights, education and other basic rights, and forced each and every one to wear the Jewish Star of David. Ruthlessly tracked down all over Europe, they were sent by sealed box-car to the death camps.

Of native Canadians, we children knew next to

nothing yet of the Cree population who lived all across the western provinces. One night, probably in 1930, a very special dinner guest appeared. Dad had brought the naturalist, Grey Owl, home with him. Accustomed to public speaking earlier in his career, Dad was called upon to introduce notables at public gatherings. Here was the guest for whom Mother had been re-warming the roast beef dinner for an hour or more.

As they came through the door, the aroma of over-done beef suddenly took on the added pungency and allure of alcohol, buckskin and pine forest, all swirling around in our small apartment. Never had any aroma taken on so much character, and offered me such exotic excitement. I was familiar only with Dad's and Uncle Will's oil-painting mix of turpentine and linseed oil.

My admiration for the great man towering in front of me knew no bounds as I took in his long glossy black braids, his buckskin outfit, the pants with the fringes and the multi-colored beadwork down the front of the jacket. Whether at this time it was also generally known that his birth name was Archie Bellamy, a native of England, I do not recall. If Dad knew, he kept it to himself. Grey Owl left us with books and photos of his beaver, his family and his work.

That Prince Albert might well have been also called Little England was obvious. It was also one of many towns across the country suitable for an aboriginal name reflecting its location, rather than the imperialistic connection it had been given. We were actually living in the heart of aboriginal country, among the

Cree people of whom we knew so little, secluded as they were around gorgeous woods and lakes nearly all the way to Hudson's Bay. Much later, both Mother and I would learn a great deal more through an encounter not dreamed of at the time, but ultimately greatly treasured over a lifetime.

Early in his years in eastern Canada, Dad had met a fellow-Brit named Dan Webster, a middle aged, reserved gentleman of the old school. Possibly they had crossed paths in musical circles when Dad was involved in entertainment for veterans of World War I. Dan had made his living by playing the violin in orchestras in Britain and Toronto, and accompanying the *silent films* preceding the era of *talking pictures.* Remaining unemployed throughout the Depression, he was not so lost out here "in the colonies" as not to find his way across the country to renew contact with Dad.

Dan was perhaps the only one of a long string of English people we knew who did not come to some resolution of his economic problems at the end of the Depression. Being taken care of by fellow musicians in old age in Vancouver, he appeared to feel that he too had found 'Lotus Land,' and marvelled that he had always made such fine friends throughout his life. Perhaps like others of his kind, a *remittance man*, he simply did not work. Was playing the violin all that he had ever known? I was too young to know anything else about Dan.

On summer weekends, I might find old Mr. Joyce sitting in the garden with Dad as the two of them pulled on their pipes, all smiles and laughs, trying to recall lines from Shakespeare, long-forgotten but exciting and challenging to bring to mind. Eagerly watching from the sidelines, I tried to make sense of it all, but we had not yet been introduced at school to the lines of the greatest bard in the English language.

Perhaps I would marry a poet, I thought, or someone one like Dad who was also an artist. Walking home with him in an early spring rain, he glanced down at a tiny puddle, exclaiming in surprise, "Look at the reflection, you can see a patch of blue sky breaking through the clouds!" I should have told him, "It's thrilling to hear things like that, Dad, just like the time you showed me how to recognize the stars!" At any rate, I hope I expressed the joy of being with him and of appreciating him.

Not one to miss a chance to enjoy recording nature around us, even if sparse by comparison to his native England, he took the cue from a jet-propelled ruby-throated hummingbird at the window one morning, drawing it to perfection in pastel crayon. It remains one of our prized mementos. When he planted a tall perennial plant of bright yellow pom-pom flowers in front of my window, I was once again astonished to think that for me he was an artist, a singer, a poet and a gardener by nature. I certainly had all the luck. He was never gruff or grouchy like some fathers I knew.

On a perfect June day, Mrs. Taylor, our friendly English neighbour, called out to us as we went by, "Come and see my roses." Eagerly we followed her to the chimney on the side of the old two-storey family home. It had protected the roots in winter, with vestiges of warmth from the interior. Roses did not normally grow so far north. Fragrant and sparkling with dew, they clung profusely on the wall. When we left, she presented Dad with a bouquet of four perfect white roses for Mother. As Dad handed them to her, I knew somehow that this was a special event, a romantic moment for both of them. Life was wonderful.

At school the Sisters of Sion, an international order centered in Paris, opened our eyes to many subjects. All year long they challenged us beyond classroom studies, with mastering oratorical, musical and dramatic presentations for our parents and invited public in the great hall we called the Assembly Room. Attending school with an international order of entirely dedicated teachers was a valued privilege, more exciting by the week.

Curiously enough another contribution to our education came to us from the glittering and famous West End London stage itself, or so the adults seemed to understand. Clifford Bould had undertaken to encourage would-be thespians in the production of theatrical performances emanating from the basement of the Anglican Church. This was where we already spent so much time in other more serious pursuits, such as Brownie and Girl Guide training.

The new activity was so much more exciting than the compulsory Sunday school for all Brownies and Guides held in the same place. The old lady reading scripture to us wore a confused, grumpy expression. One day she read a passage about how an ancient king, called Nebuchadnezzar had crawled on all fours to eat grass. I went home in a state of annoyed confusion.

We were also told that the diet of poor children at the Anglican mission in Africa consisted solely of beans. Pictures of them grinding them with a huge mortar and pestle were displayed to show their poverty. My parents, who disapproved of Sunday school, were obliged to give me a paper bag full of jelly-beans to send to the mission. This was my introduction to foreign aid. Even at eight years old I knew better than this! They needed food.

Young, tall and attractive like Errol Flynn, a popular Hollywood figure of the 1930's, 'Cliff' Bould, the actor, sent us into spasms of confusion as he supervised our rehearsals, make-up and costumes. "Don't squirm!" he would say, admonishing us loudly, in a stern voice, applying colour to our lips. Among adult actors and friends, he was known to shout out his opinions freely on all manner of subjects.

People began to chuckle. While Aunt Glad and everyone else would laugh and say "Oh! He's outrageously funny," or, "Oh, I say, isn't he a scream?" Mother would retort in a derogatory tone of voice, "I'd say, he's a howl!" Dad accepted him for the generous, light-hearted person he proved to be. Outspoken herself, Mother may have been jealous of his ability as a man, to speak out, unfettered by the "good taste" and discretion still observed by women of that very conservative era.

It was as if Oscar Wilde himself had moved to Prince Albert. Why had he come? For that matter, why had any of them come to our small town? The privileged son of a London banker, as he told us, he had decided to head for "the colonies" when his father's funds expired with the Crash of 1929. He was now a guard at the local penitentiary. Until the end of the Depression years in 1939 and a new flow of money from London, he somehow kept body and soul together all winter, with his Canadian wife Kay, in a tiny suite consisting of indoor kitchen and a freezing cold outdoor bedroom in a screened porch. Did he want to flee home to England? If so, I never heard about it or any complaints, at our table or during evening visits.

Finally, with reinstated funds from England they left to study art and drama in California, Kay returning to Saskatchewan to become one of its acclaimed artists and Clifford employed in a government office in Regina. Strangely, they never did return to live in London, although they were able to take holidays in Britain. No doubt when he saw post-war Britain, he had been shocked by the changes in the West End theatre scene from the post-war Britain of the twenties and thirties, with its emerging world of John Gielgud, Lawrence Olivier, Peter Ustinov, Alec Guiness and all the other younger actors stepping in with a new perspective on the taste of the public.

With all of them, one wonders, how it was that the Great Depression led them to seek out or even come to our small town, scarcely a pin-prick on the map of Canada, remote from any large centres and in one of the coldest regions of the country. Not the least of these was Viennese artist, Ernst Lindner. When Dad pointed him out to me as a small child, I saw a man happily floating on Emma Lake with his pipe sticking up like a periscope. We invited him to dinner. He was a long way from the Vienna woods of his youth.

Ultimately Ernst Lindner enjoyed a very successful career as an artist and teacher. Much later in a fundraising event of the 1950's he presented a superb New Year's party with a Viennese theme at Saskatoon's prestigious Hotel Bessborough. Assisting with the décor was the prelude to dancing the night away. At this point any reminder of the old days of dancing in Europe was more than welcome.

Our most frequent Depression era and beloved dinner guest was our so-called 'Aunt Glad,' or Gladys Bodington. Almost one of the family, she was a delightful friend, older than my parents, and an ex-settler from England. She had homesteaded near Lloydminster with her husband and now lived nearby, perhaps originally because of access for their two children to the local highschool. Being from privileged London backgrounds, it was not through economic need that they came to Canada.

Rather it seemed that youthful wanderlust had led nineteen-year-old Aunt Glad to join friends in a plan to defy convention, to become governesses. Brought up by such women, she and all her siblings thought of it as a career. As yet, the universities were not generally open to women. In fact, their class of society considered paid employment as unsuitable for "ladies."

After one disenchanting stint as a governess in the wilderness, or actually as a mere *jack-of-all-trades*, as she later called it, London looked inviting. However, just then she met John. So began a short-lived real adventure in homesteading. Not having to endure hardship of this kind for too long, they had eventually moved into town after having experienced the same painful early twentieth century arrival as my own family in Saskatchewan's wilderness near Lloydminster.

In 1930, in her newly opened kindergarten, she taught me to read, write and do *sums* on the blackboard. Over the years as a Brownie and Girl Guide Leader, she organized all our annual lakeside camp holidays, roaring campfire sing-songs, concerts, theatricals, picnics and country-wide patriotic Boy Scouts and Girl Guide trips to salute touring royalty.

Thanks to her efforts, she passed on to us valuable childhood experiences. Disciplined, demanding, yet fun-loving and good natured, she was born for her role. Observing the numbers of needy children and parents in the community, Aunt Glad soon enrolled the girls, supplied uniforms, and sometimes provided necessities to the parents. Having such a person to take an interest in their welfare in such difficult economic times meant a great deal to deprived families. Occasionally they became her long-time friends, whether they spoke English fluently or not.

Full of new ideas from politics to religion to folk medicine, photography and art, lively debates and laughter graced our table whenever she joined us for

Sunday dinner. Sharing the love of art photography with Dad, she joined him in entering the annual prestigious national art photo contest, one of many activities to divert them from daily economic problems.

There were countless picnics and drives in her old car to the nearest stream called the "Little Red." Although it was out in the woods and the sand hills, it was also close to home. Despite the competition with blue-jays, ants and mosquitoes, Mother's contribution of sausage roles, potato salads and tarts made them stellar events in my view. Aunt Glad found it all amusing and was eager to arrange the next Sunday outing.

So much of our family life was enjoyed with her in our midst as well as others that our living-room was one of those very "lived-in" havens, especially when it came to Sunday lunch, nineteen thirties style. As men still went to their offices on Saturday morning, Sunday was a very special event allowing Dad to set up a painting table in the centre of the sunny room, trying to recreate the studio of his dreams.

Just as I stood at Dad's elbow to ask him about the work in progress, we would look up in joyful anticipation as Mother arrived with a large tray, bearing steaming bowls of especially hearty soup and huge muffins fresh from the oven. Jokingly, we liked to tell her that she would do well as the proprietor of a soup and muffins shop, knowing well that in those days no "lady" could actually envision such a practical goal. "It wasn't done," as she and Grandma used to say. Dad stayed seated comfortably among the paint tubes, brushes and the pleasant aroma of turpentine and linseed oil, while we crowded in as best we could for the weekly one-day holiday get-together.

In that very bright and cheerful setting, flowering house plants and bulbs had been coaxed into bloom year after year on the tiered shelving built by Dad around the south-facing window. Enhanced by the blaze of January sunshine it offered, we had the impression that the plummeting near "Siberian" temperature readings of that frigid decade did not apply to us here, indoors, on our special day in all the luxury and warmth. Certainly the adults at the table would worry about the cost of wood and coal for the furnace and might even long for a fireplace-centered lunch such as they had known in England. Of such luxury I remained blissfully ignorant.

Hung from the ceiling in front of the window, the bird cage allowed us to enjoy our bright yellow canary singing away as we enjoyed lunch. A Norwich crested roller, named after Dad's home city on the east coast of England, he was a handsome fellow with the crest or tuft of plumage on his head marking him out from others of his kind.

However, one Saturday workday morning, Mother and I were as usual cleaning his cage in the midst of general house cleaning, giving him the chance to fly about the living room. Foolishly opening the back door to shake the mop, I had overlooked the fact that the bird was free to escape. Suddenly over my head, in the open doorway shot a streak of bright yellow, heading straight for the park across the street, into the hundreds of mature trees heavy-laden with great poufs of fresh snow.

Alarmed, I called out to Mother, "Oh, I'm sorry Mother, I opened the door and Norry's gone!" Hurriedly, pulling on our boots, bare-armed and lightly clad, we snatched a pot and a strainer and plunged into the knee-high snow at the back door, raced to the road brandishing our tools, waving frantically at the oncoming bus to let us pass first in our haste to get into the park. All eyes were trained on us as the passengers watched in amazement, their startled reactions mirrored in the faces pressed against the windows.

In an instant we spotted him, on a snowy perch just above our reach, seemingly unperturbed, as if taking in the hundreds of mature trees in every direction. Somehow we stretched, making ourselves taller, finally managing to tip him into the pot, just as I put the strainer in place as a lid. We dashed back across the road. As mother carried the precious pot into the kitchen she said, "Open the oven door for me; we'll let him sit there to warm up and let's hope he'll sing again, by the time your father gets home!" The oven exuded only the warmth of the dying embers in the old wood stoves of the era, just enough, we hoped, to keep him from pneumonia or sudden death.

As he failed to fly out of the oven we finally carried him back to his cage. Although he sang again occasionally, the old enthusiasm was gone. He'd seen too much of the world. Finally one day at dinner, Dad said, "In case we need replacements we could perhaps try to breed canaries." He bought a hen, a small, silent white creature. She spent her days pecking out the feathers of her mate's distinctive crest. Norry seemed to give up on life and soon died. Was it his outdoor adventure that stopped that glorious warbling, rolling sound forever? Or was he just another one of the unfortunate hen-pecked males of the world? All joking aside, we later learned that the hen may have needed different bird seed.

Recently on making contact with a relative in Norwich, England, I was surprised to learn that canaries had arrived from Holland with a group of weavers sent to teach new weaving techniques in the sixteenth century. Apparently they had always kept singing canaries in their homes to ward of the boredom of long days at the loom. In Norwich the weavers lived in the Strangers' Hall, today one of the many tourist destinations and perhaps the first place canaries sang in English homes, before technology changed our life-styles.

Emma Lake

During the summer holidays we spent two weeks at one of the neighbouring lakes, especially chosen for the fact that across the water from our cottage lay the university's summer art school. From our beach, Dad and I would occasionally tramp along the trail to visit great-uncle Will, the professor in charge. As we prepared to leave the cottage that day, Dad reminded Mother, as if it were part of an ongoing discussion, "It is high time that I showed up at the school today. Without a car, what else are we to do? And after all, Mary, a stroll along the foot-path will be relaxing, not at all strenuous." That he might be tempting fate with such a long walk in the face of heart disease was not worth considering on such a summer day.

The woods were thick with spruce, jack pine, tamarack, aspen and towering silver birch, the latter gleaming against the deep evergreens. A stump in the crunchy underbrush served as a place to rest. With no intimation of distress, yet slipping a small white pill under his tongue, Dad would continue to chat amiably with me, puffing on his pipe, drawing deep breaths, until we finally resumed our hike. An hour or so later, with the two men eagerly "talking shop" as they toured the classrooms and studios at the school, I was left to explore the place on my own.

Back at the cottage, left with my small sister, Mother was apprehensive, frightened and anxious as the hours wore on. Many years later, I realized that for her the visits to the lake were a painful and repetitive nightmare kept to herself. Understandably though, for Dad, while certainly aware of the danger of collapsing on the trail, the delights of the occasion were irresistible.

Having been committed for years to the need for an art program to serve the young people of the province, he felt impelled to visit the school himself, now that it was actually in operation. It was important to support regional youth and art, to help in the development of creative skills in the province, something which he had taken for granted in the British school system of his day.

At our beach there were a few other children eager to learn to swim as well as one or two eager to help us. Among them was little Christopher Bird, preschooler son of Bishop Bird and brother of my friend, Helen, crying with great enthusiasm, like his mother, "one, two, three, poosh!" in his unforgettably endearing Scottish accent. Later, in World War II, as a mere adolescent, he was to lose his life to a torpedo in that heroic naval struggle to protect Allied oil lanes across the North Atlantic.

But these were the happy days of childhood. We knew that we would never really die, would live in the wonderment of nature forever. Face downward on the slats of the wooden wharf, we marvelled at the millions of minnows in the crystal clear waters below. The dragonflies skimmed magically all around us, grazing our bare backs, their iridescent blue wings too beautiful to be real.

Mesmerized by the lake at all times, we were speechless with joy at being rowed along to the main beach for groceries. Deep, deep down in the water, as we peered over the edge of the boat, it seemed the filmy, fleeting clouds of summer and the shimmering, glinting water revealed a silent, magical world below. Could it be the actual, secret home of the handsome striped black and white loons? Was this their home when they were not crying, with that crazed laughter, up and down the lake at dawn and dusk? Asking Dad about it, he said he could not be sure, then continued with, "At any rate, they've been around for thousands of years, you know," as he slackened the oars a little and turned his head toward me. With the inimitable cry across these northern waters, one could easily imagine the sound echoing back and forth through the endless centuries.

One day, "Aunt Mabel" and "Uncle Keith" arrived from Saskatoon for the weekend. The next morning, we set out along the lake after the joys of a fine meal of eggs, bacon, pancakes and syrup, made more delicious with the rustic camp kitchen facilities. As old friends who had met shortly after Keith and Mabel arrived from England in 1919, they shared with Dad the memories of the days when they had all worked for the welfare of the veterans.

Before meeting Mother, then nursing World War I veterans "from the front," in Winnipeg, Keith, Mabel and Dad had provided musical entertainment and other recreation and assistance to these men. As the wife of one of them and mother of two, Mabel worked ceaselessly to obtain benefits for all the ill, impoverished veterans across the prairie, themselves included. An old story, in Canada, we have seen the problem emerge again and again, including the present time.

Because children were not allowed to address adults on a first name basis, the close friends of one's parents took on the designation accorded to a member of the family. I naturally assumed that our beautiful visitor was a relative. The laughing, brown-eyed "Spanish" lady, Mother called 'Aunt Mabel' in our presence, stepped lightly into the boat and sat down, her long, dark, wavy hair held in place by an excitingly vivid red scarf. This gypsy queen, as I imagined her to be, owed her spectacular beauty to a Spanish grandmother.

Dad began to pull away from the wharf and row out into the lake. I kept one eye on the reflections in the water of the few small cumulous clouds dotting the perfect blue midsummer sky. I hoped that we could see the loons again. After all, Dad had said that they were living here long ago like the native people preceding us. It was their lake.

At the same time, it was obvious to Mother that Dad should not have organized this trip, now laden with the weight of our guests. Thinking aloud to me for once, she had worried that, "Keith has a heart condition, was exposed to mustard gas in the trenches, so he cannot help with the rowing." Seeing the blue pallor across the cheeks of this handsome man had reminded her of his condition. I had yet to understand why she thought Dad would be tired.

As he always looked the picture of health and wellbeing, the truth was easily withheld from me. If he suffered the following week, I knew only that he slipped the little white pills under the tongue more frequently, sometimes staying home from the office. Later I came to learn that the chest pain, now admitted, was called *angina*. The medication was nitroglycerine. At the time it was the only solution available for his pain. There was no cure, nor did heart surgery exist.

The next day we all helped to bring the lunch down the uncertain, rustic wooden steps from the cottage to the narrow stony beach, taking care not to shatter the fragile butter tarts enroute. As Uncle Will had driven his Ford coupe over from the school to join in, the talk soon turned to news of the enterprise. "Uncle Keith," trained in music in England, as had "Aunt Mabel," before their farming years in Canada, dreamed of the possibility that the university would add a summer music and drama department in which they could participate.

Thrilled by their enthusiasm, but not part of it, I tried to draw the trees hanging down over the beach further on from our spot. Not content that day to try the fine brush and ink line-drawings taught at school to reveal nature at close range, I tried vainly, with my only resource a blunt charcoal stick on newsprint. If Dad and Uncle Will could draw and paint so well, why couldn't I also "see the forest for the trees?" I longed to grow up, to be clever, like all the wonderful adults in my life.

Despite the exciting weekend I was beginning to get a little cross with myself and close to tears. I had yet to learn that I was not alone. Even our own renowned Canadian artist, Emily Carr, had struggled long and hard to see into the essence of the natural world before realizing her own dream. Since the beginning of time, mankind has tried to express his talent in one artistic field or another, sometimes with tears and tragedy, before attaining a mere semblance of the perfection glimpsed in the mind. "Will I do better when I grow up?" I wondered, as I hid my work and tried to draw the wharf and boat instead. It would be something to remember when we were back in town and dreaming of next year!

The Unfinished Canvas

Dad finally succumbed to a heart attack one Sunday morning in June, 1942, during the most violent thunderstorm and flash flood we had ever experienced. It had been a tremendously courageous twelve-year struggle since the diagnosis. Was Mother suddenly and horrifyingly reminded of the winter storm and train-wreck in which they met? Following a morning of grinding pain, his face an angry blue-red, his canvas remained almost blank. He had tried to make a small start. Nothing more.

In Mother's reaction to his death she assumed a permanently stony face and pulled her attractive auburn hair into a most unbecomingly tight knot. The picture of despair, she never talked of him again. His art work vanished, hidden permanently out of sight. Presumably, we youngsters had no feelings and were therefore doomed, trapped in a perpetual veil of silence. For starters, we were not allowed to attend the funeral. His art work came to light again only after her death. This wholesale destruction of our home life had left me speechless and numb with grief. After her immigrant experience, widowhood was too much for her to bear.

There was nowhere to turn for comfort. Opportunities brought on by the prosperity that war provides had allowed friends to find work or interests in larger communities. They had all left Prince Albert behind. Even my Aunt Glad, my 'second mother,' our closest family friend, had retired and moved to live with her daughter in Victoria. Now, when we were left in limbo, her warm presence was needed more than ever. Everyone now lived too far away. Even our grandparents were retired in Vancouver. The price of long-distance phone calls was prohibitive.

On the war front, in June, 1942 the Allies had not yet begun to see a light on the horizon. Unthinkable as it was, Singapore itself, that bastion of Empire, had just fallen. The old boast that "the sun never sets on the British Empire" would not be heard again. Shortly before his own demise, Dad had been overcome by this shocking news as it boomed out from BBC, London, on the short-wave radio. The unthinkable had happened! He had struggled with severe chest pain, his face an ugly bluish-red, at the very moment that he had called out the news to the rest of us in the kitchen. "They've taken Singapore!"

* * *

My reward has been to compile a photographic
index of his work, permanently housed with it at the
Art Gallery of Prince Albert, a regional gallery in northern Saskatchewan. One of his latest drawings was an
ink study of Winston Churchill, taken from the famous
photo by Karsh from the cover of Life Magazine in
1942, during the days when his most forceful and magnificent addresses boomed through the static, across
the Atlantic cable and into our living room.

Inscribed below in black ink are excerpts Dad has printed. "We Shall Never Surrender" is followed by,

"We shall fight on the seas and oceans, we shall fight with growing confidence and growing strength in the air. We shall defend our island, whatever the cost may be. We shall fight on the beaches, we shall fight on the landing grounds, we shall fight in the fields and in the streets, we shall fight in the hills .... we shall never surrender..."

In larger print below is quoted:

"Give Us The Tools and We'll Finish the Job."
The Right Honourable
Winston Churchill

The drawing hung in the bookshop window on Central Avenue during the war. Unfortunately, like millions of others, Dad did not live to see the victorious outcome in 1945.

Tragedy and Transition

I t was 1944, exactly two years after losing Dad, that I found myself in the middle of the exciting and longed for evening of high school graduation, with the awarding of honours, the dinner, and the dance. Chosen to read the valedictory address to the assembled guests, I expected to commence English studies in the autumn session at the university.

Mother had arrived by train and surprisingly enough seemed to enjoy the whole festivity. Yet, on the way home the bubble burst abruptly. It was made clear that a university education would not be mine. Rather than a show of affection and a sense of family closeness, my attempts at discussion seemed on her part to end in a display of anger cloaked in mystery.

In her mind, my only future lay in the Registered Nurse training program. "Be sensible," she said, "we are still at war. And you will earn your salt," she added with disparaging emphasis, as if speaking to a slacker, or ne'er do well. "And you know very well that nurses will always be in demand despite economic conditions!" Dad would not have accepted her reasoning.

Then, to quash my dreams of teaching school temporarily over the summer, as permitted by the wartime regulations to permit students to earn cash for studies, she retaliated with, "Besides, you won't last five minutes. That's where they send young women, only to end up married and working on a farm for the rest of their lives!" She stopped short to draw her breath, "I won't have it! Do you understand? I won't have it!"

I wanted none of it. "How futile," I had wanted to say out loud. I knew that salaries for nurses and teachers meant mere survival in 1944. On such an income, one could not save for university nor help one's family, a necessary part of my future. Considering the immaturity of one so young, I could have no real understanding of the depth of her depression, let alone her grief, loneliness, and insecurity, the probable causes of this tirade.

"But mother, I need a degree in English literature or journalism and to study art. The nuns at school have always encouraged me. I've won the award in literature and the honour of reading the valedictory address."

"Nonsense" she replied. "How do you know there will be work and where would you get the money for any of this? It is out of the question!" The nuns had tried to help. Sister Melita, the school principal had suggested, "But Madam, leave something to God." Mother concealed her need to sneer until she came home. Had she taken this advice in a less literal sense, substituting 'good fortune' or 'chance' for "God," my future might have been saved. Having always insisted that girls

110

should attend private schools as in the England of her childhood, she had been forced to be gracious in front of the nuns.

As yet, the student loan was unknown. Apparently there was nothing that I could do but enlist in the Canadian Women's Army Corps to get the credits for university. The Army was the only one of the three services recruiting women in the area at the time. On application I learned that I would be called to the enlistment headquarters within a short time.

Consequently, I no longer spent the normal summer holidays at the lake as in my father's lifetime, but washing dishes in the hospital kitchen while waiting to enlist. In the heat of summer, it was difficult to bear the suffocating odours emanating from the steam tables, or serving counters, mixed with those of cleaning agents. Relieved to be taken down the elevator shaft away from it all one afternoon, I found myself alone in a huge freezer-room in the sub-basement. I was to pry, tug or tear entrails and eggs from hundreds of chicken carcasses now too congealed to yield readily to my aching, half-frozen, rubber-clad hands.

Normal as this type of work may have been, it was a relief not to be sent there again. Yet there was more to endure. The living quarters were reached through a tunnel reeking of laboratory guinea-pigs. I slept in a small bunker-like cell, rising at five a.m. for work at six o'clock. As I emerged the first morning, I found myself among a crowd of farm girls, well used to early hours of labour, with the ritual of standing around smoking while waiting for the dining-room to open for breakfast.

This was not the way we started the day as boarding school students. Some of these girls were topless, long-haired and dishevelled, not yet fully dressed for work. The rough straw hats worn by all suggested long days under a hot sun. Typical of the years of the Great Depression, home-made cigarettes hung limp, grey and wrinkled from the lips of those wan, unwashed faces, expressionless and old before their time, under the battered cowboy hats.

It reminded me of a set for a Western: humourless, tense, as if waiting for the sheriff. Later, when I happened to see the award-winning art photograph, of a gaunt-looking farm couple, called *American Gothic* by Grant Woods in the fifties, I was reminded of those pathetic girls as well as the period so eloquently expressed by the photograph.

To have married Clive, the young RAF cadet chosen for me by the nuns for that graduation dance, who became a frequent guest at home, might have led to a pleasant student life on an English campus as he hoped to study architecture after the war. Perhaps such traditional behavior would have been best, but we both knew that we were too young for marriage and were both ambitious for education. Besides, now that Dad was gone, there was my resolve to help my family. It was clear that marriage would never be possible for me.

Despite the war effort and the need to sacrifice, to pull together, to endure loss, I was actually quite fortunate compared to many girls. At that time thousands of young women of my age had already been uprooted from their own schools across Europe, to be dragged off by Nazi soldiers to work in the production of weapons.

However, like my own mother having been taken from her school in England to emigrate, I was even now drifting away from my own planned pursuit of knowledge and the company of my peers. They would enter university together without me, do well, marry and have children while I trailed far behind. The standard advice to the young had been, "Go west, young man." Now it was fast becoming, "Go east." That was where the great companies, agencies, government departments called out for bright young graduates. Although I could not know the future, I had the sense that I would be left out of the great adventure others rushed to accept.

When the letter finally arrived from the Canadian Army Headquarters in Regina, telling me to appear on a certain day, I made plans to take the bus across the river for a brief visit to say farewell to Mother. She was already at work as an R.N. in the position she had had to accept at the out-of-town, mandatory live-in hospital centre offering a pension plan. Specifically designed for the treatment of tuberculosis among native people, now known as First Nations Canadians, it was close to our old picnic grounds, woods and stream, allowing the patients a bucolic, home-like environment for their recovery. In the meantime my sister Janet remained in boarding school in the care of the nuns.

On that unforgivingly harsh winter afternoon in the shaky old vehicle used as a bus, I recalled our last picnic there as a family in those very woods. We had all sat there on the springy, pungent turf, that delightful carpet of pine needles and cranberries, happily polishing off the last of Mother's best walnut and raisin filled butter tarts. Amid the sudden rush of mosquitoes, ants and beetles to the picnic site, came the squirrels, wood-peckers, whisky-jacks and blue-jays to gather up the crumbs.

Now as I alighted from the bus at the entrance to the building, Mother and I found ourselves in an atmosphere which could only be described as stark, in the unnaturalness of the setting and the lack of normal rapport between us. Alone, without Dad, shocked and unable to speak, we seemed to be worlds apart, standing on that doorstep in the silence of the snowy woods. Pale, gaunt, coldly white and starched in the traditional uniform of the nursing profession of the 1940's, she seemed unable to articulate her thoughts in present grief on this final, agonizing break-up of our family and home.

Longing to throw my arms around her, yet paralyzed by fear of the strictly forbidden expression of emotion, speech was impossible. Once again, even in this heart-breaking moment, the need for affectionate embrace had to give way to discipline due to ingrained habit. Making a weak attempt at laughter, always flat, despairing and derisive, she ended the encounter with a quick nod of her head. Quite abruptly, the great oak door closed in my face, groaning on its hinges in the hands of a woman too weak to handle it or the onerous life forced upon her. I sensed the desperation of her misery as well as my own.

As if to cover for the need to share a warm emotional exchange and talk of Dad, she had chosen to disappear and perhaps to weep. There remained only heartbreak for each of us, so totally alone. In the strict British tradition, she had always insisted that feelings must be hidden. She had mastered it well but at an enormous cost.

Agonized, I retreated through the woods to the bus with the cold shadows of the declining day falling around me. As it had always done, that sad, derisive sound of anxiety, masked as laughter, haunted and alarmed me. It had often occurred when Dad was at work, never in his presence. A grim substitute for mirth, it had chilled and disturbed me all through childhood, probably since I was five, the year of his diagnosis of impending death.

Even then, still desperate to claim her as my closest friend, I had felt totally mute and lost in her presence. At this youthful point in my life, her sophistication, cynicism and adult intelligence were beyond my understanding. After all, as the doctor had said to me the day Dad expired, "You are now the head of the family." My head spun as the appalling scene flashed before me, once more. With a heavy heart I took one last look at the perfection of the woods, and thought painfully of Dad who so recently had enjoyed it with us.

I hoped desperately that she would find some way to improve her now seemingly hopeless existence. Feeling like an orphan, I could expect only a lonely and dispassionate future. "How could it all be so completely different?" I agonized, "from the one envisioned for me by my optimistic, loving and devoted teachers?"

On the way back I recalled that as children we had loved to wade along the nearby stream in search of the tell-tale, zig-zag trails left by the clams leading us to them along its squishy bottom. The clam shells, glistening with shades of cobalt and silver while wet, and therefore thrilling to us, dripping sand and water, we delivered to our indulgent parents as priceless trophies. As never before, I relived those days. A startled blue-jay darted out of the snowy branches flapping its wings to see me off. For an instant my heart leapt in joy, soared with the bird, descended. Then all fell silent. Dusk was descending.

G.I. Credits for University

Boarding the train for Regina the following day, I would find my way to the Canadian army recruiting office in late afternoon. With its faded, threadbare upholstery, the old coach squeaked and rattled its way along the track. It was a far cry from the early days of childhood when my family travelled on a Canadian Press pass. In those days the trains were furnished with comfortable blue plush seats and fresh white linen covers for the head-rests. More exciting for me were the uniformed porters from Montreal's black community, the shine of their silvered buttons vying for brilliance with the flash of their teeth and their generous smiles directed towards me as well as my parents.

Later, I learned that some of the porters, concerned about their own children living in poverty in Montreal, had insisted on developing in them their traditional talent for music. Here was a city where jazz-band entertainment always drew crowds and money. To save their sons from repeating the impecunious lives of porters on the long haul to Vancouver, they left a demanding load of musical homework to be completed in their absence. One can imagine the mothers standing over them, insisting that they practice their instruments.

As part of a train full of excited Boy Scouts, Brownies and Girl Guides I had attended a *Jamboree* in Saskatoon. These gatherings, staged across the country by the British founders of the Boy Scouts and Girl Guides movement, Lord and Lady Baden-Powell, had obvious links to the military and the British Empire. Summed up under the motto, "Be prepared" we were taught such concepts as duty, honour, and service. As my father had been a member of Baden-Powell's first troop of boy scouts in England prior to World War I, he had given me a note to deliver to his former scout master. Mustering all my courage I had marched up to the reviewing stand, a small girl shaking in her boots, wearing a Brownie uniform, and and mounted it in front of the massed platoons and spectators from dozens of communities. While Dad could neither leave his office or afford the trip himself, I was proud to represent him. When Lord Baden-Powell leaned forward to take the note, both he and the lady smiled reassuringly. His face wasn't quite as stern as that of our King George V, who looked much more frightening. It had been a daunting challenge. Happily, I found my way back to my own platoon quite easily in the vast crowd.

When shortly after this event, the Royals themselves came to call, we again piled excitedly into the coaches, ready to march proudly for our leader, our troop, and the Empire. The Baden-Powells were now also actively promoting loyalty to the Crown in the face of the dark, looming clouds of World War II. Boy scouts would soon be soldiers, airmen and sailors loyal to the 'Mother Country.' Girl Guides could also serve. We knew that we must always "be prepared" to do heroic deeds for King and country.

Singing "Onward Christian Soldiers" so earnestly from the front pews of the church on special Sundays produced a stirring sound, yet the message was confusing.. We did not believe in killing, nor did Jesus Christ. We believed in the Golden Rule, the obligation to treat others as we wished to be treated. Now we were to kill "the enemy." None of it made sense.

Finally in a blaze of colourful flags and soaring strains from the organ, we trooped out, heads held high, a long *crocodile* of Brownies, Guides, Scouts and Cubs, the somewhat confused, reluctant, yet emotionally stirred warriors of the future "Call of Empire." One began to wonder what life was about. Why was killing now so important? Couldn't it be prevented? Did we have to believe in it now? It could spoil everything.

Happily by contrast, our stirring school song also contained a line to fire the imagination in such an era. Without thoughts of war, singing "The call of duty and of honour stirs every heart that loves our school," made one proud. It seemed to refer to our normal, everyday life. Just as passionately we loved our mentors, especially that great Irish nun, Mother Melita, the school principal who approached life with so much love and enthusiasm.

The beginning of World War II on September third, 1939, brought with it a great rush to enlist, both out of conscience and need. For many young men it meant the first regular income since the beginning of the Great Depression. Here was the escape from dependence for survival on the municipal 'relief' system. I thought of this as the coaches shook their way along the tracks as if ready to scatter all their bolts and screws after four years of troop transport. Great family dramas played out on the platform, excited, worried departures and arrivals, thrilled anticipation of adventure overseas, together with brave camaraderie in these very seats had been part of those years.

Now, in 1944, as I joined the war effort, a scrawny looking peddler lurched through the coach bawling out "Orange Crush, ten cents," with a downcast air at seeing only two passengers in the car. The other occupant turned her head and I recognized the matronly form of Mrs. Rivers. She waved to me to join her.

"Doesn't your mother need you at home?" she asked, as if addressing a truant caught red-handed. Although both her sons were serving overseas, it appalled her to think that a teenage girl from a "good family" was running off to join the army.

"You'll become a hussy," she said with astonished emphasis, her large brown eyes hardening into a matronly frown of disapproval.

I told her that I needed those G.I. credits and refused to let her condescending manner affect me, knowing so well what I had to face.

By the end of the day I found myself in Regina, then driven to the army barracks. Momentarily confused at not being part of student life, I felt like a mere leaf tossed about meaninglessly in the wind. Fortunately I was ushered into a meeting area full of other excited teenagers. Next day we were issued with uniforms and put to work in low-level clerical duties to await the date of departure for the three months of basic training in Kitchener, Ontario.

By good fortune I was assigned to the mail room. As everyone liked to hear from home, I got to know a lot of other young people by sight and by name. One way or another, social life got under way, dimming the sense of loss, anonymity and confusion. Before long, four of us had formed a friendship which held together until demobilization. Holton, Devlin, Theissen and I were all from different parts of the country, hoping our present roles would lead to university. The bond between us led us to invent our own good times, feeling no need at all to search other company.

Eventually we found ourselves part of an actual 'troop movement,' joining a packed train of hundreds of boisterous youth in khaki, en route to the basic training centre in Kitchener, just as we had watched other transports on the screen and in papers since 1939. For most of us it was our first time to be face to face with the vastness of the country, to be carried away by the grandeur of endless glittering miles along the north shore of Lake Superior.

Running along the rails so close to the rocks lining the shore, we were in close contact with the

121

great rock formation called the Canadian Shield and its cover of boreal forest. Here too was a glimpse of the homeland of the aboriginals who had known it as theirs for thousands of years. Now, for a mere second in time, the Group of Seven and a few others were painting it for the rest of the world.

As the daughter of a man who painted landscape in his leisure, I had always been fascinated by my natural surroundings. I was passionately excited by line, pattern, form, color and texture. With scenery like this my eyes were riveted to the window beside my seat. Yet for many, the trip was one long card game organized to avoid the boredom of miles of 'bush.' It was something to be made bearable by ardent socializing, visits up and down the aisles for snacks and flirtations between the separate yet adjoining coaches of the young men and women.

Emerging at Kitchener on the third day I was surprised and pleased to see that the training camp sat in beautifully treed farm country, with century old farmhouses and stately elms separating the fields. Unlike anything in western Canada, it went back to the days before World War I when the early settlement had been called Berlin.

With a light dusting of early winter snow on the ground to enhance the landscape we began the all-day, every day outdoor routine of learning to march in military formation. Gaining 'good carriage' and physical fitness, and soon aglow with health, vigour and enthusiasm, we were being groomed to take part in large public events involving army, navy and air force personnel.

After the exhilaration of hours of fast-paced drill in the frosty, bracing air, appetites knew no bounds. Despite the dubious allure of mess-hall food, we were willing to devour the great brick-hard, raisin-studded yellow squares strangely called rice pudding. We joked that it must be equally useful for construction purposes. I sometimes wondered, in retrospect, if it owed its solidity to egg yoke alone, the ingredient so necessary to preparation of ancient canvases which endure today in classical art museums. "It's for the war effort" we would say jokingly, biting into yet another square.

While initially shocked by the stern commands barked out at us by the two drill sergeants, our platoon seemed to escape the severe reprimand from either of them that I had expected. Nevertheless, like regular troops, we were forced to endure the ear-splitting commands of military drills. Despite his grim, colourless demeanor, steely blue eyes, and the tall, gaunt frame, the severely demanding sergeant never did actually demolish us verbally. Amusingly different, the other NCO was plump, dark and fatherly. Demanding, but never threatening, I quite suspected that he had daughters at home and approved of us most of the time. Probably both men preferred drilling fighting men and regarded our drill sessions as just 'a piece of cake.'

Trained to perfection, to march with other members of the Allied Forces on any parade ground to which we might be sent, we were dispatched to Edmonton for the formal welcoming ceremony for Soviet General Molotov. A large physical presence, and at that time our ally, he emerged dramatically with his entourage from an immense military aircraft to confer with American counterparts in the alliance of Churchill, Roosevelt and Stalin against the Nazis.

Finding ourselves billeted for the weekend in a vast enclosure with the American Forces, we felt as uneasy as if we had arrived in Hollywood itself. In a large dance hall were hundreds of officers and men and women from the ranks, stylish civilian women, banks of flowers, perfume and enormous hanging decorations. The band pumped out a steady stream of Glen Miller's *Big Band* type of favourites.

Back at our permanent posting at Currie Barracks, Calgary, life became a routine of regular typing classes to prepare us to join the typing pool. Summoned to a lecture one day, I was excited to find that the speaker was a young war correspondent, newly returned from the most desperate Allied campaign of the moment, May 1944, the Battle of Monte Cassino, just south of Rome. It was almost as if our top Canadian reporter in Europe, Matthew Halton, had appeared. As the battle was the top news story of the time, I was astonished that such a person would address us. There had been a great deal of glamour attached to the legendary American war correspondent Ernie Pyle and a romantic Hollywood film in which a young attractive actor, played by Robert Taylor, slouched over the side of a luxury liner in a jauntily worn fedora and a fashionable trench coat, enroute to Europe to report the progress of the war.

Into the classroom strode a tall, dark, and animated young man in smartly-worn khaki battle dress and black beret whom I excitedly supposed must be the already known foreign correspondent, Peter Stursberg. Swinging his leg over the corner of the table, he perched nonchalantly on the edge, holding forth for an hour or so on the campaign in a detailed, thoughtful effort to impart some idea of the horrendous struggle in which the Allies had finally won the day.

As soon as the correspondent departed, from what must have been a practice run for a more adult audience down the road in Toronto that evening, the officer in charge initiated a discussion of his report to which, embarrassingly, I found myself the sole respondent. A classmate soon confronted me disapprovingly, "Say, how did you get this gift of the gab anyway?" The slang, or colloquialism, of *gab* for *chatter*, or *jazz* was current among young people at the time. Obviously bored, she had wanted me to *shut up* so the question period would come to an end.

A few years later, in 1953, another young individual took exception to me, as a woman being inappropriately interested in male or non-feminine reading material. I had been trying to tell him about my discovery of the book by our own renowned Canadian war correspondent Matthew Halton called *Ten Years to Alamein*. It concerned the Allied struggle for North Africa against German Field Marshall Erwin Rommel, notoriously called the *desert fox,* who was finally defeated by the British Army under Field Marshall

Viscount Montgomery in November 1942. Before the tide had changed in our favor, this victory came as a major achievement in the course of the war.

Having been brought up by my father to listen to the BBC seven days a week, I was naturally more in tune with the war than some, as he understood that the future of the civilized world was at stake. After all, Dad had died in June, 1942, shocked at the fall of Singapore and failure to stop Rommel in North Africa. Regrettably, he did not live to enjoy that victory at Alamein five months later.

Today little of the glamour associated with the career of the war correspondents remains. We recognize the bravery of as many female reporters as men, perhaps more, fanning out continually to the most dangerous parts of the world. No one would dare to disparage a woman for her involvement in it.

Our introduction to warfare was not to be confined entirely to the classroom. As to life on the battlefield, we were taken to the familiar military training area near Red Deer, Alberta, for a demonstration of the "flame-thrower." Gathered on a wide plain, as if waiting for the enemy to appear across the fields, we endured a sickening display of military might as the weapons were put into action. This may have been more in the interests of training soldiers how to fire them, than in entertaining or preparing us for possible eventual active war duty.

On the way home in the army lorries, we wondered aloud what other sinister outings we might face.

The final outdoor instruction was to learn to wear a gas mask and to flounder around for a few minutes with burning eyes and laboured breath until the exercise was over. Since the use of mustard gas by the Germans in World War I, the subject had came up on newsreels. Overseas the Allies had begun the D-Day invasion for the liberation of Europe, landing in France on the Normandy coast on June 6, 1944.

Enduring this strange existence at nineteen, I failed to think of an eventual demobilization day. Where would I go? How would I arrange my first term of university courses? I was simply lost in a totally unreal life. While I was still in shock from my father's death, more bad news awaited me. One day in 1945 I had been typing in an office near the mess hall when the kindly old Italian baker appeared at the door with two freshly baked butter tarts on a plate.

Handing it to me he said, "Here you are Miss," in an unusually preoccupied, subdued tone adding, "President Roosevelt died this morning." With that he disappeared. He had apparently wanted to share the sad news with someone. It was the twelfth of April, 1945. I wanted to cry out, "How will we win the war without "FDR" to work with Churchill?" I felt more solitary than ever. I felt lost, alone in this adult world of one catastrophe after another.

Without Dad, the mainstay of my life, and with Roosevelt now gone, how could life possibly continue? My head whirled on this truly black day. The whole camp seemed to be subdued, saddened by the death of a well-loved public figure who had supported unemployed Americans during the Depression, then joined Churchill in our joint fight for survival. It was not Stalin, the erstwhile and despised ally from the Yalta Conference who had dropped out. It was "FDR" himself. Unthinkable!

Still, life did go on as if the daily routine of our life here would never end. From the beginning of our training, we four friends, Holton, Devlin, Theissen and I continued to share leisure time, both on and off the base, playing table-tennis, frequenting movies, cafes and skating rinks. Being avid hikers, we were always anxious to explore more of the foot-hills whenever we were free to escape the camp and head for Bragg Creek, adjacent to Calgary or further afield to Banff or Waterton Lakes.

One such carefree teenage outing took us through acres of cornfields, a full harvest moon hung low in the sky, lighting our way. The rustling, golden stalks brushed against our arms and faces in the warm autumn air as we sang snatches of the popular song from 'Oklahoma,' by Rodgers and Hammerstein, "And the corn was as high as an elephant's eye..."

Tramping about the countryside induced a feeling of freedom from the army discipline we had accepted in exchange for university army credits. Passionate about long walks with family and friends from early childhood, I had proudly counted on it being a lifetime activity for pleasure and adventure and that I would finally hike my way around England, my ancestral home. Now, in the Army, I enjoyed comparing our expeditions to the story told by J.B. Priestley in "The Good Companions," that book I had read at home in childhood about a troupe of English actors and their camaraderie on the road. Avidly, I read every one of the then popular H.V. Morton travel books on his British ramblings. At least I could dream of an ideal future.

Discovering what we assumed must be the military prison called Blueberry Hill on one foray into the foothill countryside delighted us as if we had invaded enemy territory. It was *out of bounds* we were told, with the admonition to keep clear of the area. But none of us had ever been AWOL, which meant *absent without leave* or committed any other infraction. For once we had the delight of breaking the rules as if we were spies. The prison camp stood on a rise of land, behind a heavy wall of metal fencing in the middle of the rolling fields.

Could it be that the German prisoners of war saw us going by in the forbidden area while we looked up at the black apertures of the windows? Visions of wartime movies flooded the mind, such as the ever popular "Forty-Ninth Parallel, in which a Nazi submarine crew reached the Arctic determined to spread their doctrine and brutality.

From the day of our discovery of the prison to the beginning of the Liberation of Europe turned out to be a surprisingly short span of time. It also marked the end of the teenage outings and dreams of a future as bright as the tulip beds in front of the barracks. The Allies finally roared into Paris on VE Day, May 7th, 1945.

129

And so Vera Lynn was right when she sang:

There'll be bluebirds over the white cliffs of Dover
Tomorrow just you wait and see
There'll be joy and laughter and peace ever after...

Although it was wonderful that the war was over, I was overwhelmed by the breathless rush to clear the barracks. Within a few days my four friends had departed. The place was ghostly quiet. There was no sense of celebration. Everyone with a home and family had left, while the stragglers like myself were issued "fatigues" or overalls and put on "garbage detail." This became depressingly demanding physical labour, a kind of slavery, which seemed to have no end. I knew none of these other unfortunate people. Feeling utterly abandoned, I was in shock and enveloped by depression and fatigue.

There was no longer a family to be gathered around the Philco radio to rejoice together. Long-distance calls were unthinkable. Besides, the family home had been sold following the death of our father. Mother was employed as a registered nurse in another area. All the kind adults of my childhood had now moved away as a result of the relative wartime prosperity.

I was now homeless as well as exhausted, utterly lonely, and without enough GI credits to cover expenses for university. With all this falling upon my youthful head, shame set in. Lacking the maturity at nineteen years to take the train back to Saskatoon from Calgary, where my beloved teaching nuns would have helped me, I took the view that they would disown me for joining the army to earn fees for university. Although they had urged me to accomplish it by rural teaching on the special wartime permit, mother had refused to sanction it. I was completely lost.

Now I could neither face the nuns, or my mother, who had so often told me that I was useless. Depression gave way to submission, to obeying her imperative that I too become a registered nurse, someone who would "earn my salt" as she had always claimed so tauntingly that I would never do. Had I been old enough to laugh at life, to defy adversity, catastrophe might have been averted.

Yet the typical reasoning of the Depression era, from which, by 1944, the older generation had not yet entirely evolved, was about to cast its shadow over me, unless I got help. While many of them, like my mother, swore that neither music, art, nor literature would ever yield an income, defeat would have been unacceptable to my creative, upbeat father. Minimal as was the recompense for nursing or teaching at the time, most parents still saw these careers as the most important thing in life – a lifetime guarantee of employment. Apart from this pathetic view, there could be no escape for women.

Despite my obvious ability and predilection for art and literature, no discussion had ever survived these desperate pronouncements. Innovative ideas as to how women might proceed towards a satisfying life-style were few and far between in the nineteen forties. "Why must our role be confined to the sacrificial, the badly paid?" we only occasionally asked ourselves . There had to be a way out. But not yet. Most women had to wait for the post-war years of expansion, prosperity and greater equality.

From the Frying Pan
to the Fire

Shattered as I was regarding my future, I left the barracks in grief, in desolation. Ignoring my aspirations in the face of the apparent new reality staring me in the face, I walked calmly into an interview at the Grey Nuns Nursing School office in Calgary. During the ensuing medical examination of candidates, I was actually given the opportunity to withdraw on grounds of less than perfect fitness. At the same time, not being actually disqualified, I stoically ignored the advice.

As I had no home, family or friends standing by to help me formulate a way to proceed towards university studies, I saw no option but to do as people said in those days, "Stand on your own two feet." While G.I. credits would pay my expenses here for the three-year course of study, they were also the guarantee of a roof over my head and three meals a day. Eventually, I would study in my own chosen field.

With a smattering of maturity or the presence of an older friend to consult, I might have laughed it off and proceeded more rationally. After three years of well-intentioned bullying since the death of my father, Mother had won the game. The dream of education lost, my peers would go on without me. Overcome by the appalling scenario, I stumbled blindly into three years of hard labour, well beyond my physical and mental endurance. However, as a graduate I emerged, with a greatly expanded knowledge of life, a well-developed sense of humour, competence and compassion. I told myself that one day I would consider my own needs instead of those of others, proceeding towards a different goal, or so I dreamed. Clearly, I would not give up.

Since I had no insight either into the difference between the nuns in teaching and nursing orders, it came as an extremely severe blow to find that, in order to save lives, existence would be rigidly disciplined, punitive and servile. This was in sharp contrast to the warmth, kindliness and humour of the teaching nuns, part of a world-wide order, by whom I had thus far been educated.

Just in time to join a new class of about thirty students, we lived for the first three months three to a room, as probationers or *probies*. After successfully passing the classroom exams and the ward teaching sessions, we became accepted as students. The event was marked by a traditional lighted candle-carrying ceremony dedicated to the humanitarian ideals of Florence Nightingale, said to have brought light and hope to the wounded in the Crimean War. Though the "lamp" or responsibility, might be heavy, we were to live a life of dedication to professional service. Just as medical doctors were known to take the Hippocratic Oath representing ideals of ethical professional conduct, we recited The Nightingale Pledge during the event.

Our white, starched student cap served to identify us on the wards to graduates and other staff and made us more aware of the respect we must earn. Our responsibility to the patient extended from the physical to the mental and spiritual realms of existence. As a neophyte, I found such demands not only implausible but amusing. However, a year or so later, the spiritual well-being of a patient was to become an issue, in my case, threatening my status as a student. Quite satisfied with the physical care I had considered paramount in my duties, I quietly enjoyed the nuances of the incredible episode in which I had apparently contravened the demands of St. Paul.

At the end of the probationer period we would begin our three years of concentrated periods of study in medical, surgical, operating room, obstetrics, pediatrics and several other specialties in each major department, with four months of classroom study and examinations, followed by four months of ward experience, alternating over the three years.

But to begin at the start of student life on the second day of our enrolment in the school we were told to attend a lecture being given by the pathologist in the morgue. The now quite clearly defined program and strict discipline of the institution held us in its firm control. Quaking in our boots, we were issued into the hospital basement to face the aforementioned endurance test.

The tunnel leading to the morgue seemed interminable, smelling as it did of formaldehyde plus the stench of guinea pigs near the laboratory. None of this bolstered one's resolve to grasp the doorknob and to actually enter the morgue. It seemed reasonable to conjecture that such a class would serve the purpose of quickly and efficiently "sorting the wheat from the chaff," as was the term used among the nursing students and interns. How would I fare?

Earnestly resolved at all costs not to flinch, I accepted the traditionally Victorian view handed down to young people in those days that to revoke a decision was to behave in a dishonourable manner. The reverse is now the norm with today's parents suggesting, "Try it out. See if you'll like it or do well, and good luck, whatever you decide."

Within a day or two, three frightened neophytes had disappeared, never to be seen again, on grounds of illness. The truth may have been otherwise. Wisely reasoning that 'the better part of valor is discretion,' or some similar maxim, they may, on reflection, have eventually dared to choose that other career path and entered a teacher-training program. Naturally, I did not allow myself to give them a moment's thought. As a former Girl Guide I thought I knew the implications of the motto, "Be prepared" and meant solemnly to uphold it, whether or not I possessed the required capacity.

In each day's session those of us who remained fought nausea and faintness, yet stayed the course by sheer will-power. We gathered closely, as ordered, around the table on which lay a seemingly larger than life and colourfully imposing yet horrifying cadaver. The morgue was a white floodlit space of unpleasantly antiseptic odor. If questioned on our understanding of the lecture, we were to be prepared to answer in a coherent manner.

In a certain sense, the saving grace in my case, was the admiration I felt for the speaker himself, who was warm, easy to follow, informative, and good-natured. I instantly determined that I would somehow manage to endure the afternoon. Dr. Riley was large and heavy-set, past middle age, with deep blue eyes flashing with intelligence and wit. Smiling and motioning towards the walls, he began by saying, "I have hung my own vivid oil paintings of the foothills landscapes to brighten my workplace." I could see that this remark was a sure way of putting students more at ease. Clearly, he enjoyed an audience.

The image of my father flashed across my mind. This man reminded me of him, robust, tall, benevolent and smiling, like someone I would like to know, for consolation against my own shattering loss of a father, a fellow artist and nature lover. A sense of relief swooped down and enveloped me momentarily and enlivened and comforted me at the same time. I had not even seen a painting in three years, let alone one of my father's. How terribly I missed them and the seductive whiffs of oil paint, turpentine and Dad's pipe smoke wafting around the house on a pleasant Sunday afternoon.

Yet given the tension in that alien, formaldehyde-reeking, white, flood-lit space, I once again froze with horror. Hospitals were not for me even if shame forbade making changes. Given the presence of mind to leave the next day, I could have salvaged the army credits. Any of my adult friends from Dad's lifetime would have told me this, had I found a way to let them know my situation.

The lecture was starting now. My head swam with confusion at the scene around me and within. Terrified of failure to make a reasonable reply to a question, I concentrated on the lecture and the corpse itself, forcing myself with his every word to look down at it, glistening with colour, both compelling and repugnant.

Too young, too naïve to know the ways of the world, I was, of course overly earnest, tense, and serious. I was also totally ignorant of the philosophy of Mehitabel, that cat, that blasé, free-spirited nineteen-twenties American feline. Had I read the book I may have relaxed a little, understood that no one's life is perfect, and that people generally evolve through many different phases of existence and experience before finding themselves. Gaily immortalized by Don Marquis in his book of verse, *Archy and Mehitabel*, she cries out with reckless abandon, "wotthehell, wotthehell," recalling her nine lives, her reincarnation as the pharaoh's cat in ancient Egypt and as Cleopatra herself along the way.

Her philosophizing friend Archy, the cockroach, records her incredible life on a typewriter along with his own story. Unfortunately, such liberating humour was probably quite beyond the crippling effect of the Depression era mentality on most western Canadians. That one could aspire to achieve less than perfection had not yet occurred to me.

Trying desperately to concentrate on the lecture, I was profoundly grateful that Dr. Riley's paintings lent a calming atmosphere to the proceedings. The unfortunate being on the table, so recently human, with strong facial features, still ruddy and healthy looking was not at all what one might imagine in such a place.

The startling juxtaposition of colours on the walls with those of the exposed viscera of the departed coal miner on the table might well have been taken from a page of famous early twentieth century expressionistic art. As in the case of the exposed viscera of the miner, the celebrated French artist, George Rouault also used stark primary tones of cobalt blue, red and black to suggest suffering and injustice. However, this reflection came to me most forcefully later, on seeing Rouault's work in Paris.

The lecture has stayed with me ever since, deepening my sympathy for those forced down mine shafts to scrape out a living in a manner so obviously unsuitable to the modern world. The raw red and blue of the viscera glistened from the exposed torso while the broad expanse of the blackened lung tissue in the open chest cavity revealed that the miner had succumbed to silicosis, a common cause of death among them. As Dr. Riley explained the fate of the unfortunate man, the entire surface of the lungs glistened blue-black from coal dust.

Built on a large, sturdy frame, his handsome face and deep blue eyes still suggested a robust man of early middle age. Those broad, well-worn and capable-looking hands with the blackened nails showed evidence of many years of hard labour. I could not help but wonder what might have been his life and that of his family had he not grown up in the *dustbowl years* of the Great Depression. Immediately I thought of *Grey's Elegy*, a must for high-school students of the nineteen forties. A lament for unrequited aspirations in English village life of the seventeen-fifties, it was a theme which I had often related to my father's short life and my own situation thus far.

In the northern half of the province at the point where prairie gradually gives way to forest and lake country, the open tilled fields catch the eye, glinting blue-black in the sunshine, against as yet unmelted humps of snow along the roadside. Instead of growing grain in fields of his own, as may have been the case before the endless drought of the nineteen thirties, this man may have then been forced down into the mines for financial reasons, only to be overcome by the ingestion of dust particles and his tragic, untimely death.

The second of Dr. Riley's lectures introducing elementary anatomy was delivered around the small body of a young woman who had died of ovarian cancer.

Surely this session was a sugared pill, or so it seemed, for surviving the ordeal of the first demonstration, as less of the anatomy of the body was exposed.

Dramatically, he pointed to the ovaries. "These," he said, seeming to enjoy himself, "are the jewels of the pelvis, small, oval glistening gems." Taken aback, as he drew us closer to the matter at hand, I saw that they did indeed glisten like diamonds. Could there be some ancient connection between women, diamonds and the female anatomy? Perhaps Michelangelo, whom I learned of later and others of the early sixteenth century, could provide the answer, being among the first to try to understand the human body, carrying out their own clandestine studies of cadavers hidden from the disapproving eyes of the Vatican.

Perhaps, on seeing that we were all impressed with this phenomenal discovery, related to our own emerging womanhood, Dr. Riley went on at the end of the lecture to a new but related subject which gave him the chance to announce the breath-taking research which was just then saving the lives of newborns. This development meant that a way had been found to save *blue babies*, known medically as *RH Negative Infants*, accomplished by transfusing the baby with blood compatible to its needs.

In those days everyone had heard of blue babies. No doubt Dr. Riley saw astonishment written on our young, innocent faces when he said, mischievously, "Never consider a proposal of marriage without establishing that you have compatible RH blood factors.

141

Make sure that you visit a laboratory before getting on with the romance." Before him stood a crowd of late teenagers whose expressions must have registered everything from confusion to the suppressed amusement I felt. By this time I wondered whether he had perhaps tried these remarks on his own daughters to humourous effect, just as with us he had enjoyed the satisfaction of causing astonishment to a group of neophytes bound by politeness to refrain from comment. They must have burst out with something like "Oh Dad, what a crazy idea, really!"

Much later, when I had finished my classroom studies in paediatrics, I was involved with the care of several blue babies. As the deadly pallor faded to normal pink skin during the transfusion, the flaccid babe would begin to react with all the normal attributes of a healthy, squirming infant. There was excited rejoicing on all sides at each triumph until the procedure became common practice. Nothing was more difficult to endure for any of the staff than facing a parent whose child for one reason or another had not survived to be carried to her bedside either at birth or later.

After my training in children's illnesses during my senior year, I was called back to the paediatric floor to work alone on the all-night shift. This worried me in case of an emergency situation arose requiring team-work. However, I knew that should I need advice, the supervisor in charge of the hospital that night was someone on whom I could count. When the phone rang on the ward at two that morning, I learned that a sick infant had just been admitted and was about to arrive on the floor.

A limp six-month-old child with an ashen, slightly bluish pallor was handed to me by a silent, impoverished looking couple appearing on the ward without staff escort. That in itself was highly unusual as well as the fact that neither the supervisor nor the doctor appeared in the ensuing hours. After concentrating on the normal care of the critically ill child for the rest of the night I emphasized its condition in my report to the day staff before I went off duty. I assumed that the child would soon be seen by a doctor, yet would not survive the day.

At 10 a.m. I was awakened with an order by a messenger from the office of the Mother Superior to go directly to the hospital priest. Astonished, I dressed and went in search of Father Bernard. I had often wondered whether the plump and affable young cleric lacked dignity in the eyes of his superiors in the Catholic Church. As it happened, this question was settled immediately. As I walked into his office he had already assumed a suitably authoritative expression, sitting stiffly upright at his desk. Bluntly, without a trace of the usual smile, he posed the burning question I had not for a moment anticipated. Leaning forward, pen in hand, as if threatening me with the point, came the blunt query, "Why did you not baptize the child?"

He was referring to the Grey Nuns' Catholic Church ruling that all nursing staff, be they Catholic or Protestant, like myself, were to baptize a dying infant.

Taken by surprise I said, "But, Father, I was completely involved in keeping the infant alive in the absence of a doctor."

This reply did not satisfy the Pope's servitor. He frowned again, insisting sharply, "You know then, don't you, that this poor child will now grovel on the floors of hell for all eternity because of your failure to administer the Right of baptism?" Having heard the catechism taught to my Catholic schoolmates, while we Protestant students were allowed to "turn a deaf ear," this doctrine was known to me and offered no surprise.

Presumably irritated by my failure to show emotion, he read me a long account of what St. Paul had had to say on the matter. The interview ended with his admonition that "You will probably be suspended for a period of time and will graduate after the rest of the class, having to make up the lost time at the end of your studies!" As I had guessed, ultimately I was not suspended; rather, they preferred to have my labour on the night shift. Recently I saw a small report in a newspaper to the effect that since the accession of one of the recent popes, Church dogma on the status of such infants has changed for the better.

As a sign of the times, infant care was about to become a daily concern. In 1945, I had stood on the street and watched the Calgary Highlanders return victoriously from World War II, to the roll of drums, the skirl of bagpipes and wildly cheering crowds. After so long a separation, couples began to have families.

Before long the maternity ward staff could scarcely keep up with the hectic pace of deliveries. Every inch of space had to be negotiated at high speed, night and day, to maintain the service.

By three o'clock in the morning one could expect a rush of mothers-to-be coming by wheel-chair from the front door of the hospital, with the babe sometimes arriving en route to the maternity ward. It was on-the-spot training for the outpost work we might face as graduates. Recalling their own earlier days in rural areas, the older doctors were always quick to remind us of their earlier experiences.

Memorably, in our time as students, one young, popular obstetrician, who worked night and day, succumbed to a fatal heart attack while on duty. More often than any other specialist, Dr. Maxwell would rush in after midnight to take over from us at the end of an often long, difficult labour-room struggle to bring forth the squalling, protesting babe. As if it were his first delivery, he would hold the infant up for the mother to see, bursting into a great smile of obvious triumph. Noticeably overweight for a young man, he may never have found time for fitness. Ironically and tragically his own life came to a sudden end.

On the wards, joy overflowed into noisy, boisterous crowds of friends and family arriving on the wards to visit the mothers and babes. On the other side of this euphoric scenario were the tragedies one can never forget, when mother, child, or both were lost before or after birth. In some cases the infant was abnormal. To break such news or to be a part of the scene at all was a nightmare itself.

Having to deal with one such parent in mourning, I stepped into a private room, a world apart from the public wards. Standing at the window was a tall, striking brunette in a long green satin gown of great luxury awaiting a visit from her husband, a high-ranking military officer. She was surrounded by vase after vase of exotic blooms and ornamental bottles of such fashionable scents as the then very popular, yet costly Shalimar.

So this was how "the other half" lived. In the days which followed I noticed other things new to me, such as Vogue magazine and the glamorous new publication called Flair. There was also a popular novel on wartime France, leading me to discover that crème de menthe and calvados were French liqueurs, the latter being the choice of the hero. I determined to try it if ever I got to Europe.

In that room I saw the gleam of emeralds for the first time, heard of such streets as Rue de Rivoli, Fauberg Ste. Honoré, as well as the famous fashion houses of Givenchy, Balenciaga, Schiaparelli and others of the era. My vision of life in Paris became enmeshed with imagining the life of a correspondent. I saw new worlds take shape before me. The whole concept of a life spent close to art, music and literature came alive as I saw photographs of Paris. Having surrendered at the outset of World War II, it had come out architecturally unscathed from the war, despite Hitler's later monstrous command that it be razed to the ground. It was there, irresistible, waiting to be discovered; not to follow through would indeed be tragic.

When not studying for the next set of exams, I read whatever I could about France and the world, devouring important novels of the day concerning grave contemporary issues. There were fascinating parallels between reading about the war and observations made in the course of a day in the operating room. This was particularly noticeable when tempers flared. Two of the most colorful surgeons and their registered nurse assistants had recently returned from *the front* and worked as a team. They were all possessed of verve, zest and intensity, so different from the subdued student behaviour, dogged by the constant fear of reprimand by supervisors.

To me as a confident student in my senior year, working as the surgeon's assistant, this was life at the front and I was part of it, a welcome change from the usual hushed subservience of our training school. These people appeared to have an amazing degree of what today we call *pizzazz*, working with fervor and good spirits without heed to the frequent visits from the nun responsible for the operating theatres. In this post-war atmosphere, she refrained from comment, keeping her head bowed as if in pious contemplation.

Other post-war changes reverberated around us. In 1947 we heard comment on the news of a noteworthy explosion in a field somewhere near us. It was the blowing of an oil-well, the discovery of Leduc oil field, and the beginning of the oil industry in Alberta, as we know it today. It dominated the headlines and the newsreels for days and was talked of everywhere.

As a result, there were soon more than the usual number of severe burn victims to be treated. There had always been the very difficult challenge of saving the lives of such victims from the explosions in the nearby Turner Valley coal mines at Drumheller. If more than two thirds of the skin were burned, these patients usually died. The technique at the time involved applications of vaseline-type ointment and tight bandaging. Skin grafts were also used, yet more often than not these poor men endured much pain, with little success despite the intensity of our efforts to see them rise from their beds and go home.

At the same time immigrants suffering from a number of chronic, disabling illnesses were arriving in large numbers from Europe. Tuberculosis and poliomyelitis were treated elsewhere. Osteomyelitis, an infection of the bone was prevalent, and like tuberculosis, was difficult to treat without antibiotics. Even though penicillin had been developed in time to treat the Allied troops, it was released for use in our Calgary hospital only in the late nineteen forties.

Penicillin was first administered on our wards in injectable form. Working with only a Bunsen burner to melt the pellet of penicillin in peanut oil, we then forced it, with difficulty, through an out-sized syringe and needle every three hours, day and night, into the buttocks of the unsuspecting patient. Invariably a hard, painful lump developed at the site of the injection, requiring the application of hot compresses for several days to encourage absorption of the congealed oil. While quite laughable today, it caused no mirth for our patients or the battlefront medical units.

Despite wrapping the syringes in hot towels, it was practically impossible to carry a dozen doses of the waxy penicillin mixture along the hallways and into the wards before it cooled, hardened and was even more difficult to force through the syringe. Fortunately this was a short-lived period of misery for the patients as the antibiotic soon became available in easily administered injectable clear liquid form. Streptomycin made is appearance shortly afterwards and as time went on other antibiotics were developed.

Thanks to penicillin, streptomycin, and other antibiotics, tuberculosis soon ceased to be the deadly scourge of the ages. While we did not treat such patients at our hospital, everyone rejoiced that the drugs were so effective as to eventually eradicate the disease in Canada. Control of poliomyelitis, also treated elsewhere, had to wait for the Salk vaccine in 1952. Heart, stroke and cancer victims, and many others with untreatable diseases, spent long periods of time as full bed-rest patients, with no research developments yet available to improve their situations.

The resulting proliferation of blood clots, pneumonia, bedsores and emotional problems, together with the lack of modern nutritional practices or development in physiotherapy increased their misfortunes.

Consequently the medical wards presented an enormous challenge to provide adequate care for large numbers of long-term patients whose physicians were as yet without recourse to modern laboratories, x-ray, pharmaceuticals, or surgery.

Relief of severe pain was accomplished by laboriously grinding rock-hard tablets of morphine or other narcotic to a powder with mortar and pestle. Adding water to it on a spoon to dissolve it over a Bunsen burner, it was then ready to draw up into the syringe. In time, the pharmaceutical companies began to supply these narcotic drugs and many other medications in tiny glass vials. Taking only a second to saw the top off the vial, draw the prepared dosage into the syringe, one could proceed much more quickly to the patient in desperate need of instant relief.

Lesser painkillers, or sedatives such as the barbiturates caused a number of unfortunate side effects. As one MD making his rounds on the ward remarked with deep disgust in a loud and irate voice, "The barbiturates should all be dumped into the Pacific ocean!" With that he made his noisy, complaining, and angry departure from the floor. We all felt the same way, being forced to administer them to our long-suffering patients with whom we sympathized.

As someone quipped, "What about the poor fish in the ocean?" Finally, modern pharmaceutical companies developed a whole gamut of less stupefying sedation. Before the dawn of modern scientific research into the major scourges of mankind, medical care of long-term patients was a tough challenge for everyone involved.

For young, healthy students, previously unaccustomed to the sight of degeneration of the body, that aspect of the human condition came as a major shock in learning to deal with suffering. At the very idea that we could ever suffer from age ourselves, we told each other hilariously, "It could never happen to us, of course not!" We felt sure that we were young and healthy and that we had been given a better start in life than all the down-trodden people whom we had tried to help, both older and worn out by the immigrant experience and the years of the Great Depression. In a way we were right. Medical progress in the last half century has made it possible for us to avoid many of the scourges of the past and to enjoy living longer, more fit, privileged lives.

As I was about to graduate in the closing months of 1949, my return from a day's leave made me think of my regard for the old building in which I had worked so exhaustively, pushed myself to the limit, and learned so much about life. At the moment caught up in watching the magic of the sunset playing on the dark upper windows of the facade, my mind darted from room to room, behind those windows, to the patients in the beds. On the outside, so deceivingly quiet in the fading light, the building was in fact a seething inferno of intense, highly organized effort to make suffering bearable, to save lives.

By this time I would have done anything to become a physician, to be entirely capable of controlling suffering, of bringing a return to health. A few nurses across Canada actually went on into medicine over the years. I knew however that I lacked the tremendous stamina also required of an intern, apart from academic and financial considerations. Later, I was to learn that the Soviet Union picked some of its future medical students from the ranks of its most experienced and satisfactory senior nursing staff. It would seem to be one way to ensure the complete dedication essential in such a career.

One evening as I walked towards the building, thinking of the suffering patients, the image of a familiar wartime newsreel scene flashed momentarily across my mind. A Nazi aircraft released its deadly cargo over a roof clearly marked with the insignia of the "International Red Cross." Immediately, of course, I realized perhaps more vividly than usual, the struggle between compassion and brutality, the folly of our civilization. We struggle to save humanity, even one life at a time, only to see multitudes struck down as if life had no meaning. While it was much too soon to begin to forget the images of World War II, there was a certain idealistic dream alive then, in 1949, the fragile hope of a world without war.

Surprisingly, after all my most demanding struggles to succeed, to keep up the pace physically as well as professionally, I felt a small tinge of satisfaction and even gratitude at having been part of the intense, daily and universal effort to save lives despite the grim news from the killing fields. I felt as if I had completed an enforced national service, as the British had done in wartime. I was gratified in having gained the finish line.

There was now only one dream for the future in my thoughts. Of course, for a long time it would be impossible to enter university. Yet I could imagine that this new post-war world might lead eventually to the reward of a degree and a writing career. For now, it was essential to refuse all offers of marriage, or of nursing positions reported every day, being offered to the graduating class of 1949, be it in the north, in California or wherever else. As someone now older and wiser, it was time to work out a serious plan for the next twelve months.

Ali Baba and the Sea

A week after the registered nurses graduation exercises in 1949, I happened to meet some old friends from school days, excited to be enroute to study in Paris on an art scholarship. It was the first time I had ever heard of scholarships for ordinary Canadians. With the intention of following it up with a "shoe-string" or low-budget tour of Europe, it seemed an excellent plan. Why had I lacked the curiosity to explore scholarships three years ago, before disappearing into a world of hard labour?

Another close friend of mine recently graduated from university was working in Geneva. With my background in the French language, and now with friends located in two French-speaking countries, I soon convinced myself that I must join them for a year or so before devoting myself to assisting my family. Through membership in the International Nurses Association in London, I was free to work in hospitals in western Europe. Needless to say, I had always dreamed foolishly of someday becoming a professionally trained journal-

ist on overseas assignment. Now, at least, on the typewriter I might have the brief opportunity to observe and
to record my impressions of post-war Europe. Being my
father's daughter, it was an obsession I could not shake.
I would not give up.

A year later I had arranged a working passage on
a ship. At that time, every adventurous young person
longing to see the world, chose this traditional route, air
travel being considered new and impossibly expensive.
The contract issued by the Department of Health and
Welfare, Canada, was to medically assist and provide
isolation technique for a patient with two infectious diseases being returned to Britain. Described officially as
an 'alien' in the government terminology of the post-war
era, this fifty-year old Arab seaman had been diagnosed
with tuberculosis and advanced or third-stage syphilis
causing mental confusion. Impossible to transport by
air on either count, he would travel by ship. I had been
chosen, in part at least, due to my prior experience in
working with tuberculosis control among the aboriginal
population, as well as my contact with the different attitudes, customs and languages of a minority group.

During the months of waiting for the ship to
arrive, I had been astonished, like everyone else
involved, at the sudden progress in the treatment of
tuberculosis. As part of an operating room team, of a
state of the art surgical unit, I had assisted with the
new procedure to remove sections of lobes, or entire
lobes, of tubercular lung tissue. The recent availability
of penicillin and expert recovery-room care meant that,

in a short time, young long-term care patients were no longer left to die but were returned to good health. No longer would we see poor sixteen-year old girls dying on the wards looking like old women. After this impressive, important experience, it was with a certain degree of reluctance that I embarked upon the next great adventure of my life.

Ali, the tubercular, syphilitic patient for whose well-being I was now assigned was actually beyond recuperation. As a stoker on British merchant navy ships based in Liverpool, he had spent his life shoveling coal all day and allegedly slept with rats gnawing at his toes. With his ship in port at Vancouver to pick up cargo, he had been examined by the health authorities, diagnosed and then held with others of his kind in a special unit in New Westminster, B.C. How many times this essential health work went on in all the ports of the world in modern times gives one cause to marvel.

On the appointed day I set out to meet the patient. I wore the smart-looking, full-dress Canadian registered nurse regalia, mandatory at that time, with knee-length, black, scarlet-lined wool cape, cap and stiffly starched white uniform, matching white stockings and shoes. Shown into a large cheerful-looking hospital ward, I saw dozens of brown-skinned men of one nationality and another, sitting cross-legged on their pristine white beds over steaming bowls of rice. Each wore a colorful red or multi-colored cap or fez. As I took in the incredibly exotic scene, they in turn seemed to look curiously, yet pleasantly in my direction.

Ali Ahmed, or 'Ali Baba'.
Sketch: M. Lanham.

Then my eyes fixed on the far walls, only to behold
the flowing white garb of their jailers, three young nuns,
arms folded and smiling, as well as a doctor who had
prepared the medication and the orders for me to use
on board. Just then one of these nurses approached me,
her prayer beads tinkling pleasantly on a cord from her

waist. She led me down an aisle of tightly packed beds to meet Ali Ahmed, or 'Ali Baba' as we were to call him affectionately amongst ourselves on shipboard.

Now that he occupied the spotlight, Ali was of course at a loss for words. Later I would find out what a chatterbox this silent, middle-aged man could be. He was of small, stocky build, dark and swarthy, with a lined face denoting the hardships of a life of labour, of deprivation, yet there remained a certain colour and vitality about him. As he sat upright in bed taking me in, I tried in vain to get him to speak with me. The nun then led me to the doctor to arrange for the medications to be delivered to the ship. I thanked the nuns and departed.

As directed, I went to the port baggage office the following morning to pick up Ali's burlap sack of "loot" collected on this last trip around the world and then took it by cab to the dock to find the berth occupied by the Motor Vessel Cape Hawke. A small ship of only three thousand tons, it was somewhat difficult to locate in the line-up of larger vessels. However, quite suddenly I was being helped up the gangplank by a member of the crew with Ali's sack, and shown aboard this typical old World War II British freighter. Waiting to welcome me, once I alighted from the gangplank into the ship, was the fatherly Captain Peter Wallace. As I surmised then and later confirmed, he was a gentleman, a disciplinarian and an admirable figure of authority.

After being shown to my cabin in the officer's quarters, on the raised section of the vessel towards the prow, or forward end of the vessel called the "Bridge," I was asked to then report to the Captain's sitting-room on the same hallway. It was a leisurely, dignified discussion which allowed him the opportunity to assess his new working passenger, also, of course, designated as an officer, rather than crew member. It was clear that he expected a good performance on my part.

Of prime importance to him was reassurance that the 'isolation technique' for tuberculosis which he had been promised by the government would be rigidly applied, with strict confinement of the patient to the 'Sick Bay.' Should help in restraining him at any time be required, two able-bodied young seamen would be sent to control him, allowing me to administer sedation. As an Arab had the right to carry a knife, possibly hidden in his sack, I was to alert Captain Wallace to confiscate it if trouble arose over medication or for any other reason.

As he had now voiced his concerns about carrying out the government contract from his point of view and mine, he asked very pleasantly if I would care "for a little something" from his liquor cabinet. I could see the satisfaction on his face when I declined. He could now be sure that I would observe the rules of his "dry" ship. The interview ended with a comment about life at sea, the long months alone, writing letters, reading and waiting at every port for mail from his wife and teen-age children in Scotland. Dismissing me finally with a smile and a handshake he said, quite softly, "And I want you to leave this ship just as you are now." Certainly a gentleman and a man of admirable tact!

I went back to my cabin down the hall to unpack before the evening meal when I would meet the other officers. Already assured by the interview that we saw "eye to eye" and that the trip would probably go well, I soon learned that Captain Wallace and others on the ship were veterans of the gruelling five-year wartime merchant navy struggle to keep the sea-lanes open for the oil supplied by the Allies. As they said, he was well acquainted with the kind of old Liberty ship which he now commanded on this last lap of one of his many nine-month global navigations. Quite recently I learned that Captain Wallace had followed the family tradition of more than a century of service at sea. At the time, I had no idea of the heroic Sir William Wallace of thirteenth-century Scottish and English history.

On the second day, Ali Baba, more correctly Ali Ahmed, was carried onto the ship on a stretcher. As if on a litter borne by slaves, he wore colourful striped pyjamas, a red striped fez, and was set down by the attendants in the Sick Bay bed, looking as I imagined, somewhat reminiscent of a potentate from some mysterious far-away kingdom. To those of us in 1950 not yet used to the sight of men with coloured head-gear, eyes outlined with kohl, the neck embellished with a chain and dangling silvered perfume amulet, it was an amazing spectacle.

Knowing the importance of his burlap *sack of loot,* as it was called in the Merchant Navy, the attendants assured him that it would be safe, placed at the back of the room. To Ali, and his kind, his sack represented the financial success of his year in ports around the world, just as if he had been a sheikh travelling with saddle-bags and chests in transit on the desert. Given that Arabs on this ship were permitted to carry a knife, one could not be too careful in one's dealings with them. Earlier in the day I had set the stage for his arrival as an 'isolation technique' patient by setting bowls of disinfectant, gowns, masks, gloves, syringes and medication along the opposite wall from his bed.

The year before, I had run into one other such exotic patient in the middle of the night in a hospital emergency room in Victoria, B.C. Suddenly, on a stretcher before us, under the harsh lights of the examining table, was an Asian, an old man with a long white beard, dressed in what we would call an ancient costume, complete with prayer beads. He was exactly like the traditional Oriental figurines of the day, often displayed beside the ginger jars in the windows of Chinese neighbourhood shops around the city. As he spoke no English, looked at us in fear and astonishment and then expired, we were too late to help him or to get to know what had appeared to be an intriguing figurine come to life. The police said they had noticed a rotting orange in the window of an empty shed. Opening the door, they found the poor old man, possibly starving, whom they could only surmise had just recently arrived on a *junk* from across the Pacific.

And now here was Ali, another most unusual character whom I certainly meant to keep alive and as comfortable as possible for the estimated six-week voyage. The would-be reporter in me decided to use my typewriter on the deck to write about him. The nuns had sent him along well-sedated, calm and quite ready to enjoy the morning's excitement of getting settled before lunch. No doubt he was delighted at the prospect of returning home to *Libberpol* or Liverpool.

As if we were old friends, the silent man of yesterday's visit suddenly burst out with a volley of Liverpudlian-English hitting my ears at first like some sort of unintelligible gibberish. Given that he was such a chatterbox, I was soon surprised and gratified to be able to make sense of it. Perhaps his most frequent and impassioned refrain was, "My god jus' like yo' god, Seesta," said with an unexpected sort of delight and persistent enthusiasm.

Always politely using the title "sister" for nurse, as in common use in Britain at that time, Ali displayed an unfailing spirit of good-will and comradeship to his remarks. Being unable myself to discuss the "Almighty" with any suitable comment, I could only nod, smile and keep on agreeing with him as ardently as possible. This response seemed to suffice. At the time, 1950, I was scarcely aware of the importance of Allah to a large part of the globe.

Totally unaware of the Muslim world, except for the European confrontation in the Crusades, nearly a thousand years ago, I was not aware that the Arabs were among the earliest known navigators and traders, plying the unknown seas from Arabia, to Africa, to India and China. In his passion to collect *loot* from ports around the world, he was in a sense a latter-day version of those who went before him, rather than merely a stoker on an old, battered World War II cargo vessel of the British Merchant Service.

Ali.
Sketch: M. Lanham.

With some perplexity at his unexpected enthusiasm for discussion, having just met, I was also touched
by and appreciated this first contact with the Muslim
world. I not only wrote his comments in my journal,
but did sketches of him, one or two of which have hung
on my walls throughout the years. One can never know
whether or not his desire to pour out his thoughts was
normal or drug-induced. In any event it was a precious

encounter with another, then seemingly remote, exotic part of the world.

Remarkably, despite his excitement he never let slip an inappropriate word, nor did he ever remove his hand-crocheted fez, striped with red, green and yellow. Not only was it a matter of religion, but it had been made for him by his wife. Whenever he talked of her, he would politely draw my attention to the poster of Yvonne de Carlo, a glamorous and exotic film star of the era, which he kept in a small drawer beside the bed.

"Seesta, Seesta, my wife, she look jus' like dis', I buy her in de market in Libberpol from her mudder when she tirteen, Seesta, she bery good wife, Seesta."

I pinned it to the wall for him. This reminder of home made him think of the things in his attic. I had only to promise him that I would go to visit at "tirteen, Upper Barlement Street," or Upper Parliament street, and he would exclaim enthusiastically, " my wife, she give you six, ten, twelve yards bery good silk, Seesta, what you like." He would spread his arms, the legs of his striped pyjamas hanging over the side of the bed or knees drawn up tight in front of him, extending his arms even wider as he dreamed of the luxuries he offered.

Perhaps as he talked he became a merchant showing off his diaphanous treasures in the market back in Aden, in the Gulf of Arabia, a latter-day Sinbad the Sailor, of the Arabian Nights. The black, kohl-lined eyes would widen dramatically as his delight at his seafaring deals, his acquisitions from the previous trips came to mind. Although I would have been reluctant to look for him in Liverpool, I remained curious about his address. Sadly, I have never found anyone to tell me about it. Perhaps I would see a complete redevelopment of the area and go away trying to envisage his world as it was, customers going and coming throughout the day.

Between the prescribed morphine induced sleeps he would regale me with the story of the golden coins, among the things in that sack at the back of the Sick Bay. As well as fine silk, his Liverpool attic boasted coins he had traded and made smart deals for, all over the world. It seemed like a tall tale, but he claimed that there was no trouble getting them through customs offices as long as the coins were sewn into the heels and soles of sandals. During this latest trip the ship had docked at Caleo, Peru, on the way north to Victoria. He had had tremendously good luck in getting his hands on the most valuable silver coins and in getting them stitched into the soles and heels of ladies' platform sandals. Caleo had treated him 'bery good!'

Sandals, Seesta! I find shoemaker, he cut open heels and soles like dis," he said as held his slipper to demonstrate, "I give you when you come my house. You come my house, Seesta!"

I had heard from the officers and the Chief Steward that the delectable crayfish on my plate that night was also from the *victuallers* in Caleo. They had all enjoyed the visit so much that they repeatedly expressed their regret at not being able to take me there. Presumably their interests in the place were different from Ali's.

When it came to ports he had found intriguing, it was evident that he would be pleased enough to call Marseille home, rather even than *Libberpol.* "Now there was the city for a man, the city of dreams," he might have said, had he been fluent in English. It was a great place to buy a good knife, a dagger, the kind a man must always carry. The very best were to be found in certain special, secret parts of the great port seething with all kinds of dangers which he could face when carrying one. I could just imagine the deadly tool tucked away in the sack of loot in this very room. Fortunately he did not then suggest showing it to me.

My floating hotel, Officers' quarters, dining room, sun-bathing, star-gazing and storm-watching.

There were long, confused tales of his intrigues, the great dangers in being involved in the trade of cocaine and other drugs. He had bought, sold and used them himself. The eyes narrowed and glinted as he recalled the especially fine daggers to be found in Marseille, even under bridges where the women, too, waited to ply their trade. "Bery good daggers, Seesta, and ze womans!" He was an old syphilitic who had probably stopped in many of the lairs, caves and dens of the world. What else could a man do when one had to sleep in the boiler room of a dirty British freighter for months at a time, with the hard work, the cold, the poor food and the rats biting the toes? His dark eyes flashed as his voice thickened to a growl with anger. It was time to sedate him with more morphine.

We had lifted anchor in Victoria on the second evening, as I had been told we would do, taken on lumber further up the coast to add *ballast,* for buoyancy of the heavily laden vessel, and then steered into open sea. Meanwhile I had taken the precaution of walking back and forth around the vessel to become accustomed to the gentle rhythm, the movement beneath my feet, it being crucial not to succumb to sea-sickness. Unlike a passenger, I had to fulfill definite obligations as an employee on the ship. Delighted to find that the magical pitch and roll of the waves suited me as if I had been born on water, the many moods of the sea were to make me love it passionately.

With every passing day the joy of gliding south over that great, calm, incredibly blue Pacific ocean increased my amazement. At the same time it would fulfill the dream of going to London, Paris and who knows where. That I was alone seemed unfortunate, but I knew that many a traveller had endured solitude in the quest for knowledge or a reward of one kind or another. I was on the way now, with no way of changing the course of events had I so wished. The Motor Vessel Cape Hawke and the sea were now my masters as we skimmed along toward Panama at an easy-going eleven knots, leaving me nothing to do outside the Sick Bay but gloat over the view from the deck. Spellbound on a dazzling blue saucer without a shore in sight, I recorded it all with my typewriter. In the face of the enormity, the magnificence of the cosmos about me, the sketchbook was a poor tool in my hands.

By the time we approached the waters off California, a warmer sun began to caress the skin as I sat on the deck after lunch during Ali's morphine-induced siesta. Skipping over the sparkling deep blue waters, dolphins began to make their appearance, first a few, and then large numbers bounding toward the ship in military formations, like patterns of geese at migration time in northern skies.

Not only were they eager to reach the ship, but also to rub themselves against the sides of the small vessel, grinning up at us, extending their bodies upwards so that we could all but touch them. Ranged out over the semicircular expanse to starboard of the great blue rimless saucer, literally hundreds of dolphins plunged and rose in perfect geometric forma-

tion, like a well-designed and spectacular performance, leaping, racing towards us from as far away as
the eye could see. A breathtaking sight, as if identical
platoons of winged seahorses, glinting in the brilliant
sun, had come to life, soaring out of the indescribable
deep blue depths.

But suddenly they stopped short, precisely, on cue,
as if brilliantly choreographed. In less than a second
most had vanished back into the deep. The remaining
few raced to the side of the ship, rubbed against it, leapt
up with heads held high as if to make eye contact, to
grin, to wink as if to say, "Come on, please, stroke my
snout." Irrationally, quietly, I begged, "Don't go. Please
stay a minute" as I tried to reach them with my outstretched finger tips. With the speed of lightning they
disappeared into the sea again. The incredible act of
magic was over. The curtain fell. The sea was empty.
No amount of applause could induce an encore. Then,
one day, suddenly it would happen again, and again,
and again.

Folklore has it that dolphins have been known to
try to assist shipwrecked humankind. Apparently now
discredited, the tale has a certain appeal, considering
the bond, the mysterious affinity one feels from such
a show, much as one does with a friendly dog, such as
a black Labrador, for instance, who also grins, wags,
makes eye contact and seems to show great enthusiasm, warmth, and intelligence.

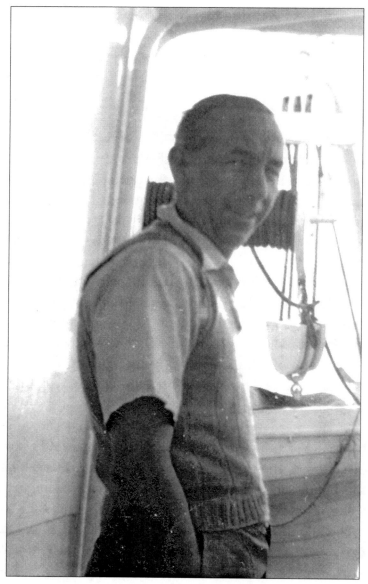

Captain Peter Wallace tells me a tall tale.

En route to Panama. Sliding softly over a great blue saucer, the Pacific Ocean.

Seeing me out on the deck one day, Captain Wallace told me to hurry to the fo'c's'le head, or forecastle of the ship "to see the flying fish fluttering about on their great gauzy rosy-orange wings." Skeptically, I asked "why can't I see them on this part of the deck also?" I was joking of course. Obviously he found it difficult not to break into laughter at this point, rare as that was for so serious an individual. I glanced at the "forward" deck and saw that they were about a foot long, slim, silvery-blue fish with fragile, elongated wings to match. Especially in the early mornings they were numerous, carried by the breeze and the spray, fluttering daintily on to the boards, like imaginary silvery creatures in a book of tall tales.

Clearly I was not the first of the 'lady passengers' put to the test; the Captain's wife and daughters having travelled with him may have also been victims of his teasing. Others may have known the old Rudyard Kipling song with the lines, "On the road to Mandalay-ay, Where the flying-fishes play..." building up colourful fantasies appealing to imaginative women.

About that time, in the warm waters off Central America, I happened to be standing at the starboard railing alone one afternoon at the right moment to be taken by surprise at a flash of glinting iridescent emerald green immediately below me on the surface of the water. Taking another look, I saw a giant sea-turtle, swimming by within a yard of the side of the ship, with the water rippling over its shell, one could take it that this creature was intent on a race. Otherwise, with the vastness of the ocean, why did it choose to stay so close to the side as if it wanted company? Were we usurping its usual route, pushing it further away from the shore than usual?

Although this was not at Galapagos, west of Ecuador, I was reminded of the world of Charles Darwin and his book *The Beagle* in which he recorded natural history. On such a small freighter as this we were so much closer to the creatures of the deep than on an ocean liner and able to enjoy them at close range.

"How fortunate I am," I thought, as usual scarcely able to believe that this was anything but a dream.

Yet much more was in store. Later, when reading Melville's great work, *Moby Dick*, at university, those poetic lines written by a master, with pages and pages of them about the sea itself, its moods, colours, rhythms, I was able to relive the experience. Often skipped over by those who seek to know only the story at the heart of the great literary work, a great deal of its value to those who love the sea is ignored.

The next day we travelled so close to the coast of El Salvador that for the first time I was able to see the shore clearly. I raced to the cabin to bring my art supplies on deck. The mountain-sides were on fire with blossoms. A blaze of vivid orange-red flowering vegetation glowed in the deep green forest of a mysterious land. Hurriedly I sketched the arresting sight in pastels. I was eager to show it to Ali, who was, after all, never without comment.

It was time to leave the deck, to prepare treatment for him and to wake him up for 'tea' and dinner. He rarely begged to go on deck, unless extremely disoriented, which then required several strong seamen to restrain him for further sedation. Whether or not he had any idea of the fascination of sea creatures or exotic coastlines, I never knew. As he had been so happy to tell me, *fishing for loot* in foreign ports was his real sport.

When I entered the Sick Bay I saw the familiar sight of the short, round body hunched forward on the narrow hospital bed, softly intoning his prayers to Allah, the red striped fez in place as usual. Realizing that he was in a calm state of mind, I decided, as I had always intended, to make a quick sketch of him. I offered him paper and crayons in case he would like to amuse himself with colour. Not surprisingly, he declined such a strange new idea, while being obviously pleased at the attention being bestowed on him. As usual he reminded me that "My God, jus' like yo' God, Seesta!" I agreed just as cheerfully.

Sitting upright in bed, he was the perfect portrait sitter. Working quickly so as not to try his patience, moments later I had a coloured sketch of him in profile. Holding it up for him to approve or disclaim against, he burst out with an impassioned, "Seesta, Seesta, why fo' you not make me like Ingliss gen-l-man?"

"Well Ali, because you are wearing your own hat, your fez," was all I could think of saying, trying with difficulty, not to show amusement and astonishment at his concern. He had expected much more of my talents!

Had he not left me speechless, protesting loudly and gesticulating wildly about the shape of Inglissmens' hats, I might have said the truth, that I liked his colourful red, gold, green striped fez so much better. One often thinks of these things too late. Probably he had found me heartless not to have drawn him as he may have seen himself in some mad dream of 'Inglissmen' in a bowler hat, rather than as he had been, down in the boiler-room of some derelict freighter. Had it occurred to me at the time, amused as I was, I should have rectified the omission, with a corrected drawing, complete with the preferred haberdashery.

It wouldn't have been much to offer a poor, fatally ill human being still trying to wring some pleasure out of his existence. After all, he had always seen himself as a merchant-king on the high seas, perhaps a tradition passed down to him from antiquity to search out trade across the world's exciting ports of call. Like all of us, they wanted to get the most out of the great voyage of life. For Ali, it might have been only a hat, or imagining himself in a different role. Why not turn the tables for once? Why not pretend to be a rich "gen-l-man" in London in a bowler hat? Who knows what was in his mind?

*Andy appeared in full dress uniform of his rank when
greeting the pilot taking us trough the locks.*

Panama

A soft, bumping sensation woke me at dawn the next day. We were moored on a sandbar, only to slide gently off it in a few minutes. Looking about me from my cabin port-hole, I saw an amazingly attractive landscape of palm trees, exotic blooms and a small sandy looking formation which the Captain referred to as a "sugarloaf" mountain. Apparently we had reached the area of the Panama Canal during the night. "Wonderful!" I said to the tropics, "just gorgeous!"

I was aware too of the sound of heightened activity around the ship. As I hurried onto the main deck I saw a billowing sunrise casting a long green shadow on an almost apple-green and white Panama. A large green fortress-like rock island lay in front of us, with continuous lines of mountains to the left, the city of Bilboa to the right. Despite our having arrived there in time to be taken through the locks at the appointed hour, plans had changed due to the schedule for annual cleaning of the mechanism itself. Our passage had been postponed by twenty-four hours.

Approaching the lock.

To the lock.

Waiting in a line-up of ships at anchor all around us, I was jolted into the reality that the everyday world was once again very much with us. Evidently, it was a crowded ocean after all! We had not been alone with nature on that magnificent blue Pacific as I had thought. Closest to us was a reeking sulphur ship with rusting hull, a *red devil* logo on the side and the poverty-stricken looking crew lolling about the railings. Non-descript vessels of all kinds, were in the line-ups for the locks, including ocean liners with passengers on the decks waving and smiling as if in need of new company.

Displayed on almost every square foot of wall in the canal area was the American flag announcing the U.S. presence so strongly as if to almost suggest at first glance that we were entering a war zone. Nearby lay a gleaming white banana boat and two freighters similar to our own. Three small craft, marked U.S.A., pulled up on our starboard side, the first, disbursing the pilot while the second held the crew. The third, a speed-boat flying a Panama Canal pennant was piled high with huge bunches of green bananas. Standing nearby was a tall, loose-jointed native wearing a padded orange life jacket marked U.S.A. shouting orders to our crew waiting on the deck to lower the rope ladder for the pilot.

Climbing up and onto the deck he was now responsible to guide our ship, the small three-thousand ton Cape Hawke, through the locks to the Caribbean. It was then the turn of boat number two to come to the side, allowing its crew from Panama to scale the rope ladder and come roaring over the side, a seething mass of swarthy workers in search of breakfast on our ship. Apparently this was a normal ritual and no surprise to anyone but me. Piles of eggs and bacon had been laid out for them on the deck by chief steward Albert Dobson, as a routine part of passing through the canal.

Warned to keep away from them, I looked down from the bridge to see swarms of small, dark men attacking their windfall meal ravenously, whole fried eggs dangling from mouths in the rush to get more food than others. Small, very agile, they were known for their ability to strip a ship of its belongings with lightning speed and dexterity. Consequently the captain had given repeated orders that all belongings must be secured and the portholes and doors locked with special care.

Ali was aware that we had reached a port. At about eight o'clock, after trying to convince him of the impossibility of getting off the ship to talk with the U.S. immigration officials as he had imagined, I locked his door and left him with his breakfast for a few moments. Dashing to the deck for a quick glimpse, I saw that we were proceeding slowly towards the locks. Breathtaking scenery with palm trees, bursts of waxy, scent-laden blossoms, cerise, purple and golden orange were momentarily nearly close enough to touch as we moved along. Red flat-topped buildings were perched on the sides of ravines and in clusters along the canal.

In the lock.

After I had given Ali his next dose of morphine to allow him four hours free of confusion about getting a shore-leave, I ran up to Monkey Island, the top bridge on the ship and watched the procedure of guiding us through the first of three locks. The pilot directed the *mule drivers,* propelling the ship along the canal and elevating it, in so doing, from lock to lock. The iron mules or electric cars were pulling us through the narrow confines of the canal. These machines plied quietly ahead with what immediately reminded me of the undulating rhythmic locomotion of a caterpillar moving along a branch. Colourful in stripes and straw hat, the pilot would raise his arms to right and left, signifying orders to the mule drivers.

Into Gatun Lake.

About noon, in quiet and orderly fashion we were delivered through the first three locks and went skimming into Gatun Lake, gliding close by small palm-treed islands, all afternoon expecting to see a crocodile. Re-entering the locks to return to sea level began at supper-time and as the tropical evening quickly overtook us, the operation proceeded in darkness under a myriad of glittering coloured lights, the mules red, the water in the canal a light iridescent green. By ten o'clock we had cleared the locks and took leave of the pilot as he prepared to depart in the waiting craft.

It had been an eventful day, yet unfortunately, for Ali not a happy one. By necessity, he had missed the excitement and was still insisting that he get off the ship.

Meanwhile, the crew were intent on taking on 'stores,' lassoing crates of carrots and other produce from the natives standing by in the small waiting craft full of provisions to haul up over the deck. A noisy altercation ensued between the natives below and the jovial young 'Birken'ed boys' of our crew from Birkenhead, England, as a crate of oranges broke open and spilled into the sea along with sundry other bits and pieces. Tired of this noisy interchange, Captain Wallace, Andrew, first mate, and James, the second mate and I stayed on the bridge to enjoy the simple pleasure of the silence of the warm, tropical night until the lights of Colon Cristobel faded away. We were now well out into the Caribbean at last "where the trade winds blow." Even so, it was sad to have left the Pacific behind.

One of several tiny islands in the lake.

Almost ahead of time, the breeze had come up to relieve the heat of the day, though so too had the moon. Marvelous as it was, my day having begun at dawn, I was eager to visit Ali and retire to my cabin. I hoped that by morning he would forget Panama. In another two weeks or so he would see that wife of his. "Seesta, Seesta, she look jus' like dis picture, Yvonne de Carlo," he would say to me again and again. Then he would add with great enthusiasm, "She give you twelve yards pure silk, Seesta," holding his arms wider and wider as if once more to display his shimmering wares back there in *Libberpol*.

By the next day we were cruising along the coast of Venezuela heading for the fuelling station at Bullen Bay, Curacao, Dutch West Indies. As soon as we dropped anchor we were enveloped by a sickening odor of oil from the station itself. Even Andrew, the normally good-natured first mate was disWillted to be stuck overnight in such a place. Newly married, he was anxious to get home to Glasgow. Furthermore, there would be no shore leave to go by cab to the capital city of Willemstad. Apparently, everyone was irritable at the thought of not being able to at least relax ashore with a 'pint' or two.

The real trouble was that on the way to Victoria, British Columbia, the officers and crew had spent a few days loading in Cuba which they and their passengers had greatly enjoyed. In addition, they had always, up to the present, offered time in port to passengers. This time, it seemed, one had to settle for the Dutch fuelling station for lack of an interesting port nearby.

Although I felt no need to go ashore anywhere, I had begun to think that I would find no coffee before arriving in Britain unless I went ashore. As an addict, it came as a shock to be forced to settle for the steward's 'cha,' or weak tea, ever since leaving Canada, there being coffee plantations all around us in the tropics. Eventually, Captain Wallace decided that like previous passengers I was to be allowed one port stop, even if it were not to be Cuba, their own preferred haven. I was to be taken for a walk along the ocean front that evening, after Ali went to sleep, and into Curacao's main town of Willemstad in the morning.

Our only funnel hissed and puffed as if to claim a certain degree of respect, or so I was told.

While this discussion had been going on I had been looking over the side, trying to ignore the stench of the fuelling station beside us. Suddenly I caught a glimpse of a shaft of brilliant light in the dark water beneath me. Between the pier and the side of the ship, sheer iridescent emerald in the fading light reflecting the coral bottom, the elegant black shape of a shark's fin cut through the water. It was the only one I saw on the entire voyage.

Uhmm..... a delicate rustling sound in the moonlight.

Selecting first mate Andrew Goldie as tour leader for the passenger excursion, Captain Wallace asked me if I agreed with the plan. And so, along with James, the second mate, I climbed over the railing, as Ali slept through his prescribed dose of morphine. With the tranquil green, yet possibly shark-ridden sea below, I descended the rope ladder and enjoyed what was surely one of the great walks of a lifetime. Moonlit, with the Southern Cross and the Milky Way overhead, a light soft breeze rustled almost imperceptibly in the palm trees along the path beside the pink sand of the beach. Lightly treading the well-worn way, words came in hushed tones of wonder. As a northerner, it was difficult to imagine that especially in January such a spellbinding place could exist.

Two tall, white, long-legged birds stood among the moonlit palm trees, drinking from small pools dotted around the vegetation on the other side of the road. Here and there one heard the munching of a single cow, while nearby lay perhaps a dozen sleeping goats lined up in a row, cheeks on the cool road surface, long sleek bodies on the grass. Beauty and harmony were everywhere.

Further on, a small, attractive black boy strolled towards us carrying a basket, then a late model sports car purred along very softly, turning into a driveway. As the driver did so, his lights further illuminated great waxy blooms, scarlet, crimson, orange, tumbling over the walls. Set well back from the road was a row of luxurious houses, softly-lit behind the greenery at the roadside. The French doors stood open to let in the cool scented enchantment of the night while the sounds of Beethoven's Ninth Symphony fell on my surprised and grateful ears.

"Are these the homes of the Dutch administrators?" I wondered aloud. "Or oil company executives?" It didn't matter, but signs of an imperial past can be interesting. "Perhaps tomorrow I will get a glimpse of how the native workers live before we sail away?" I asked and was confirmed in the supposition by Andy, not that anything mattered on such an evening walk, regardless of Cuba or cups of coffee.

Once down the rope ladder again in the morning to a waiting cab, Andy, myself and two seamen enroute to a doctor were driven to Willemstad, while Ali slept through his next prescribed sedation. Spread all around us on the hilly, mountainous terrain, were goats, children, and a random scattering of homes. Either low, square and shuttered, or high-fronted and fantastical in the Dutch style, they were multi-coloured, plastered, painted in delightful shades of orange, cerise, salmon or yellow, often with a bright green trim.

Once free of the two ill seamen, Andy paid off the cab and we strolled down the picturesque winding streets hanging with tropical vegetation. Pleasantly free of cars, this left ample space for tourists to bargain at the shop fronts as well as along the way through town. Colourful old women, chattering and gesticulating loudly at us in their own language, proffered items for sale from the baskets clutched to their heads. In sharp contrast were the stout, ruddy-faced Dutch merchants standing about in white shirts and Panama-style straw hats on every corner, like ghosts from the early days of Dutch control of Willemsted, known for its slave trade and general commercial interests.

Wandering into the part of town near the river we came upon the hotel district, with the high, narrow, Dutch inspired facades in many colours. Among these unusual structures stood the modern Hotel Americana and next to it, the 'Summer Garden.' We sat down then and there where Andy finally got his restorative pint of ale, the first since docking at the British Columbia port of Victoria, Canada. Finding the thought of trying the local orange liqueur, aptly named 'Curacao,' quite irresistible, the subject of coffee eluded me!

By the time we had made a stop for my request to buy a cheap straw sun hat at a stall to shield me from the tropical sun, it was time to return to the ship. However, as Andy warned most prophetically, "Don't go to Britain in February without a bottle of rum. It'll help you to survive the lack of central heating." Thus warned, I climbed back up the rope ladder precariously clutching these two items. We had arrived on board just in time for an unseasonal hot Lancashire pot pie and another cup of Steward Dobson's watery 'cha.' It was always offered to me with a broad grin, as if he knew it had few qualities to recommend it. "'Ere you are lass," he would say, as it swilled into the saucer. Coffee was grown all around the tropics, and yet I was still without a single bean, much less a grinder!

From Bullen Bay and Willemstad it was not long before we dropped anchor again, unannounced, at least to me. I found that the ship would bob around delightfully, like a cork in a tub for an entire week, while the chief engineer and his men gave the ship's engine a thorough overhaul. As Ali slept away the glorious weather in his medicated routine, I could sit on deck and work away at the typewriter without thinking of anything else. Another week in the tropics was quite acceptable, and as James, the second mate, loved to proclaim, "You'll never be as healthy again as you are on the sea, Miss." No doubt he said the same to all passengers. He told me several times quite seriously that over the years a number of them had mentioned the desire to write a book about it, so that eventually I sensed that he too perhaps felt an urge to write about the sea. As he was older, I did not dare to ask him about himself.

The hustler.

The street scene.

The blissful days drifted by as if this was an established summer home near the equator. Songs in Spanish faded in and out on the ship's radio from time to time. There was an air of unexpected privilege in my case about the passing around, by steward Dobson, of lime juice spiked with gin. This was a British Merchant Navy tradition to help withstand the heat in the stalled vessel, a time-honoured custom at sea served even on 'dry ships' like the Cape Hawke. No one mentioned the true seriousness of the engine-checking operation at hand until one day after we had lifted anchor again I asked Captain Wallace if we were near Bermuda. "Would we get a glimpse of it?" It was a great cruise destination for wealthy Canadians at the time.

"Oh no," he said emphatically, "when we've passed all the islands we'll begin to feel the cold weather ahead." I was amazed at this statement, having imagined a gradual change in temperature as we proceeded north towards the British Isles.

Yet the delight of the tropics and the trade winds did come to an abrupt end as we faced into the Atlantic with its leaden skies, heavy seas, and slightly cooler temperatures of February. No one mentioned that the Atlantic could whip itself into an unrelenting fury. Enraptured as usual, I continued to gaze around at paradise with few other thoughts. Known as "the graveyard of ships" down the centuries, the Bay of Biscay lay before us off the coasts of Spain and Southern France.

Despite the effect of disease, disorientation and morphine injections it is probable that Ali also knew what lay ahead, having spent many years at sea. He was obviously quite naturally irritated by the length of the trip, and confinement to his bed, after the week of repair work on the stalled motor. Considering his situation, he had been easier to control than one might have anticipated. Only once had I been forced to call in two strong young seamen to restrain him. He had not otherwise been antagonistic towards me despite the incessant medication. Considering his desire to continue to do business at every port of call, as he had done earlier, his drugged insistence at going ashore in Panama had been predictable, yet it soon subsided into another deep, drugged sleep.

Finally, however, he took a definite stand against his bedtime sedation, a loathsomely thick, white barbiturate mixture. Efforts to disguise it in cocoa failed miserably. No one could have ever volunteered to swallow such a potion. Fortunately it is now replaced by more modern choices from the pharmacopoeia. One evening I was met with a barricade when I arrived with the medication tray.

As I turned the key in the lock I found the door was now roped shut. As I persisted in trying to get in, the knife blade, probably the one from Marseille, was thrust through the tangle of rope. The open sea lay below the railing giving me a space of only a few feet in which to negotiate this encounter. It was no place for a struggle. I went immediately in search of Captain Wallace, as previously directed in case of need, yet I am sure that Ali intended only a warning.

Quietly, deftly and without a word of annoyance from the captain or cry of protest from Ali, the knife was removed from the web of rope around the lock of the Sick Bay door. Sure that it was alive with tubercular bacilli, and as infectious as cholera, which is not so, the Captain handed it to me, imploring me to soak it in antiseptic solution once outside the door of the Sick Bay.

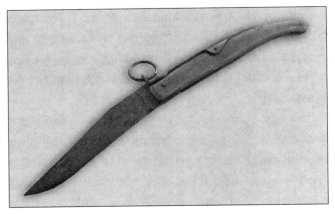

Ali's rebellion! Captain Wallace triumphs!

I have the knife to this day, thinking fondly of Ali and Captain Wallace each time my eye falls upon it. Apparently, Ali had the wisdom not to hold a grudge. Nothing was ever said about the incident, even in his moments of discontent and confusion, his soliloquies cheerfully concerned rather with the fact that "my god jus' like yo' god Seesta," and that there were piles of coins and silks waiting for me in *Libberpol.* He seemed to accept authority in a practical manner.

Only occasionally would he rail and cry out *No kanzir, no kanzir,* which we understood referred to pork, forbidden by his religion. We had never offered it to him. Instead, as I brought in his soup bowl, on a tray, its contents swilling about to the increased roll of the ship, he looked darkly at the barley grains from his spilled soup bowl now rolling rhythmically back and forth across the floor in time with the rough Atlantic waves tossing us about. I could get more soup from the kitchen, but I could not read his mind. Like almost everybody else on board except me, he knew what a rough sea could mean. For the moment though, we were still enjoying relative calm.

Fits of temper being easily controlled, the days occasionally ended with his perfume ritual, before he began his Muslim prayer sessions on the bed. Ali would sit straight up in bed, carefully lift the delicate glass stopper out of the silver amulet he wore on a chain around his neck, reach up to my ear-lobe and touch it most delicately with the tiny attached glass wand as if he knew very well that such behaviour was actually taboo. It was a delightful, subtle scent which I imagine came from the Middle East. I would of course show no emotion, saying only, "Thank you," acting out a serious professional tone as I departed, making sure, as usual that he had everything for the night. Perhaps he once presided over a perfume stall in an Arab market or watched the habits of vendors and customers. All these years I have been hoping to find that scent in some exotic hide-away, as a reminder of the remarkably likeable Ali Ahmed.

The ship's cook, Armand, was an exuberant, amiable young black man with a ready smile. Tall and loose-jointed, he spent the mornings just outside the galley making bread, while singing volubly and passionately, punching the dough down in an enormous metal bowl and tossing it about expertly between each kneading. Although the grey, dense slices were not at all like bread one finds ashore, it was certainly not for want of effort on his part.

As I passed along the side of the galley one day near

the end of the trip, he appeared before me. For the occasion he had exchanged his cooks' uniform for a freshly ironed white shirt. Visibly ill at ease, embarrassed and unsmiling now, rather than his usual cheerful self, he seemed in a hurry to blurt out his message to me, knowing that the crew were not allowed to mix with the officers.

Nervously shifting his weight from one long leg to the other, he asked in a husky voice, "Seesta, you know 'bout Madame Tussaud's Waxworks in London? I show you Chamber of 'Orrors. You come wid me? I show you everyting!"

The very thought of visiting these "Orrors" chilled me. They had been so well-publicized and photographed for their novelty after the war. In perfect truth I told him that I did not know my itinerary while saying, "Thank you very much," before retreating quickly to the officers' quarters.

I had no idea whether Patrick, the ship's radio operator, had been annoyed by Armand's incessant vocal attempts outside the galley or not. However, we all noted that nothing enraged him so much as he approached the officers' table as the sight of the plate of bread slices. Perhaps it was mere subterfuge to avoid greetings or conversation. He would instead take out his obsession against the bread in violent action. Throwing a slice on his plate, he would squeeze and pound it into a ball, curse it, punch it with his fist, finally slamming it down on his plate again. Neither the other officers or myself ever complained about the food, simply accepting it as the menu one found on a British freighter if not on an luxury liner.

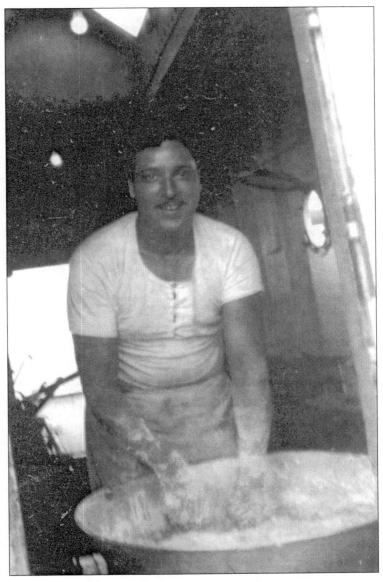

Armand sung passionately, "Mammy,
how I love ya, how I love ya.....dear ol'Swanny!"

Armand, the cook, posing for a photo in the galley.

Being moderate men like Captain Wallace, none of my colleagues tried to challenge Patrick into conversation. Perhaps he felt alone on the sea from his 'perch' in the radio operator's cabin above the officers' quarters. As an Irishman, he was in a sense alone among the Scotsmen. Patrician in manner and speech and with his tall stature and good looks, he could have been handsome, had his features not been unfailingly contorted with anger or irritation.

At that point in my life, with the exception of George Bernard Shaw's plays, I knew nothing of the works of Irish writers. Since I was innocent of the love of the Irish for a pint of Guinness, a pub crawl around the Dublin of James Joyce, or the chance to tell a good story to one's own cronies, he seemed to me to be nothing but a hopeless neurotic and a curious misfit.

On one occasion only, as far as I know, he came onto the deck in the evening. I had just left the Sick Bay for the night and stopped for a moment to glance at the magnificent sunset. He frowned at it, failed to see it, being still full of complaints. I mounted quickly to my cabin on the bridge to let him lash out at the universe in the solitude he seemed to need. However, I concluded from his overall seriousness that he was regarded as a competent ship's officer. We were to need him later on.

The second mate, James, was middle-aged, unsmiling, and mysteriously dour. In a deep, rugged voice he sang the same song incessantly as if to avoid intrusion on his privacy, the last line ending emphatically with "And Clancy lowered the boom." Perhaps he hated every minute on board, or had not been able to pass the exam to claim his 'master's ticket' to become a captain himself. It was said that he had had many a close call with torpedoes during the war while hauling oil across the North Atlantic and in the heroic struggle to keep the sea lanes open to the Allies, he had seen his father pulled under by a shark. Reticent as I was about speaking to him, I regret never having asked Andy about him.

Two other young officer cadets told me in detail about the sacrifices of their own fathers or relatives, and of the trials of the relatively unknown or unsung

British Merchant Navy during the war. We had all been standing at the railing in the tropics and looking down into the water described as shark infested at the time as they told me what the ocean could mean to them, beside the perfection it represented at that moment. Fortunately, I had been aware of the importance of the British Merchant Navy which was occasionally mentioned in the news during the war.

In a light-hearted moment, Andy pointed out that "The lifeboats are useless, being corroded with rust to their moorings." "And apart from that," he added with a rare glimmer of fun in his blue eyes; "in any event if the sharks don't get you, the rule is that the men get to be saved first. Women have more fat to keep them warm! You'll find comfort, of course, in the uselessly corroded life boats with the de-salinator and the supply of nourishment – barley sugar candies! You survive for seven minutes in frigid waters, not more!" Andy was too young an officer to have given service in the war and could therefore enjoy this moment of teasing me. At the same time, he was as usual providing food for thought in a tactful manner. Probably he chose suitable moments such as this to make his comments to all passengers he encountered.

Unfortunately, it appears that for years to come, the valour of these men, not members of the regular fighting forces, was also not recognized with reasonable financial reward. They were apparently among the many tragically unsung heroes of World War II. Knowing all this, one could imagine that perhaps James and others carried the raw memories of these fairly recent tragic events around with them aboard ship.

At any rate, one could more easily understand his strange manner, his volleys of loud, monotonous whistling or tuneless singing whenever he worked on deck. After yet another long confinement on board, another nine-month trek around the globe, hauling freight to and from one country and another, these men could be excused for showing exasperation now and then.

Had I learned the meaning of the song, I might have gained understanding and amusement about James' situation as an Irishman on a strictly operated Scottish ship. In so far as I was concerned our daily life revealed serious, old-fashioned and militaristic undertones despite Captain Wallace's fair-minded attitude. Nevertheless I cannot imagine that he, Andy or the very superior yet Irish radio operator enjoyed any of the six verses of this popular song. In it, although "Clancy was a peaceful man," he clashed with his mates in the pub on being found to have drunk one of their drinks, on finding the iceman kissing his wife, as well as his involvement in a wedding brawl. In each case, of course, "Clancy lowered the boom. Boom, boom, boom, boom."

Unknown to me, James may have been the life of the party among the engineers and crew of the ship. Possibly he was suffering from homesickness for Ireland, consoling himself with a song from home. At the captain's table my acquaintances included only Captain Wallace, the first mate, Andrew, and the Irish radio operator, Patrick.

Andy on duty at the wheel while soaking up the sun.

Like the 'Old Man,' as they called Captain Wallace, the first mate, Andrew, or Andy, was always mild-mannered, serious and thoroughly pleasant. To these two dour Scots I owed the assurance I felt of being part of a well-run team of people working together as intended for the common good of everyone on board. After the difficult years of study, Andy was about to receive his Master's ticket. Tall, handsome and gentle-manly, he confided in me that now as a married man he might not choose to remain at sea.

Captain Wallace had told me early in the trip that it was Andy, the officer responsible for the needs of passengers, including tours while in foreign ports of call, on whom I should rely. He had always treated me in a perfectly courteous and thoughtful manner. As he was on watch on the bridge in the afternoons while Ali slept, I could take a book, writing or sketching materials up there for interesting or amusing snatches of conversations under the sun. I could not have sailed with more pleasant, cooperative and fair companions.

A rotund, middle-aged Liverpudlian, Mr. Albert Dobson, the chief steward gave me the impression that he was an old 'sea dog' himself, another veteran of the war on one of these old ships. With his broad grin, missing front teeth, blue eyes and curly grey hair, he was also the soul of good humour, fatherly, and with children at home. His smile seemed to say, "I did my best, lassie, to make a good meal, even if the stores are runnin' short, an 'ere's yer cha," as, with a chuckle, he set down yet another great swilling cup of indifferent weak tea. The one time he tried to make coffee for me, I was sure that it was cocoa. He blamed the pot. Amused, I declined to inspect it.

Liked by everyone, Albert had earned the reputation of making a fast-track to the best markets in foreign ports to buy highly rated gourmet fare. This included the crayfish he bought at Caleo, Peru, en route to Canada, and the tins of fruit and custard from Australia. None of us had ever tasted anything like these special finds. Certainly, unanimously, he was forgiven for all those plain English meat and potato meals through which we sat with relative good cheer when his special items were depleted. After we turned North into the Atlantic a murmur circulated around the table to the effect, "Oh no, Dobson has done it again. He has begun to run short on the variety of things we normally have!" Fortunately, Andy found it amusing, if only for the moment. Everyone liked 'Dobson.'

Around the table it was suggested that our steward had not calculated the food supplies used during the extra week we had spent on the motor repair in the Caribbean. Yet little did they know at the time just how fortunate we were. They still ate those large protein-laden English breakfasts. As I was the only one to eat cereal instead, there had been, on Andy's part, an amused respectful restraint in making allusions to the added protein-value of oatmeal. This was a sly warning to me and a joking allusion to the cockroaches found in ship storerooms.

Once, in the "flash of an eye," as they say, I had seen Captain Wallace, master of a "dry ship," dispose of a couple of incriminating empty beer bottles over the starboard railing. In this comic act, Charlie Chaplin could have done no better. That day, in fine weather, he strode purposefully to the side, wearing a winter cap with ear-flaps flying, supposedly to hide his face in profile, opened his windbreaker from the bottom instead of the collar, and let fall into the deep the forbidden objects. Just as smartly he turned, strode back towards his quarters. I have no doubt that on leave with his family and friends in Scotland, he could relax that level-headed stern guise in favor of great moments of previously repressed levity.

Painting rigging, a risky assignment.

The potato peeler.
How many bushels?

Holding their paint
brushes.

As our lives depended on him above all else, Captain Wallace meant a great deal to all of us. However, the day before we landed I met the engineering staff. The captain took me down the steep steps into the depths of the ship to look at the propeller shaft running the length of the vessel. There I met his colleague, the chief engineer, on whose shoulders also rested a great deal of concern for our safety. Apparently the engineers' quarters were apart from our own.

It would seem that between these two most senior officials also lay the responsibility for the dozens of unilingual Gaelic speaking teenage youths enjoying their first taste of life at sea. I saw these shy school-boys only once. Although I never found out why they were on board, I am sure that during the nine months of the world tour some one must have had to keep them in line and deal with their homesickness, illnesses and loneliness. Did the captain, the chief engineer or Andy, the first mate, speak Gaelic also? Apparently, I had not dared to pose many questions to my dour Scottish hosts. In hindsight, it occurs to me that Captain Wallace and his fellow officers had more than enough to fill their days.

There were also the two boys known as the "Birken'ed boys," one rotund, the other lean. Always grinning, comical fellows, one could almost name them the ship's mascots. With pails of white paint, they could be spotted aloft, brandishing their brushes, while hanging precariously from all sorts of positions day in and day out, sometimes simply coating the railings. Their carefree, devil-may-care manner suggested that they were perhaps just youngsters out to see the world. Another youth, an Australian whom I never met, peeled potatoes all the way from Sydney, Australia to Paris to enter chef's training.

One youngster, an officer-in-training called 'Wee Willie,' followed me around because he had attended art school and enjoyed the evening sketching sessions I offered. He insisted that I must wave to his mother whenever we finally sailed up the Clyde River into Glasgow. He knew that she would be standing on her porch on the hill in Gourock to welcome him home. It was to be a colourful moment for me, considering that I had seen the photos and newsreels of the warships launched from the Clyde in preparation for World War II.

It was now the last week of January, 1951, as we left the Caribbean behind and sailed north into gradually cooler Atlantic waters. And it was then, as we entered the Bay of Biscay that Ali Baba became concerned in trying to save my life. Had I recorded the exact day, I should have liked to remember this event every year on that date for the rest of my life.

The North Atlantic

Preparing Ali for supper, I entered the Sick Bay as usual at four o'clock to give him his next dose of morphine and other medications. As expected, at this time of day he was on his knees, bowed low over the mattress in prayer. What was unusual was that he began to moan, in a long, low and desperate howl. Glancing up at me from under the bushy eyebrows and the striped red fez, he appeared not only frail and old, but terrified. Injecting the morphine with difficulty I asked, "What's the trouble Ali?" I did not know that we had entered the Bay of Biscay, the graveyard of countless ships down the centuries that men have sailed the seven seas.

Between the sobbing sounds I heard, "Go back, Capitaine, Seesta, bery bad storm come Seesta, bery bad storm! Go back Capitaine, now!" His voice was throaty, full of apprehension.

Instinctively my senses jolted to attention. My ears filled with the roar of a strong sea wind. I was aware of the leaden sky at the porthole, despite the fact that it was only late afternoon. Ali was certainly terrified, although he must have seen many storms in his hard, poverty-stricken life as a stoker on other aging freighters. Nevertheless, despite his advanced mental deterioration, he had had the presence of mind to be concerned about the safety of his 'Seesta.' He would not stop wailing until he had persuaded me to get back to the officers' quarters.

The unflappable Captain Peter Wallace of the Good Ship Cape Hawke.

"Ali, I'll be right back," I said naively, and as matter-of-factly as possible, "as soon as I ask the Captain what to do. Ali, don't worry!" Opening the door of the Sick Bay not more than a few feet from the railing, with the angry, gunmetal grey sea before me, I turned and faced into a wind so stiff that it threatened to impede my progress back along the deck toward the prow. As soon as I found Captain Wallace I could tell that he was preoccupied with the matter at hand. Without looking up from his work, he instructed me in a few terse words to arrange with steward Dobson to have Ali's supper taken to him in a bag by a crew member. I was to head for the officers' dining room and wait for orders to be issued at that time.

Those orders came with the realization that I would not see my patient again that day, or perhaps for some time to come, given the shocking revelation that in a freighter no inside passage exists for emergency use. It was a disturbing thought! At the same time, as a sign of things to come during this brief meal, more than the usual back and forth swoosh of plates on the table demanded attention. Although a two-inch vertical strip of wood had been attached all around the edge of the circular table, with the sudden tilting and clattering of the dishes sliding about, we were scarcely able to keep the food in place.

Warning everyone to remain fully clothed and to leave the lights on during the night, a sober Captain Wallace explained over the hurried meal, "This is an old World War II Liberty ship. It is welded together and could split in two pieces in such a storm as the one upon us now, here in the Bay of Biscay. "You all know that it is known as the graveyard of ships down the centuries."

He had said all this very calmly and quietly. For me, he added, "For the first time we are carrying a cargo of wheat in the hold. Grain can shift, unlike the motor cars we usually bring back after delivering the whisky we haul from Scotland. It could cause us to capsize. That is why we piled lumber all over the deck, twelve feet high, after picking you up in Canada, to add buoyancy to the ship carrying such an unstable cargo."

As ordered, I went immediately to my cabin. The officers also dispersed with the captain to meet the challenges of the night. Whatever that might entail, I knew nothing personally about storms at sea, yet none of it disturbed me as it did not yet seem to be quite real. I did not envision a disaster. I had every faith in the Captain and the officers, an issue I had settled in my mind early in the voyage, worrying instead about the fate of Ali, way off at the other end of the vessel. As it turned out, the officers were all trained to give medical attention of the kind required and as he did not cough would surely not contract tuberculosis from him. They moved him out through the back of the Sick Bay, through the adjoining crew's quarters and into a spare room available for emergencies.

Roaring in more forcefully upon us with every passing hour, the storm increased in velocity at an alarming rate. The noise was deafening. We were being tossed about like a cork by a colossus. Just when survival seemed to depend on being able to see the storm and the ship, utter darkness was now everywhere beyond the portholes. While the officers below worked feverishly to keep us afloat, isolation enveloped me. I realized that it would be a long night 'flying solo,' with no phone and no information.

Soon losing awareness of these normal reflections of interdependence, of rationality almost, I now stood in a state of controlled terror, fingers tightly clutching the porthole frame so as not to lose my balance against the violent pitch and roll of the ship. Seemingly detached from the lumbering old barque, it was as if my cabin bobbed helplessly over the giant peaks and troughs of water in the limitless, merciless ocean, the rest of the ship having dropped into the deep without a sound.

And yet again, in the next moment, I was desperate to get my bearings, to understand the dark world beyond. I tried to make out the swirling, shadowy hell out there beyond the porthole. Peering feverishly out into the menacing dark, I could barely make out the fast-moving mountains of black water slamming now over the galley and then on to the roof of my cabin, so high on the Bridge, submerging the whole ship in front of me, then again suddenly real and visible.

In hour after hour of merciless battering by the elements, the waves pulled back, roared in again with a pattern of endless repetition, without even momentary pause. For a split second of intense concentration I could make out the lighted galley a few feet in front of me, the pots in their racks dancing a mad, frenzied tango as the wall of water pulled away, exposed them for an instant, trounced in again with a deafening roar, lambasting us with tons of water as if to completely shatter the galley and whatever remained of the ship.

Meanwhile, the inferno of clanging, booming, ear-splitting racket seemed to increase in volume with every hour of darkness. The metal railings clattered down noisily onto the deck, both shrill and staccato by turns, as one section after another were pulled from their sockets. It was a dance of the piccolo, the tambourine and finally the tuba as the piles of spruce planks piled on deck for buoyancy joined in, surrendered their role and hit the deck in a low grumble, one or a few at a time. They bumped, bounced and finally plopped over the side. These were the highlights of the deafening oceanic concerto, with the cacophony, the diabolical orchestration, alternately terrifying and amusing, without a single pause for intermission. While I could not see the extravaganza, the sound was everywhere, confusing, deafening, magnificent, permanently implanted in the mind.

As the storm continued to intensify during the night it seemed more and more as if I were bouncing around clutching the porthole frame in a watery bubble of some sort. Deep in the ocean itself one moment and then tossed around on the surface, myself a hapless captain, on guard, I clutched an imaginary steering wheel I dare not let slip from my hands lest, like a cork, I would be thrown with force about the cabin.

"No time for broken bones," I thought out loud. So great was the noise of the crashing of tons of water over us, forcing us down, down, down, then suddenly up again, a part of nature as never before, free of past and future, the second by second survival was existence itself. Transformed by nature, no longer a part of the material world, caught up in the realm of the sublime, for one moment, rather than the caverns of hell; terror, beauty, magic and enchantment had become one, part of the many moods and seasons of the sea itself.

Oddly, the morning of the third day at dawn issued in sunshine and a strange sense of reality. I gave up 'the watch' and the steering wheel position at the porthole. The sea was rough and not yet entirely safe, but there was a sense of relief, a fragile hope of finally reaching port. There had been no time to think of anything but the heaving universe around me. No hands had been lost in the desperate effort to keep the ship from capsizing. However, the cargo of wheat had shifted on the first night, causing the vessel to tilt, or 'list' to a forty-five degree angle. In the ensuing struggle down below to keep us afloat, the drinking water and food stores had been quickly jettisoned, apparently causing strong words and dissension between the captain and the chief engineer.

Hardest hit had been the crew's quarters, with a foot of water around the bunks. I was deeply shocked and disappointed to think that without railings there was no way that I was to see Ali or to help him. I knew that he had probably been difficult to deal with during such an ordeal, particularly if no one had been free to administer sedation during the worst of the storm.

Even before breakfast the news had spread that Captain Wallace had ordered a lifeboat drill. Everyone immediately assembled on the deck. As I foolishly tried to descend one or two steps in curiosity, I heard Captain Wallace talking about releasing the lifeboats. Courage failed me on the spot, as I wondered if we were sinking and about to abandon ship. Here was something utterly beyond my ability. Andy had taught me that long ago, jokingly, to make me think about it.

Seeing me faltering at the top of the stairs, Captain Wallace prevented my further precarious descent. Picking up a thick coil of rope, he wound it around my waist and tied me safely to the bridge to watch the procedure in progress. Within a minute my clothes and hair were white from sea-spray. The life-boat drill had been organized to release the boats from the cranes or *davits* which held them in place. Everyone knew that due to corrosion they had been useless for years. Given the recent difficulties, however, the mandatory drill must be carried out.

Captain Wallace and Andy tied a long, very thick rope around the mast and proceeded to unfurl it across the deck toward the side, winding it around the waist of each chosen seaman to form a human chain of about a dozen crew members. The wind was brisk, the waves menacing, causing the now frail, storm-battered lifeboats, which hung pathetically, like broken toys from strings, to thrash around in the wind. Nevertheless the lead man in the chain was obliged to approach the edge of the deck, arm outstretched over the raging sea to pull a life-boat in over the deck. Eluding outstretched arms, each wrecked craft fell, plank by plank, like so much kindling, all at once, or in a spray, in bits and pieces into the jaws of the still heaving North Atlantic.

It was a horrifying exercise, despite the rope around the waist, especially as Andy was the lead man, teetering at the edge of the deck, knowing that survival time was calculated to be seven minutes in freezing, surging waves. His seemingly light-hearted remark, mentioned in the tropics, had been convincingly and dramatically re-enacted, without loss of life and with great courage. Presumably Captain Wallace would have to show proof in writing that lifeboat drill had been carried out, yet deplored the whole dangerous and futile performance.

After the forty-eight hours of havoc, the winding down of the storm was not only a relief to all, but left me with a sense of having reached yet another milestone of experience. Together with the entire voyage, I would savour it for years to come in all its extraordinary facets. The lifeboat exercise had been done quietly with what to me appeared to be amazing precision, bravery, and very few words, like the dour Scots they were.

Most unfortunately, even the footing on the deck must have felt extremely uncertain, James having oiled it heavily the day before the onset of the storm and the loss of all the railings. As for the possible perils for a captain, rather than his officers and men, I learned that they are given the training to take on certain medical duties, including the delivery of a newborn. He must also face the duty of 'going down with the ship' should the vessel begin to sink, after helping everyone into lifeboats.

During the previous winter of 1949-50, while waiting to take on my working contract on the Cape Hawke, another vessel, much reported in the European press, had also listed badly and finally arranged to discharge its passengers to a waiting vessel. The Captain remained to the end, cutting a heroic figure in a newsreel in which he is standing alone on the tilting deck. Whether he actually perished or was rescued I do not recall.

When we sat down to the first seemingly more normal meal, without fear of losing the plates from the undulating table, it was clear that Mr. Dobson's victualling, or food service at sea, would not resume. Most of the food containers had been lost on the first night of the storm. Gone were the hearty breakfast plates of eggs, bacon, sausage and ham beloved by the British. The diet would be limited to oatmeal, complete with the added protein of cockroaches, joked about in better days, damp, packaged sliced white bread, strawberry jam, most unappetizing stale tinned corned beef and eggs, tinted deep orange with age, probably made barely tolerable only with a thick blanket of pepper. Having spurned the beef and the eggs, it was a slim menu for me.

Guiding us up the Clyde.

The 'cha' was now made with desalinated sea water, resulting in a flat and unpleasant end to an extremely frugal repast. It was a hungry ten days until we reached Scotland. I doubt that Patrick, the commercial radio operator, made any more dramatic assaults against the bread, even sliced, commercial and damp. In any event I have no recollection of any serious complaints during the last ten days of the trip in our battered ship, said to be listing to forty degrees, the occupants blissfully thankful to be alive.

218

On February fifteenth, nineteen hundred and fifty-one, we were edging, gliding blissfully and slowly along the estuary of the Clyde River toward Glasgow. It was an unusually balmy morning, according to my beaming Glaswegian companions standing on the bridge all around me. A light 'Scots mist' caressed our uplifted faces. I was especially delighted, as if the sudden, slightly effervescent tingle on the skin were a special welcome to Britain, to Europe, to a new chapter in my life! Although the thought was mixed with the sorrow of leaving the sea, the concern for Ali and the events of the moment took precedence in my mind, especially as at that point a pilot came over the side, just as in Panama, to lead us through the narrow sections of the historic waterway.

Spontaneously, a palpable though tightly controlled excitement arose on the bridge, and on the deck, followed by a burst of euphoria, as celebration gave way to the triumphant strains of an appealing Scottish song. Unknown to me, it may perhaps have been a tribute to a fine captain or a general thanksgiving for a safe return. The Clyde River held me in thrall now as we inched closer and closer into port and saw in detail the life all around us on the banks.

For hundreds of years vessels must have plied these waters to pillage, to trade or to return from war. Here it was, exactly as I had seen it on the newsreels with my parents in Canada, the Firth of Clyde as a naval hot-spot of prime importance in World War II. All homecomings had not been so free of care. Still, the banks were alive with people waving us on in the midst of the normal industrial dockside activities.

The youngest officer in-training on the Cape Hawke was that nineteen-year-old junior officer-in-training known as 'Wee Willie Ross,' mentioned earlier, who now implored me to join him in looking at the distant point high on the bank where I would see his parents' house in Gourock just as he had told me earlier. We began to wave. Sure enough, I could just make out the form of a woman standing on a back door-stoop and waving a white cloth. What a great relief it would be to her to welcome her young son back from his first tour of duty, the circumnavigation of the globe.

The pitch and roll of the vessel, the sea breeze, and the sound of it all had been a delightful and benign intoxicant now difficult to relinquish. Thoughts flooded my mind. But what had gone wrong? As I suddenly realized that we were now approaching the gang-plank, how could I see Ali? Just then I heard voices muttering, "make way, make way!" Suddenly Ali appeared! As he leaned forward from his stretcher, he was all too quickly hustled out to the public health officials waiting to drive him away.

He looked very old and ill. First, it was the storm and now officialdom that prevented me from carrying out my responsibility, my undivided attention to his needs as a dying man. According to my originally assigned duty, I had expected to escort him to a designated government facility. At the very least, I should have been given an hour to listen to him, to find out

how he had been treated. He appeared to have deteri-
orated markedly as he was hustled away by crew members. Just then spotting me in the crowd, he reached out
toward me. His baleful glance spoke volumes. But he
knew, of course, that after the railing had fallen into
the sea there had been no way for me to reach him. A
disaster. What had he suffered?

As if it were yesterday, I fondly recall those dark
eyes, full of expression, full of stories, of love for life.
At pathos, Chaplin himself, in his silent films could do
no better. For Ali who was dying, it was all too real.
He looked as if he were longing to say, "You come my
house, Seesta? My God, jus' like you God, Seesta. Come
see my house. My wife, she give you twelve yard, silks
... Seesta, silks and gold coins ...." I was utterly crest-
fallen not to have been allowed to bid him farewell, as
he too would have wished, would have expected of me,
if there had been any way of reaching him."

I am fortunate to have both my sketches of him
as well as his knife as precious mementos of such a likeable character. Undoubtedly, he had missed the normal,
calm routine of medication, care, companionship and
an audience for his tales. It is still difficult to realize
that these merchant ships had not been designed with
auxiliary inside passageways alongside the cargo sections of the vessels.

All hands being required to save the ship, he may
have suffered withdrawal symptoms if the timing of
the morphine injections were not regular or other medications, isolation and hunger were involved. How could

I follow up on his demise? I wondered if he would ever be allowed to go home to his little "Yvonne de Carlo" look-alike wife again at 13, Upper Parliament Street, or 'Barlement,' as he called it, for a short visit, to exult over all the treasures in his attic. No doubt she regularly sold them at the market for her merchant-king. I was devastated at the time and was never able to go to Liverpool to enquire.

After I had met the families of the captain and of the officers, waiting for them at the dockside, I was approached by the owner of the Lyle Shipping Company who had come to apologize for the perilous trip I had endured on the Cape Hawke, promising me lifetime transport at cost, wherever I wished to travel on their ships. He then invited me to be a weekend house-guest with him and his family.

I thanked him, declined, due to my pre-arranged itinerary, and joined two or three others, including Wee Willie Ross, still following me, to look for something to eat. After all, we had subsisted on the bread and jam rations for ten days. It was now a winter twilight with wartime lighting conditions left unchanged after six years. There was the glow of what appeared to be forty-watt bulbs to light the street corners. The restaurant offered nothing of any substance, as rationing was still enforced. We went away extremely hungry.

Finding my way to the YWCA, shocked about losing contact with Ali in so summary a manner, I arrived in time for a stone-cold supper of something untouchable called 'blood sausage,' alone on a white plate, with white bread. It was followed by dry cupcakes and tea. Desperate for food and warmth, I approached the massive, glowing fireplace with excited expectation of at least fulfilling the latter pressing need. There were several long benches drawn up around the centre of heat, the only source of it in a drafty old building in a country without central heating.

Surveying the benches out of the corner of my eye, I hoped to see a spot where I could plump down and feel welcome in Scotland. I needed to thaw out from sitting in the cold dining-room with the cold, unappetizing food I could not eat. Sitting hunched up towards the fire, one old woman turned her head in curiosity, just enough to take me into her inquiring gaze. "You're not British?" she called out questioningly and unpleasantly. "I can tell by your clothes."

"Canadian," I explained, adding quietly to myself, "Well give me a break, it's part of the Commonwealth," a popular colonial link in those days. I had hoped to chat with the women around the fire, having had nothing but entirely male company for six weeks! It was thrilling to have at last arrived in Britain, the country of my heritage. I also had a good story to tell of life at sea. But she quickly retorted "Anyway, Canada didn't send us any beef during the war!" Perhaps I should have accepted the ship's owner's invitation to spend the weekend with him and his family, had I not been expected in London.

I chuckled, as my family and so many others had sent innumerable packages of tinned beef, ham and other foods as often as finances would allow. I could well remember the work of wrapping and mailing them according to regulations. As there were neither empty seats nor a welcoming atmosphere, I took the only recourse at hand, climbing the stairs in search of my bed in the chilly dormitory. On the stopover in Curacao, Andy had told me "a bottle of rum is guaranteed to ward off the chill of our unheated British bedrooms," I pulled the small, dark brown bottle out of my luggage, then climbed into an upper bunk. After one or two cautious sips of this strange comforting potion, I slipped into a deep, warm sleep.

Breakfast consisted of lukewarm oatmeal, cold white toast and tea. No coffee was served. Under my plate was a piece of red and green folded tartan paper. On opening it, I found a note inviting me for a day trip to Loch Lomond the following morning despite February winds, rain and cold. The writer was a medical student with an exam to write that day. While I was delighted with her kind offer, my pre-arranged commitments made it unfortunately impossible to accept.

Obviously happier then about my amusing, yet strange welcome to Scotland, I took the train to Edinburgh to board the 'Royal Scot' for the all-day ride to London. I missed the roll of the waves beneath my feet, the invigoration of sea air, Ali Baba, and everyone else to such an extent that I was at this point scarcely aware of the intervening hours since descending the gangplank. It didn't matter at all even though I was also desperate for food.

Wee Willie brought his pet along to see me off in Edinburgh.

Front and centre in my life, my six weeks at sea represents one of the finest experiences of a lifetime. On shipboard I had typed out the story of life on the high seas as far as our cruise through the Caribbean. Painstakingly I had recorded it all in the rich, regional speech patterns I heard around me, largely Glaswegian, Liverpudlian, Irish from both Dublin and Belfast and Jamaican. I had great hopes for the thick, crumpled and damp wad of coarse yellow newsprint I proudly carried off the ship, meaning to work it into a book, yet ignorant of the work involved.

Back in Canada, visiting friends, the cleaning woman found it on the floor, took it to be garbage, and threw it out. Undaunted, six decades later, I have perhaps not been able to fully replicate the exact tone of voice, the exact accent of the delightfully mingled colourful speech, bringing these priceless characters to life again.

I trust the reader's imagination to imbue the seamens' remarks with all the vibrant colour inherent in the everyday speech patterns of men working harmoniously together on a British Merchant Service freighter, circa 1950's. Not having heard a single inappropriate word expressed during the entire voyage, surely our dour Scottish captain deserved a medal for his concern that respect be shown the "lady" officer on board.

Arrival in England

To glide down the length of Britain by rail from Edinburgh to London on 'The Royal Scot' was to get a most appealing first glimpse of the country. Almost immediately it was announced that we were approaching Hadrian's Wall. By leaving the compartment for a moment to stand between the coaches it could see it clearly. Built by the Romans it served to deter "those wild men to the north," as the Scots were described. Indeed, it seemed to be almost beneath the wheels for one moment then stretched off over the irregular terrain into the distance. Returning to my compartment, I watched the endless panorama of England as "that green and pleasant land" as Milton put it, began to flash by my window seat. Free of industrial wastelands, reminders of bombing from the war or anything to spoil the image of perfection, it was spread out like a great map, as streams, villages, ancient stone bridges, rivers, fields and vistas rolled by, mile after mile, for eight hours, on each side of the train.

Was I too entranced to think of lunch? Probably not, as due to British rationing I had not yet had a

normal meal, except for bread and porridge. I do, however, remember leaving my compartment to claim a
cup of coffee, being still in search of one after six weeks
at sea. At a table with a clean white starched cloth, a
good-natured fellow was noticeably pleased to tell me
that he had now mastered the technique of making this
strange "American brew."

Standing erectly over the cup as the coach
jumped and rumbled on the track, he held a pot of
hot milk in one hand, the silvered coffee pot in the
other, trying to pour them simultaneously into the
cup now bouncing around on the saucer. Apparently
designed to please the most discerning of customers,
it was also a game of skill and good humour, played
over white linen on a moving vehicle. But then, think
of the Scottish Games. Who but the Scots would "toss
the caber" or play the bagpipes in the rain? It was a
never-to-be forgotten cup of excellent coffee, presented
with a smile.

Still totally absorbed in the countryside flashing by my window seat in the late afternoon, I had not
realized that we were already approaching London.
Suddenly it occurred to me that the February dusk was
closing in. At that moment the trainman came through
the coach as the speed slackened to announce the exciting fact that we were now arriving at Euston Station.
This was a name I knew well from wartime bombing
reports and much else. Suddenly both confused and
wildly elated, I tried to gather up my belongings and
push my way into the line-up in the aisle toward the

exit. Now the coach slid toward the stop silently and slowly under my eager feet.

"It is no longer the sea under my feet now; it but is actually London!" I said to myself, unbelieving. For so many years, I had awaited this thrilling moment. Astonishingly, in the next second, as we waited for a full stop and for the doors to open, the windows revealed the brightly illuminated dome of St. Paul's Cathedral.

Lit by a full moon low in the sky above it, here it was. Miraculously spared from bombing raids by members of the Home Guard, intrepid Londoners and technology here was Christopher Wren's eighteenth-century masterpiece at its most spectacular. I froze with amazement at the unbelievable sight, fumbled with baggage in the line-up, then found myself in a crowded waiting room. Where was my hostess, Georgie?

As arranged from Canada by Aunt Glad, her sister Georgie would meet my train and offer hospitality in London. She was to recognize me by the red beret I would carry. Expecting to encounter a motherly type like Aunt Glad, I was surprised to see a slim, delightfully elegant woman step forward from the crowd, come up to me, introducing herself as "Georgie." She picked up one of my bags, laughed and quipped, "a romantic trip I am sure, on the high seas with so many Scotsmen!" Anticipating what the next remark might imply, yet did not, I managed to somehow laugh it off light-heartedly, replying "not really," as we hailed a cab to Georgie's street in Knightsbridge, in central London itself.

Lights blinked around us as if all London shared my excitement. This was a contrast to the dimly-lit streets of Glasgow. As we drove along, Georgie mentioned our route, via Chelsea, then for the morrow, promised Mayfair, Harrods, the Admiralty and the Marble Arch. Feeling almost at home already as she mentioned these familiar names, common to me through all the war years gave me a sense of *déjà vu*. The bombs fell on these very streets. Thanks to my father's concern for his homeland, all this was familiar to me through regular graphic coverage in the illustrated British papers, from the slums of the East End dockside areas to this central heart of London. I couldn't wait for daylight, to see it as it was now.

I knew that Georgie had more than done her part in the Home Guard, on those very thoroughfares, and as we proceeded through them in the cab I asked her about it.

"We were picking up people by the teaspoon, an arm or leg," she recalled, leaving further details of such heroism for later as we drew up in front of a grey stone row house on Pont Street.

The apartment reflected her life as an artist and traveller, with mementos used to good effect, in a unique and charming open space. Before her divorce, she and Tim, Sir Timothy, in fact, had travelled a great deal on the continent. This of course enhanced her taste in art and furnishings. They had first met at the exhibition of her miniature portraits at the Tate Gallery. Not only was there a vogue for this kind of painting but none other than the famous Russian ballet dancer Pavlova had sat for her, creating a most talked of exhibition as she explained to me over coffee.

Those were the great years of her life. Eventually there were two sons, a divorce, then the war, and now a lapse in her creative output. However, she was proud to say that her son Marcus was an established London portrait painter. As she prepared the meal, I was invited to explore her shelves. Full of Italian ceramic tableware and other pieces inspired by ancient Mediterranean themes, here was a hint of the enticing world of their pre-Roman countrymen, the Etruscans, of whom I had read as an introduction to the history of western art.

Marcus, in his thirties, tall, handsome and distinguished looking, shared his nearby Kensington studio with a long-term and older companion. Much later I was amused to learn that Georgie had hoped that he would transfer his interests to me. This came as a surprising idea, considering that I had so ambitious a career plan in mind and felt marriage to be the domain of the beautiful, among whose ranks I did not belong, and had also to think of my family. To promote her campaign she had apparently persuaded Marcus into inviting me for a Saturday night supper at their Kensington flat.

Here I thought, was the bohemian life of the artists, just as I had read about it and seen it in illustrated British papers. Overly impressed and supposing Marcus to be a 'Greek god,' as the expression was, I refrained from mentioning myself, my ability to get a likeness in portraits or the fact that there were artists in my family background. Had I done so, my education may have taken a giant leap forward. Put in touch with young people, being referred to a good art school and to friends of his, I could perhaps have become a Londoner and remained there permanently.

As it was, with no declarations forthcoming from either Marcus or from me as to interest in each other, Georgie set out to introduce me to all the friends she could hope to assemble at her table. To feed a dozen of us, the first thing she must have was my ration card. When we escaped the line-up for cards, emerging with the precious paper, she almost raced me to the street market. As we approached it, the odours on the breeze announced, like the bunting festooned across the road from side to side, "Have a nice meaty herring!" Still the stuff of dreams, six years after the war in February 1951, a normal meat supply was not yet available. Once again I had walked into the real-life version of what I had so often seen in photographs of a hungry wartime crowd gathered around the fishmonger's stall as samples of the catch of the day were held aloft.

Being a consummate cook after her years in Europe with Tim, Georgie prepared a delightful gourmet meal to introduce me to a dozen of her friends. Some of them were the sons of friends in high places or wartime Home Guard veterans of her own age with whom she shared grim memories of hardship. Apparently possessed of a romantic nature, she had kindly hoped to start an instant love affair for me, if not with her son, then perhaps from her guest list.

As I recall, conversation failed to develop far beyond admiration for her fine culinary use of my ration card and the party soon dispersed without new acquaintances being made. With a few more women in the crowd, the prevailing British reserve might have broken down to allow for friendly conversation and an exchange of ideas. As it was, they went home without at least hearing a good sea story. Truth to tell, I feared that my "going to sea" would suggest the image of the "bohemian" as well as the "colonial" in their midst. How could I leave Georgie to live that down? I was sure that my world would be abhorrent to them. I had observed this reaction in my own English relatives.

Since the end of the war having developed the habit of strolling over to Harrods, for an 'elevens,' she introduced me to the delights of espresso, croissants and brioches of the famous luxury department store, before touring the luxurious displays to be found on every floor. Personally I was not especially drawn to Harrods, being a young and penniless person who needed nothing much more than a haversack on my back and sturdy shoes.

However, as my hostess was anxious to show me the delights of London I was determined not to disappoint her. I would go along with her kind suggestions for a while at least before moving on to my work in Paris. Getting to know Britain would come a little later, before my return to Canada. Fortunately, one of her great interests was to introduce me to typical court scenes at the historic Old Bailey, for which any Dickens fan, myself included, would be grateful.

Had I been alone in London I should have gone to the British Museum or the Albert Hall that day. We went instead to gradually explore Green Park and Hyde Park, adding the Serpentine, Kew Gardens, Baker Street, Germyn Street and Fleet Street over the ensuing weeks. As to the latter, I mentioned reading earlier in Canada that in the eighteenth century the venerable old Cheshire Cheese establishment was, among such literary gentlemen as Dr. Samuel Johnson, famous for its lark pie. Recently it had been announced that women could gather there.

We tried it, only to be chased out most unceremoniously by a testy old fellow gesticulating wildly and shouting, "Off with you, off with you, get out of here!" We had had time only to quickly glimpse the scrawled testimonies by celebrated writers on the ancient walls as to the perfection of the dish. As to whether it was still served, he gave us no time to enquire. Recalling this thoroughly unpleasant Victorian behaviour, one can only think of it as a very mild version of a scene from today's Middle East. At that time I had no idea of the systematic abuse of women in particular as a major issue in any part of the world and simply saw the incident as the hilarious antics of an octogenarian.

Georgie had one or two acquaintances among the clerics at Westminster Abbey, as well as a special seat of her own which she persuaded me to use for a

Sunday morning service. When I demurred, due to my vagabond appearance, she insisted magnanimously that I borrow from her wardrobe. When I see this section of the Abbey on TV, I can still see those pews, in fine detail, the polished wood, fine leather and the lamps. One day she determined to show me some of the historical items which had fascinated her over her lifetime of visits to the Abbey. The great building was largely empty in 1951, the modern age of tourism not yet underway. Approaching one of the clerics perched on a stool to answer questions, she asked, "Sir, where is the Stone of Scone now?"

Amused by this, he replied in an attempt at a comical accent, "Don't know mum, me 'obby's gardening."

We were all standing beside a quite plain old chair known as the ancient Scottish Throne. The Stone itself was definitely not in place under it. The story of the theft had caused amusement in the press as a Scottish student prank. After five years of war, Britain was ripe for a bit of fun, ostensibly upset at the disappearance of it from the Abbey. It had been installed in 1655 for the coronation of Charles II, last of the Stuart kings. The present scandal was short-lived and the royal stone was restored by the radical student group involved. We had heard about it on the ship's radio when it was missing.

On another outing we bought tickets on a barge for a trip down the Thames to Roehampton and Kew Gardens, just as was done by kings and commoners over the centuries. Unfortunately, no one played Handel's Water Music; yet it was a memorable day, steeped in history.

My kindly hostess made sure that we attended every possible West End theatrical performance. In the endless line-ups for matinee tickets at Covent Garden, I saw not only visions of Eliza Doolittle's flower stall but many excited young people like myself. To watch a performance by Sir Lawrence Olivier, or any other great actor of the day, seemed like a "once in a lifetime" chance before TV or budget-priced airfares existed.

Walking home after a George Bernard Shaw play, I waited for the lights to change at a small residential crossing when suddenly I saw the two young princesses a few feet away. Elizabeth, Margaret Rose and friends were enjoying themselves in an open carriage, oblivious of anything but their own conversation, I was struck by the radiance and spiritedness of the two girls, free for once of the need to assume a public presence.

On another occasion I set off to find the legendary Kitty Foyle's Bookshop. Wandering through its labyrinths, the high shelves packed with books along the narrow aisles, I encountered and chatted with various student types among the clerks and could have daydreamed about joining their ranks for a few months, in order to learn more about literature and deepen my familiarity with London and its people.

Georgie would have been delighted to have me as a paying guest and also to retain my ration card. The real issue was a matter of ideals and the goal in life to be worked out now that for the present at least, the original plans for university had failed. No, I reasoned,

I could not stay in London, at least not yet. I must prove myself in the operating room setting in Paris as arranged, just as I had done in Canada the year before taking the government contract on the high seas.

Still too immature to break with the past in favour of a new beginning, I would leave London behind despite all it offered. Totally oblivious to the fact that Britain had begun to provide free universities for ordinary people, in addition to the 'public schools' of the privileged classes, I saw no future there. Moreover, education was free in Paris. The very different mentality offered untold cultural opportunities for the observer, or so I told myself, trying to believe in such a future. Close to the truth too was the fact that two of my friends were in France. In London I had no contemporaries.

Among Georgie's fairly frequent visitors was her friend Claudia Grainger. A top civil servant, a woman somewhat younger than herself, she appeared to be an authoritative, sophisticated aristocrat. Although it was a somewhat daunting proposition to a young penniless traveller, they now invited me to attend plays and concerts with them. One evening Claudia arrived unexpectedly in her smart new black MG, suggesting that if I would agree to sit in the rumble seat, a common enough practice at the time, we could all go for a tour of her favourite West End haunts. Amused at the prospect, I agreed to give it a try. I had no idea that there was anything more to the suggestion than appeared at the moment.

On such a fine spring evening the mood of the crowd was euphoric, rushing for the theatre or the concert hall. As the renowned Dr. Samuel Johnson remarked in the eighteenth century, "He who is tired of London is tired of life." Once again, for me, however, perched on the rumble seat, the small slice of London I saw was almost déjà vu, just as I had seen it all these weeks as well as in the *Picture Post* back in Canada: the friendly street scene, London in the spring, flowers in boxes, natty English sports cars with rumble seats, the good life among the affluent members of British society as it had always been. I knew there was another London, poor war-torn London and so much of interest to be seen in a great city.

At home in Canada, I had also seen hundreds of photos of working-class London, but now lacked the courage to seek it out on my own. Certainly, a prowl of East London would have little appeal to my present companions nor would Georgie understand my interest. I had read George Orwell's *Down and Out in London and Paris*, in the world of 1933, and had seen the newsreels of the aftermath of the bombing raids. Such excursions would have to come later, on another foray into English life in the company of young people like myself.

It was time to get to work in Paris, to take over the student lodging of my Canadian friends as planned. When I broached the subject of Paris with Georgie, her immediate reaction was to bring on another visit from Claudia the next evening. In the meantime, she explained to me that her friend hoped that I would agree to travel to Rome with her in a month or so.

Despite my shortage of funds, I reasoned that it was probably a once in a lifetime opportunity not to be missed. As Georgie explained, "She wants to go to Italy before the election next month. She thinks that if they get a majority vote, the Italian Communist Party will take over the country, refusing visas for tourists or government visitors from Britain. She may be on a fact-finding mission. It seems likely at this point. After all, she is in close contact with sources at the BBC. Fortunately she is welcome to stay with an old colleague."

As she poured the coffee, I exclaimed in amazement, "How exciting for her!" not yet believing that I was involved. After all, Paris was my next stop.

Georgie took a sip and went on. "Yes," she said, now frowning a little, "but the trouble is, you know, we English are prohibited from taking any currency out of the country this year. It is absolutely prohibited. Six years after the end of the war we still have this severe food rationing and drastic currency restrictions. There is considerable resentment of the government because of it, you know."

Georgie got to the point of all this as she continued, "You want to see Italy, so here is your chance. You shouldn't miss it. At the same time she will be able to go, only if you agree to pay some of the expenses, starting with the cost of getting the MG across the Channel, as she, being English, is not permitted the resources to pay for the trip."

I was immediately hooked. Afford it or not, employed or not, I would go. My mind in a whirl of astonishment, I wondered aloud to Georgie, "How many other impecunious young western Canadians will get to fulfill their dreams of Italy this year, with a car trip across France and Switzerland along the way." It began to occur to me that I may have been offered the ride in the rumble seat so that Claudia could decide whether or not I would be a sufficiently good sport on a trip. It was also clear that without me the regulations would prevent her from paying with English pounds, shillings and pence in this year of enforced restrictions.

Georgie continued to elaborate this very enticing proposal. "You know, she was in Italy when war broke out and was caught there for the duration. She worked in the *Underground* and became very fond of the people and the language. Her family's military influence had a lot to do with it. That's why she must get back to Rome before the present government falls into the hands of the Communists."

While she spoke I began to wonder at the wisdom of being in close quarters with a woman of her experience, age and social class. Might a little upper-class snobbism towards 'colonials' like myself cause friction along the way? I set about washing the lunch dishes for Georgie who in all her good-nature and generosity had obviously set up this trip for Claudia and for me, just as her sister, Aunt Glad in Canada might have done in her place. I would, of course, have to ask my future employer for three weeks grace as to my employment date.

Paris

Finally I left the sheltering luxury of Knightsbridge and struck out for Paris to keep my rendezvous as previously planned in Canada with Max and Jessica. Just as it was known to behave, the English Channel was choppy enough to send most fellow passengers on the crossing running for the white enamel basins piled on a corner of the deck. Having earned my sea-legs so recently, I was able to devote myself to the thrill of seeing both the white cliffs of Dover and those of the French coast on the way to Calais.

Suddenly whisked off the ferry and onto a crowded train full of excited young people stowing away their haversacks, I was soon bounding across the colourful French countryside, leaving the white cliffs far behind as the panorama of fields, orchards and vineyards appeared before us. Nearest to me, a group of South Africans in a most convivial fervor were embarked on what in those days was called, "the trip of a lifetime," modern budget-priced air fares as yet unknown. They had planned this trip because, from far-away Africa, and penniless as they were, they could not ever expect to return to Europe. So typical of the era, I had seen them get on the train, bent double with the weight of the haversacks on their shoulders. My own trunk remained in London.

While the South Africans made it clear that it was for them a novelty to meet a Canadian, I in turn had never encountered their unique, attractive accent, nor their warm, outgoing ways. Probably evoking wartime habits, we all wore pins or badges with Commonwealth insignia on our clothing to facilitate recognition and contacts in foreign countries.

My undivided attention to the conversation was soon diverted by the inviting countryside before me. This was the land of the Impressionist painters and so much else that I could scarcely contain myself. Not so, in the case of a gangly English youth beside me whose attention was drawn to some chattering pre-school French children and their mother. He wondered aloud to me, "Out of the mouth of babes; how do they master this impossible language?" Looking at these lively toddlers prattling away at such a rate, one might well wonder. "I say, it won't be easy, I can see that! I'm going to attend the Sorbonne to learn French, I hope!" I was thankful to have been acquainted with it from an early age, one major reason I was en route to Paris myself.

In the last letter received from Max and Jessica before leaving London, it had been arranged that they would meet the afternoon train from London, at St. Lazare Station in the Montparnasse district of Paris.

As the train slowed for arrival at the stop, I was quite aware of entering a foreign country. Compared to the Underground in London, newly updated, efficient and fast-moving, this was all very different. I alighted in the late afternoon sun to find myself in an imposing nineteenth century edifice with domed glass roof, the air heavy with Gaulois cigarette smoke and an overlay of soot from the trains.

Suddenly I saw Max and Jessica waving and coming toward me through the crowd. Jessica had taken on a pleasantly European presence, enhancing her already considerable beauty. Max was as dour, blunt and unsmiling as ever. He wasted no time in announcing, "We won't be seeing Europe with you. I've got a job teaching art in Canada. As soon as we can afford to pay the return fare, we're off. Right now, we're working for the American government at Orleans. We'll pick you up every weekend. Have to get going before dark tonight, so we'll get you settled now."

It was a profound shock. When the plan was first discussed in Canada we had planned to work, study and travel around Europe together. They had completed their scholarship in Paris and were not even slightly interested even in France, longing instead for home. I felt frozen to the spot. "What am I getting into?" I wondered, already imagining myself all alone that night in strange surroundings. I offered no comment, appearing to be equal to whatever fate threw in my way. After all, it had been my luck for years. I was speechless.

I enjoyed the fact that the long sequence of buildings
I called home were so typically Parisian in style.

We left the station and proceeded by taxi to 12,
rue de l'Observatoire, near the junction of boulevards
Montparnasse and St. Michel, in the heart of the Latin
Quarter. Already reeling from the first shock, I was
now to receive another. I was charmed as they stopped
before a block-long row of nineteenth century greystone
apartments with wrought iron balcony grills facing the
boulevard and a fine row of plane trees, but they then
led me to the back of the building. We faced a roughly

built seven-floor outdoor wooden staircase leading to the old servants' quarters, now converted to students' lodgings. On the way up to the top floor, Max tried to impress me, pointing and commenting with one of his strange uneasy grins, "Suicides occur from these landings, you know. Foreign students sometimes become despondent."

To myself I said, "He could do with a bit of colour around those pale blue eyes and colourless hair when he makes such inappropriate and ghoulish remarks."

Arriving at the seventh floor, I was aware of the aroma of cooking oil, garlic and other enticing, mysterious aromas. "Here we are. Home at last," chirped Jessica. The way she said it told me that she knew what a shock it would be to me, just as it must have been to her.

Any frank remarks we might have made were cut short by Max's booming retort, "And if you don't like it," he said, "I'll rent it to the first idiot I find!" How could I not comply, when he spoke like that, I wondered. Clearly, he was embarrassed.

The room was one of two facing each other, with another marked *lavatoire* in between. I was ushered into a cement bunker, a single electric light bulb dangling from the ceiling. A tap had been blasted through the cement in recent times. Little more than one small cot remained from my friends' furnishings. What I called "the Bunsen burner," such as we used in the chemistry lab in high school, was the only equipment to heat water, make coffee and prepare food in stages in order to assemble a plate of food. A small, strangely low table as well as a basic pot or two completed the furnishings. Apart from all this, I would have to spend the night alone here, totally unaware of my surroundings, or of the residents, with no telephone to contact Jessica if necessary. It was difficult to imagine that they had toughed it out here for the whole year as art students. The difference was that there were two of them. "Oh well, I am used to challenges now. I have managed to handle them myself thus far," I thought quite proudly.

As she opened the door onto the corridor again, Jessica was explaining, "We must hurry along to the food supply, set you up for the week and for lunch. We need to have it as soon as we get back here, to keep us going until we get home to Orleans."

A short walk took us to their customary food source, a small, typically Parisian shop around the corner, in Montparnasse near Clos de Lilas, run by a kindly old woman, as were many of the small shops in the early fifties. Wearing worn denim smocks which hung from their shoulders, these employees looked as if the war had ended only very recently, as if they had suffered hunger and were not quite at home in these well-stocked shops.

Probably due to the Marshall Plan set in place to restore the European economy, this shop was piled neatly to the ceiling with unheard of luxuries. At least that was my impression, from the point of view of a stranger from America to the epicurean palate of the French. As these thoughts were going through my head, Jessica quietly pointed out the basics of oil, bread, cheese and wine, as well as the things we would need for our lunch.

As we left, a little bell tinkled over the door. Jessica called out, "Au revoir Madame, merci Madame," in a pleasantly deferential tone of voice used in those days towards older people. The shopkeeper replied in kind in a lilting tone which Jessica had obviously learned to exemplify, both on entering and leaving the premises. She sounded convincingly French herself, rather than just another clumsy foreigner at a loss as to how to cope politely. As I was to learn, to be taken for a Yank in 1951, could invite resentment. Too many Yanks in uniform crowded the most popular thoroughfares, making their presence felt so strongly that Parisians sometimes felt as if they were almost pushed off their own sidewalks. Too many large American cars blocked narrow streets, sometimes making it difficult for pedestrians and motorists alike to find their way in familiar neighbourhoods.

Back at the bunker, without benefit of three chairs to sit on, we stood up to drink red wine to honour the occasion and to sample for the first time in my case, the delectable, crusty, soft-centered French bread, or *baguettes,* topped with good country ham and cheeses. Max applied himself to providing three very strong, wonderful cups of coffee laced with chicory, a national favourite, over the 'Bunsen burner.' Meanwhile he announced that, "Before going back to Orleans, we'll all get on the motor-bikes to tour a few landmarks to introduce you to this part of the city. That way you won't be so lost, trying to find your way around."

Having never ridden on such a vehicle before and fearful at the thought, the ride was a memorable, unexpectedly light-hearted and grand welcome to Paris. I clung to Max's jacket with Jessica on the other bike, as we swirled around Avenue George V in the slight traffic of the early evening darkness, passing close to the beautifully flood-lit bust of Rodin's Balzac, past the Louvre, along the Seine, over the Pont Neuf and back into the Quartier Latin, up Boulevard St. Michel and home.

"I'll arrive from Orleans to pick you up at about six o'clock next Saturday morning on the bike," promised Max, no doubt prompted by Jessica worrying about leaving me alone on the first night in the city, rather than with them. They did not know, of course, that a night alone in a cabin on a freighter, ploughing through a violent storm at sea offers even less security. In the morning I would have to find the hospital and prepare to start work.

As I got ready to leave the next day, my usual ambivalences began to surface. I had come to the heart of Europe; I wanted to be involved in work which would teach me about the country. "Oh well," I thought, as I picked up my keys and left my bunker, "I'll do my best. I have the advantage of having come to see what Europe has been through," or 'to see how the other half lives,' as for years the press had queried. With BBC short-wave war reports flooding into our living room in

Canada in Dad's lifetime, everyone had asked, "How will they survive it? What would we do in their place? What will be left of Europe after the war?" That at least would be my own private off-duty type of reporting on humanity outside the operating-room.

Thus occupied, I descended the seven story staircase and made my way into the Port Royal metro station. Just as Jessica had described, there it was, the charming wrought iron Art Nouveau style archway and lettering spelling out the name of the station.

I was to head for the directional wall-guide with the map of Paris overlaid with lighted indicators in keyed directional colours. It showed not only the metro routes through the city but also their point of intersection or *correspondence* so that one could anticipate in advance the required transfer point to another line towards the desired destination. I bought a *carnet des billets,* a book of tickets and proceeded along the platform of the cavernous tunnel to wait for the train in question. It would be clearly marked, *Direction Étoile.*

The station at Port Royal, badly in need of a post-war updating, like all the others, was poorly lit, shabby, reeked of garlic, Gaulois cigarettes and other indefinable odours. A few beggars lounged on the sidelines, coming into view only when the surging crowds rushed forward into the fast-moving coaches and took off. The Metro crowds exuded the essence of Paris in 1951, surprising the senses with strong perfumes, the aroma of soft, odorous cheeses, gorgonzola, Polish sausage, Gaulois cigarettes, unwashed bodies, popular hair tonics and other not so subtle vapors, exotic and otherwise. Paper being in short supply and plastic not yet in use, food was still scantily wrapped, if at all, in small squares of newspaper without string or tape, while personal hygiene was difficult to maintain without universal modern plumbing.

At a time before this was common practice in Canada, students on the Metro embraced enthusiastically as they stood half in, half out of the packed aisles of the coaches, the painted ends of their long, thin crispy, unwrapped loaves protruding into the aisles from one arm, books in the other. In the midst of these urgent love-ins, extricating oneself from the bottleneck in the aisle in time for the next stop could be a battle of wits and perseverance for a newcomer to this seemingly novel form of rapid transit.

However, one soon felt fully alive and part of a warm, compelling and often amusing surge of humanity here in *le nombril du monde*, or centre of the world as it was known. "What would the nineteenth-century caricaturist Honoré Daumier have made of it?" I wondered. How would he update his well-known depiction of public transit in the horse-drawn coaches of his time to show the likes and dislikes of people, the humour, the interaction between classes and their assumptions about each other? He would not find this in the euphoric coaches of the students but perhaps in other parts of the city.

On a rainy morning I set out to find the hospital for a preliminary interview, following the written acceptance I had received in Canada. Strangely, I found that the streets were full of stranded employees trying to get to work. Signs posted at every corner announced *La Grève Nationale,* or general strike. Old army trucks plied up and down Montparnasse Boulevard at long intervals. It was a colourful though confusing introduction to Paris. People were feeling stressed and irritable. When the truck suddenly rolled up at the corner, one had to choose the route very quickly. Obviously this was an impossibility for a newcomer.

Without benefit of that remarkable lighted directional chart in the Metro, I had to let two or three vehicles pass by before hazarding a guess as to the areas they served in relation to my destination. The bored truck attendant would keep on calling out, *Allons y,* or "let's go" in a thin, whining voice as he pushed people up the high back of the lorry, without benefit of a box, portable steps, or time to give directions. As I scrambled up into the vehicle before it jolted off again, fleeting memories of another scenario came to mind. Memories of the newsreels showing the brutal herding of Jewish prisoners into boxcars in the war or even of the carts full of victims in the French Revolution. As local colour this was tiresome, not dangerous.

Yet before long I felt completely at home in Paris discovering my own neighbourhood, the Latin Quarter, to be one of the best. As I passed La Sorbonne, or l'université de Paris every day I could daydream wildly of one day being a student there with the benefit of free education. Thrilled to live near le Boulevard St. Michel, Blvd. Montparnasse, le Clos de Lilas, St. Germain de Près, the famous Café de Deux Maggots, le Pont Neuf and Chatelet. I had of course also discovered the Impressionist painters' gallery in the Tuileries.

"Surely I will never leave Paris, an impossible thought," I muttered to myself like many other naïve newcomers have done down the centuries. Whenever it occurred to me that I had a duty to go home eventually, the thought sent me spiralling into abject depression. I must savour every moment of my present existence and hope for the best. Nevertheless, loyalty to family must never be forgotten. In agony I wondered fruitlessly how it would all end.

Not being a tourist, it was important for me to obtain a work permit, or *permis de séjour,* signed by my landlord. This gave me the chance to enter the front of the attractive old building in which I lived. Reminding me of a wrought-iron bird cage, the ornate nineteenth-century elevator for that section of the building wafted me unsteadily to the third floor. An ominous barking greeted me when I rang the bell, suggesting the presence of a large and formidable creature. This observation was followed by the muffled sound of feet approaching the door and hands struggling with heavy locks. This might seem to be a wise general precaution which had become a habit even after the end of the war.

Once I was admitted to the apartment by the elderly Madame Gregoire, struggling to secure three large brass locks, with severely arthritic fingers, and holding a German shepherd tightly by the collar, the old lady led me into the living-room to meet aged, Monsieur Gregoire. Reclining in his threadbare upholstered chair, he shook hands with me and exchanged pleasantries. He explained with effort that his son would take me to the work permits office in the morning, his usual practice with tenants in need of a 'permis do séjour.'

Madame expressed the hope that as a registered nurse, I would give her husband his monthly injection ordered by the doctor. Pleased to agree to this proposal, hoping in time to get to know them a little, to soften their very reserved old-fashioned manners. Here were two kindly old people whose bearing seemed to reveal forbearance and pride in the face of much past suffering. Such people had endured two world wars within three decades, being forced to meet the onset of old age and the second of two great conflicts simultaneously.

When their son took me to get my work permit or *permis de séjour,* I learned that his sister had already married a U.S. serviceman and now lived in America. In order to assess for himself the opportunities of "the new world," he was about to follow her. It seemed quite tragic that the old couple would be left on their own. I wondered what had been their story. By 1938, for those with children, like themselves, life would have been daily more frightening as the threat of war increased, once again, just as in 1914. While the Chamberlain government in London sought a "non-aggression" pact with Hitler, in the interests of a "appeasement," of "peace in our time" France put up a system of defense known as the *Maginot Line* to hold the Nazis in check. In the enthusiasm which followed, I recall that the BBC acknowledged the French project by playing, 'We'll hang out the washing on the Siegfried Line,' perhaps in an effort to bolster flagging morale at home too. It was said that Winston Churchill had initially expressed admiration for it as an important defense.

As I learned much later, rumour had it that one of the other reasons for Chamberlain's visit to Berlin had been in the interests of gaining a year to update the London water supply system, before bombing raids led to massive fires. Within a short time we had been dismayed to hear the BBC announce that the German army had breached the Maginot Line. The newsreels had brought us face to face with the shocking spectacle of the attempted escape of Parisians streaming out of the city only to meet death on the roads. On that morning in early September, 1939, Mother had come to the breakfast table with the dreaded news that, "The skies over Europe today are black with Nazi aircraft." I was now beginning to see first-hand some of the effects of it all.

The visit to the Gregoire's had left me in no doubt as to the privation and fear that had been felt in the four walls of that faded-looking apartment turned veritable prison over the entire five years of the Occupation. While it had been the same or worse for millions of people, the difference was that I had had the privilege of meeting the Gregoires in their own home. With no means of escape, they had been forced to endure five years of coercion and hardship. In all likelihood they had stored-up memories of World War I in their youth, and of their parents' stories of the Franco-Prussian War of 1870. I had heard that these were still remembered by grandparents.

In early 1951 almost every light standard or wall space around the centre of Paris was marked by graffiti announcing the common affront, "Yanks Go Home." The perception of the advertisers of the day indicated the need for endless repetition of an image and a name. Consequently the Metro stations were also plastered with hundreds of advertisements for *Monsavon,* or 'my soap,' one after the other at each station. The printed billboard images were of a standing cow with a bar of *Monsavon* soap under the udder rather than a milk pail. On each bar was scribbled in large black hand lettering, "The U.S. is milking France dry!" Despite the American Marshall Plan of assistance to help restore the economy, as in Germany, these detractors were bristling with resentment at the large foreign presence in the country. Nevertheless, American G.I.'s continued to crowd every street-corner and thoroughfare and were stationed on bases in France.

Consequently, rather than be taken for a member of that great concentration of Americans, Canadians made sure not to appear in public without a Canada badge or pin attached to jacket collars or shoulder bags. There were, of course, many jokes related to the subject. One of them concerned the incomprehensible need of the Americans for a glass of milk in preference to wine. Apart from the notion that it lacked a manly image to drink something in public regarded as food for infants, bringing cries of derision from the French, there was the contention that such a practice, if started in childhood, brought about a "softening of the brain."

While they sat around the sidewalk cafés in their traditional way, with wine and Gaulois cigarettes, young Frenchmen knew for certain they were right. From infancy they had been given wine, watered at first, in small amounts. Their cognitive faculties had not been undermined. Intellectually, they would say in those student bistros in which I heard such ill-founded comments and remarks to the effect that, "Those Americans are a sorry lot!"

Before long, I was to run into the same amusing reaction to foreign ideas in Italy. In the satiric and hilarious song, 'Buvati di Latta,' or 'Drink Milk,' the impact of the reclining, sensuous form of Anita Ekburg of 'Dolce Vita' fame as a billboard advertisement for milk was used to ridicule supposed attempts to Americanize the land of the grape.

Expressions of gratitude toward those who put in place the means of economic recovery as well as assisted in the liberation of Western Europe were naturally expressed outside the arena of such popular comment. Given that for its size Canada had played a large part in the liberation, we Canadians were everywhere very popular, very well-treated. Being a small country at the time, our political presence was not felt to the same extent.

It was quite natural then that as individuals we did not seek the company of Americans, but tended to mix mostly with other members of the then Commonwealth and to accept the goodwill of the French and other Europeans when offered. Besides, how could one observe the old world of Europe, and try to play the reporter privately, if one responded as well to the many overtures of the ever-friendly Americans.

The year 1951 was a now well documented and important time to have come to Europe, just six years after the cessation of hostilities. It was a time of ferment, of the stirrings of a transitional phase before massive changes to the economy, and public attitudes transforming France and other countries with a new pan-European mentality altogether. Fortunately I had arrived in time to see a little of Europe before the winds of change rebuilt societies, created new political alliances, removed ruins and rebuilt cities. I was not disappointed; the scars of war were still at hand, as well as much of pre-war France which remained untouched.

From the safety of Canada we had wondered, "How did the 'other half' survive?" Just to be there at that precise moment in history was an incredible privilege in itself. It was a daily learning experience. Carrying out my own form of youthful rebellion against the status quo without adequate resources was perilous, yet exhilarating, to say the least. Young people began to declare themselves "Citizens of the World," a very new concept at the time.

Yet for me, there could be no thought of turning my youth into one of "wild abandon." Work awaited me on the operating room team at the hospital. I had been extremely fortunate to have secured such a post. It had gone well from the initial enquiry by mail from Canada to my final acceptance through the offices of the International Nursing Commission in London and to my acceptance by the nursing director of the hospital. Qualified operating room nurses were apparently difficult to find. It would be demanding, exhausting work as in any operating room. Canada had a good reputation in this field.

To my great surprise, a young Asian businessman once said to me from his recovery-room bed, "It is wonderful you know, you young women go around the world helping the sick." Obviously, this was long before the recent era of Doctors Without Borders and related groups including nursing staff taking immeasurable risks in dangerous places.

I was astonished to be able to postpone the date on which I would begin work until after the date of Claudia's return from Italy. I went back to the 'bunker' to find pen and paper to let Georgie and Claudia know the good news. Shortly after, I returned to London to prepare for the unbelievable. Within a week or so, I would cast my eyes on Italy.

Italy

On a fine, warm, early spring morning in 1951 Claudia and I left for Italy by car. In those days before tourists began to flock to Europe in great number, Italy still floated on the imagination as an experience much to be desired, but quite out of reach for most young people. In all likelihood this would be my only opportunity to see it. Scarcely able to believe my good fortune, I tried at the same time, to take Claudia's worries to heart, her fear of being unable to cram everything into the rumble-seat of her new shiny black MG and close it. "If anything shows, it will draw attention to the car," she worried. "The *banditti* will give chase, especially if they see baggage. And then there are the British license plates. They hate us, you know. The Italian Communist party is leading in the polls." She went on distractedly, yet finally, with trial and error, we managed to secure everything out of sight.

Apart from Claudia's great affection and familiarity with the Italian language and people, her trip may have been one of political urgency, to gather information from her counterparts in the Rome office of her government headquarters in London before the Communist takeover of Italy. Perhaps she found some relief from the tensions inherent in such a commitment that morning, by venting her frustrations on me as a baggage handler.

Off we went, cruising easily, slowly, my excitement barely suppressed and with difficulty, down the road through early morning London via Dover to the ferry. Claudia being unable to use British currency, I paid for the car and would continue to do so as arranged. The channel crossing was completely uneventful, with no sign of the usual choppy waters and seasickness.

Since I was struck by the remembrance of the importance of these places in World War II, the privilege of passing through the still sleepy early morning towns of Dover and Dieppe was not lost on me. From the ferry terminal, the latter looked like nothing but unremarkably muddy flat lands, rather than the site where thousands died in the failed Allied Commando raid of 1942. As Dover had also played its part during the war, I was delighted to see it now as charmingly British as I had imagined.

A practical woman engaged in testing the performance of her car on the poor stretch of road through the fields, Claudia remarked, "I hope you know that you will be the navigator." Having never driven a car and knowing nothing of Europe, I was more than surprised, but ventured to say that after all her trips across Europe over the years I was sure she knew the roads.

Being half her age I then kept silent on the matter. Perhaps she was only trying to draw me into the project but had been at a loss for conversation.

However, before long, she suggested that we stop for lunch in a field, and not a moment too soon as suddenly in the distance Rheims Cathedral came into view. The fields before us were dotted with bright red poppies, enchanting in the soft, slightly overcast light of northern France on that fine peace-time morning, despite the sad wartime connotations of Vimy, the memories of Canada's John McCrae and so many others. "In Flanders fields ... if you break faith with us who die ... we will not sleep, though poppies grow...."

We slid down from the low-slung bucket seats of the MG into the grass and wild flowers for the first of many picnics of baguettes and cheese for which I would remember France. Although pleased to be there, it seemed inappropriate to picnic on a battlefield or close to one of such monumental carnage, albeit in World War I.

But Claudia's mind was elsewhere as she suggested, "You could help give us a pastime for the trip if you were to recite blank verse in the days ahead." Fond as I was of poetry, I was forced to admit that memorization was not emphasized in my high school education, nor had I yet attended university. She assured me that she had learned such things, "In a good Swiss finishing school." A little later, as we set out again, she asked that I tell her about "those shops, which you call drug stores in America, rather than chemists' shops."

I was a little hurt, feeling that what she was really thinking was, 'Well, if as a colonial you cannot cope with poetry, you must at least be familiar with the vulgar American culture." Clearly, I was not the travelling companion she would have wished to have, or vice versa, had each of us been free to choose. I hadn't dared to mention Dr. John McCrae or any other Canadians, and yet of course the lines kept going through my mind.

As beggars cannot be choosers, I had the strong conviction that the less I had to say, being young and a colonial, the better it would be. Yet in all fairness, she may have wished that I were a great talker, instead of a dreamer intent on taking in every aspect of the passing countryside. She was from a military family; I was an artist's daughter.

On the first night in France we stopped at a walled medieval village known to Claudia, alighting at a delightful ivy-covered stone hotel, very like a small castle. Tired after a long day, Claudia fell asleep immediately in one of the two deep feather beds. A nightingale sang passionately in the moonlight, perched on the ivy creeper growing around the window. I recognized it as the bird my grandfather had described in his memories of England. Innocent though I was of any serious romantic liaison, I was amused at my fate; alone in a room with a female, superior officer-type travelling companion in this setting associated in traditional poetry with the flowering of young love.

As adolescents we had not missed the allure of the line in the popular wartime song, "A Nightingale

Sang in Barclay Square," wondering about the meaning of love. It was the sort of question one never asked. I wondered then, on this peerless night in France, with so much good fortune since leaving Canada, if I would spend my life alone, or would I actually meet a soulmate? First of all I must become the person I wanted to be, creative and successful. I could survive my misfortunes but not failure.

I began to wonder what had been Claudia's fate in her youth, or in the war, that had left her alone now. "Had she been close to someone who had been killed in the war?" Could she perhaps be listening with closed eyes and a sad heart as the bird again poured out its impassioned song? As I drifted into sleep, I could not see across the room from me whether she had awakened or not. It had been a delightful welcome to rural France, the land I was to learn to love, borne sublimely on the wings of song.

On the way downstairs to breakfast, I had noticed a rack of outdated post-cards of supposedly alluring French girls of long ago, their tresses garlanded in deep red roses. Finding the cards so banal I bought one to send home and laughed aloud as I said, "Oh, these are really hilarious!" They recalled the World War I songs old people sang, "The roses are blooming in Picardy still" and "Mademoiselle from Armentaires, parlez-vous, parlez-vous?"

A rather angular and stern figure, her dark hair cropped short, Claudia dressed in solid black pants and shirt long before this was common. Concealed behind sunglasses, her expression was unsmiling, determined and autocratic. Claudia had earlier mentioned the "opulent beauties" of Rome, whom she deplored, perhaps with some measure of envy. Far from being amused at my youthful mirth, she now seemed to fear for my sanity, supposing me to be a sentimental, ignorant colonial, who liked such songs.

Certainly we had elements in common with Don Quixote and Sancho Panza or other such ill-matched duos. Had I been aware of the great Spanish tale by Cervantes at the time, the humour of the situation would have amused me and tempted me to laugh now and again, most unwisely. Being always one to keep the peace, I returned to my most serious of demeanors, suitable for a servant toward a master and got the car packed up for another day's progress towards Rome.

Once upon the road, Claudia again reminded me of the true seriousness of the trip, which I appreciated in full, given my interest in politics. As she said, "It is unthinkable that Italy could be cut off from Western Europe, but it will happen if the Communists win the election. People say that it is only, after all, 'soft communism,' whereas it could still keep us out of the country."

I could understand her apprehension. Georgie had hinted that Claudia had worked there in the *underground* all during the war, spoke the language, and worked for the Allied cause through her special standing as a member of a military family. She finished by announcing that we would take all the obvious shortcuts across France and Switzerland in order to reach Domodosola, the northern point of entry by way of the Simplon Pass in record time.

Sometimes when we stopped for lunch on a bench with our packed sandwiches in a village park, villagers gathered around us. They had noticed the MG, the British license plates and even my Maple Leaf pin. Before long the tears would begin to flow as they poured out their wartime memories as well as their gratitude to us, as British and Canadian Allies and liberators. There were to be many such expressions of grief across the country as the people recounted tales of courage, starvation and desperation, which, despite this idyllic spring day, remained in their minds as hideous and vivid memories.

Having seen much suffering during the war in Italy, Claudia was quietly kind and responsive to them as they looked to us as women hoping for a sympathetic response. Everywhere we went the years of extreme suffering showed its mark upon the often overly thin haunted features of young and old. The conveyances they drove were nothing short of extraordinary, sometimes without resemblance to a car. There were obviously no fixed rules. Necessity being the mother of invention, it might even consist of a bicycle with a wide, unwieldy cabin built over it.

Crossing the country in a south-easterly direction we finally reached the border into Switzerland near Basel, where we came upon a village celebration of some kind, the farm-folk proudly resplendent in colourful, traditional costume. On horseback, or in elaborate horse drawn carriages, passing in procession over the brow of a hill, and thus silhouetted against the sky, the occasion gave the impression of being a gala, time-honoured event. The peacefulness, prosperity and orderliness of those mountain valleys suggested paradise, a land that had come through the war unscathed.

Recently I have heard Switzerland referred to as an imaginary country. The more I got to know it over the next year or so, the more I felt its charms intensify to such an extent that had I then known the term I should have used it with delight. Proud of its own folk culture, it boasts a record of eight hundred years of democratic government in its three linguistic zones, French, German and Italian. Despite having escaped invasion by the Nazis or any other conflict in modern times, the Swiss built well-concealed fortifications and kept themselves in position of preparedness through compulsory annual military training for each male citizen.

Somewhere in all this magnificent mountain scenery, we came upon a region boasting small, colourful onion-domed churches, not at all similar to those in Russia, but unique in our experience. Unfortunately, I did not find out their significance, distracted as I was by this land of delightful chalets, pastures full of "make-believe" looking cattle, contentedly munching the grass and wild flowers at their feet. Large, sleek, light-brown beasts with long curled horns, prominent dark eyes beneath thick lashes, each was further embellished with a decorative bell hanging from the fine leather collar around the neck, so that its whereabouts could be heard over some distance. Likewise, in former days, the sound of the massive, trumpet-like wooden krumhorn set down in a pasture served the same purpose.

In the nineteen-fifties, the blowing of the krumhorn was the occasion for country merriment, each participant proudly dressed in his or her traditional cantonal costume. As Catherina, one of them with whom I later met and chatted, expressed it as she whirled around in her finery, beaming with delight, "It is so *champètre*; so countrified. I am so proud to be *champètre*." Never having heard of western Canadian farm people of the *dust-bowl* years who spoke of the experience with anything but extreme distaste, I was completely startled by her love of the countryside. I was shocked and speechless. It took me a moment or so to make a suitable comment!

Catherina, on the other hand, had every reason to speak with such glee about life in the French Swiss Alps around Lac Leman, or, in English it is known as Lake Geneva, with Montreux and Vevey on its shores. For one thing, every inch of her surroundings on the slopes was green, productive, and suffused with wild flowers. The villages themselves offered a variety of charming old fountains, parks, chalets, cafés, ancient wrought iron décor, with great pots of flowers, geraniums, *golden globes* or *trollis* from the slopes and many other seasonal wild flowers embellishing every balcony.

None of the charm of these villages was threatened by cars, highways, advertising or the noise of industry.

Like the fine cheeses, chocolates and other gourmet specialties of Switzerland, its wines have earned accolades in the world market, although little of the latter has the chance to reach the outside world, due to its popularity at home. A glass of Swiss champagne, preferably served beside Lac Leman, was an experience to be treasured. Unlike the poor Depression-era Canadian farmers I knew of, these rural people, Catherina's family included, had their own flourishing vineyards and were concentrating on increasing *la fortune*, just as was done by the ancestors with the assets they talked about with such obvious pride.

Claudia paid little attention to the passing scene, feeling that the absence of Roman influence and architecture had doomed these people to be known only for their "appalling shops full of nothing but cuckoo clocks." In her opinion, "One simply did not notice Switzerland." It is a society based entirely on folk culture, hide-outs for German spies during the war and of course the all-powerful banks in Zurich." Needless to say, we made few stops as we passed through these bucolic alpine scenes en route through the French and Italian cantons to the Italian border. Indeed, we had no funds for indulgences of any kind, nor did we stop to admire a single cuckoo clock.

Warning me that the rail-trip through the Simplon Pass into Italy would be long, hot and dark, Claudia emphasized the need to guard our purses and to remain strictly aloof in our seats during the long crowded stretches of complete darkness in the tunnel. My only possible complaint might be the poor ventilation and heavy snoring for a few minutes before we finally emerged unscathed at our entry point of Domodosola.

After a long line-up before the Italian Customs officials and a great deal of good-natured banter rippling back and forth through the crowd under the wonderfully hot mid-day sun of April, we claimed the MG without incident, and made our way to the autostrada. Before doing so, Claudia inspected the baggage once more, complaining, "The *banditti* will follow us. We simply cannot let any of our baggage show, you know, we have to make sure that the rumble seat is secure."

While the autostrada is said to have been a gift to the people from Mussolini in his early years, it was also referred to as part of the necessary build-up for the Abyssinian campaign of 1937, a testing operation for "Hitler's War." Exhilarated at the change from the secondary back roads we had enjoyed on our short-cut route through Switzerland, Claudia swept grandly onto a stretch of 'Il Duce's' super-highway. As the breeze rippled through my hair in the open car, I felt a thrill, a fresh sense of anticipation. Without another vehicle in sight for the moment, my companion looked quite pleased to try her new, sleek black MG under ideal conditions.

Within minutes we heard the roar of two police motorcycles close behind. Suddenly, to my utter amazement, I felt a warm, fleshy hand closing softly around the back of my neck. As 'my' policeman came level with the open window at my side, I saw out of the corner of my eye that he was a very young, rotund fellow with a thick mat of curly hair and large, cherubic, blue eyes, reminiscent of what one might see on a baroque frieze. Perhaps equally startled, Claudia watched from her mirror an older, thin, stern-looking *carabiniere* riding alongside at her window. No doubt he had glimpsed her matronly profile and dared only to drape his smart grey leather-gloved hand over the open-window as he drew alongside.

Hearing an exchange in rapid Italian, I took it for an argument, only to find that it ended peacefully when Claudia handed over a box of Camel cigarettes made popular by the Americans during the war. With a sudden flourish of approval shown in the ensuing roar from the motorbikes, the two stalwarts of the road surged ahead of us.

"They wanted to race us down the road. The new car attracted them," Claudia explained.

"Race?" I asked incredulously, assuming that the duty of the police is to enforce the speed limit.

"Italy has no speed limit," she explained, matter-of-factly, without a trace of amusement, letting me in on one of the first of many surprises to follow. Again, it left me speechless. To say she was taciturn was putting it mildly. She had that certain worldly quality of disdain suited to her background. I hoped not to be the recipient of more of it than I could take. I could not entirely suppress my enjoyment of life around me at all times.

At this point we saw that in order to impress us, our strange, improbable police duo were now executing exaggeratedly graceful swan-like arabesques, a kind of ballet on wheels, back and forth across the road. In retrospect, I recall the same sort of behaviour in Shakespeare's comedy, *Much Ado About Nothing* in which Dogberry, the constable in charge of the Watch, and Verges, his partner, sixteenth rather than twentieth century bumpkins, make an equally drawn out and awkward exit from an exchange with Leonato, the Governor of Messina. After he pays them to leave him alone, they mount their steeds and depart in an outrageous, embarrassed and pompous manner. We at least, had gotten away with a mere box of cigarettes. Here was a most amusing and original introduction to Italy and its uniquely creative spirit.

Was this perhaps a sample of a kind of Commedia del Arte? Was Claudia amused? I did not know, having never known her to relax the *stiff upper lip* of the Empire. Although the distance between the interlopers and ourselves began to lengthen as we held back, I thought it wise to look for a side road. Fortunately, it led to our first glass of Chianti and pizza from an outdoor oven hidden from sight under the trees. As Shakespeare's Leonato had said, "Neighbours, you are tedious." We too hoped we were free of such characters and had taken the right precaution. Hilarious as it had seemed to me, we had no need of a police escort or any other such entertainment.

Lago d'Orta

For several hours before the light of a perfect spring evening began to fade, we drove light-heartedly south through Piedmont and Lombardy towards Rome, eventually swerving off the autostrada onto an enticingly beautiful old side road. I noticed that it was becoming more attractive with each kilometre. By midnight the MG was purring its way slowly along a moonlit strip of ancient cobblestone between old stone ramparts decorated every few feet or so with flower-filled niches.

Above the wall, creating an image of utter fantasy in the magic stillness of the spring night, a row of gorgeous old villas was partially screened from the road by mature lemon and orange trees laden with large ripe fruit and waxy-looking green leaves. One might imagine hearing the voice of an Italian opera singer wafting down from an open window or even echoing from the velvety black distance of some village lane. Indeed that scenario actually occurred during our stay there at Lago d'Orta a short time later. Above all, it was an experience to be remembered forever.

Then, without comment, or any sign of elation, but surely pleased, Claudia calmly nosed the car around a narrow corner to the left, coming to a stop in a beautiful, fully lighted square. Intriguing dark waters glinted ahead of us from the light of the cafés and shops on either side, indicating a body of water at the far end of the square. As we alighted to enter the hotel, my nose picked up the freshness of a lake. As if she were at home, Claudia was already giving orders to the porter. The warm air wafted around me, pungent with the aromas of espresso, ripe cheeses, hams, olive oil and fresh Italian bread hanging at each side of the bead-curtained doorways. It could have been an opera set at intermission.

"Where are we?" I asked. "This is incredible, I can't believe it, Claudia. It's amazing."

"This is Lago d'Orta, a smaller lake than the others, Lakes Como, Stresa and Maggiore north of us. It's less frequented by tourists. I always stay here," she said, without appearing to look around or smile at the prospect. With that I climbed into one of the inviting old four-poster beds and fell asleep instantly in a state of delight.

The next thing I knew a tumultuous peeling of bells all around awoke me in time to see the soft light of dawn. Raising my head a little I vaguely recognized my surroundings and saw across the room a wrought-iron balcony straight in front of me. I glanced at Claudia. As she did not stir, I guessed she must use ear-plugs. Tiptoeing to the railing in a state of unbelieving delight,

I saw the now misty lake, last night lost in darkness. It was now the source of the jubilant sound filling the air. Astonished, I saw that an island formed the opposite shore. Later in the day Claudia explained that it bore the name of San Giulio and was home to a seminary.

Handsome villas lined the water's edge as far as I could see in each direction. Resounding joy rang out all around me, to left, to right, everywhere. It was music to lift the heart! I felt that I was caught up in a timeless expression of adulation of some kind, perhaps to welcome the joy of spring itself. Somewhere among those villas there must surely be a monastery as the round-a-lay bounced, reverberated to left, to right, above the villas and over the lake and in each direction as if expressing the perfection of creation in the early morning air. The magic sound pelted down in utter joy, like melting drops of golden colour, here one minute and over there the next, exploding into the sky with a warmth and richness of meaning perhaps preserved by the monks for hundreds of years.

Mists were floating along the lake in the soft, subtle and ravishing light of the northern lake country at dawn. Becalmed, without a ripple, the surface was imprinted with the mirror image of the ancient villas along its banks. It was an etching more entrancing, more sensitive than the reality of the very stones of the buildings it reflected. The lake itself, that now limpid body of water, from its depth enhanced, augmented, magnified the sound as it swung back and forth and all around us, travelled in and out among the background hills, then peeled its way along the shore, gradually falling silent at last beneath my feet at the edge of the square.

One after the other, as if in measured harmonious time, three fishermen in boats came gliding out of the arched boat-houses at the foot of the villas lining the island shore, skimming slowly, effortlessly along, as they may have done for decades. The perfectly etched glassy surface of the lake below me rippled only momentarily before they slid silently along the shore and out into the lake. Then, glancing below to the rose garden between the hotel and the lake, I noticed the back of a picturesque old man in suspenders, under a floppy straw hat pruning the bushes in a relaxed, contented way, despite the early hour.

Here, I thought, was "the best of all possible worlds," for him. What more could one wish for? And yet, it occurred to me that he and the whole village may very well have been caught up in the war, if not actually part of the well-known battles of Ortona or Monte Cassino to the south. Perhaps this idyllic place, this paradise, had seen the ravages of war one way or another, giving the monks, or priests the added incentive to put so much feeling into their music-making, to celebrate freedom again.

In search of coffee, I left the balcony and made my way past my sleeping companion and downstairs to the square. As I sat at the nearest outdoor café table in the cobblestone square, I was soon enchanted by the delightful aroma of the place, the unique flavour of Italian coffee, rolls and butter, and as a tantalizing new sound wafted through the air a great choir of young voices, could be heard in the distance, gradually gaining momentum and proximity. Where were they? I paid for my breakfast and walked to the entrance of the square where we had come in last night from the row of villas behind the lemon and orange trees.

Something new had been added. Perhaps I had not been able to see it in the moonlight. The large windows of the villas were now lavishly and ingeniously decorated. From the sill of each upstairs window hung a very large, white, embroidered tablecloth or other treasured linen, affixed to which were lavish bouquets of flowers, a foot or so apart. What could be the occasion of all this celebration, I wondered? As I lingered on the road, I heard the voices of an impressive, well-trained body of singers, sometimes faintly, sometimes more clearly.

Suddenly several hundred teenagers, young men and girls, came into view around the bend. Walking in a column with their youthful priest bringing up the rear, they carried a decorated likeness of the Virgin Mary on a litter. As I was to observe in such religious rituals, the plaster saint often swayed precariously, yet remained upright. Eventually reaching the square they scattered rose petals on the lake to the applause of dozens of bystanders before enjoying a well-earned breakfast with the crowd in the square.

Finally, hearing the uproar of cheerful voices from below, Claudia came down and sat with me at my table, mentioning none of it. She had apparently needed her sleep too much to appear earlier. Knowing the Italian language and the customs, she was soon able to explain the festivities, the round-a-lay, the singing and the shower of petals she had enjoyed on previous trips. It was the Feast of Corpus Christi, or the Blessed Sacrament, as we also soon heard from the general conversation in the square.

Over breakfast it was decided that we would stay a day or two. "Perhaps my stern companion has begun to relax," I thought. And then it happened! About noon, we were jolted back to reality by the sudden invasion of the square by swarthy workers moving wooden chairs from the back of a truck, shouting, dragging, scraping and bumping them into place in a rising crescendo of noise until the whole medieval joy and serenity of the morning evaporated. The chairs were placed in rows beneath a charmingly baroque wrought iron balcony on the wall of a building on the far side of the square. One might take it as a perfect place to play Juliet's famous scene.

At the same time, with the harsh, malevolent roar of motorcycles, the imagined romantic image suddenly morphed into that of Mussolini in his early speech-making days. I shuddered. At that precise moment, the motorcade of black-jacketed ruffians arrived and took over the square. This was the cue for the balcony door to open and the speaker to step forth, clutch the railing, glare down at the crowd to silence them before shouting Italian Communist Party propaganda for the next forty-five minutes.

Just as suddenly as the musical morning at Lago D'Orta had been disrupted by a cloud of dust and noise, they swept stridently off to the next village in the same obnoxious style. Claudia had been alerted to Italian politics once more and reminded me of the urgency of the trip to Rome. Despite the lure and proximity of the great tourist attractions of those three large lakes, Como, Stresa and Maggiore, we must press on to Rome. Inevitably, though, as if to stall off departure, we paused to buy a bottle of Chianti and sat briefly sampling it under the trees on the hillside.

As she had pointed out so many times, the mood of the country might not be the best and there were still many miles ahead of us on the way to Rome. There was nothing to do but to face up to whatever was in store for us. I had scarcely glimpsed the famous lake country but told myself that I would return with young people and a haversack. As I said to Claudia, "I'll be back next year, providing that the Communists are defeated." "So will I, I hope," she replied most emphatically in an unexpected moment of frankness, knowing that barring the expected takeover, she could well afford to live there in elegance, once the British financial restrictions were lifted. With that she finished her glass of wine and we departed.

For my part, I tried not to think of ever going back; going back to 'America' as everyone seemed to call our part of the planet, as if it were some sort of a disease about which they would "rather not know too much, thank you." At that point I wanted no part of it either.

Very reluctantly slipping out of Lago D'Orta, we drove south toward Genoa, following along the Ligurian Sea coast, one of the most scenic in the world. Winding our way across Piedmont, we began to notice the election notices posted in endless repetition on every pole or wall along the highway. The coastline itself gave way to industrialism and election propaganda even more frequently as we approached Genoa. Rather than try to get a glimpse of the ancient port city, we were forced to race by it to avoid the pelting stones rained down about us by the pro-Communist workers outside a Fiat plant. Presumably, on their lunch break or shift change, they spotted the smart British car, an MG no less, and gave chase with stones, lacing the air with epithets. Fortunately, we sped quickly away unscathed.

Before long arriving at Rapallo, the perfect beach resort on a warm blue seafront, even Claudia snatched a few moments of enjoyment, Italian style. As we waded into it, I dreamed foolishly of staying a week or two. In due course, heading for all points south we were met with another barrage of stones and insults while passing the great Fiat car production centre of La Spezia. Yet, once again we easily outran the shouted epithets and stones. The propaganda plastered on every surface seemed a portent of worse to come.

Eventually passing into Tuscany from Piedmont, stopping on the coast at Santa Margharita and then at Viareggio, we joined hundreds of others wading out in the sandy shallows of the ocean for perhaps a mile or two, warm and silky, without a ripple to disturb the surface. The crowd, utterly bewitched, subsided into near silent delight. From time to time, the sea murmured the slightest refrain. Eventually and unwillingly we regained the shore, enchanted with all things Mediterranean.

Skimming through Pisa, giving only a nod to the famous leaning tower, we lunched in Firenza, or Florence, taking a prolonged stroll through the famous straw market and the Ponte Vecchio, the medieval bridge with shopping stalls along its span. Florence itself would have to wait until another time, magnificent as it was; there was simply no time to stop or any way of paying for that pleasure.

Claudia had reserved a room in Siena for the night. Arriving there by early evening we saw the cathedral just before the sun went down on this unusual sight. The outside of the Greco-Romanesque stone structure was striped in black, the inside lavish with ornate baroque decoration, including pillars gilded in rose, black, blue and gold and impressive mosaics at our feet. As we left the cathedral after this hasty glimpse, the sunset was now casting pinkish rays against the striped walls while we strolled into the Piazza del Campo, Claudia's ideal setting for a meal.

Shaped like a shell, the Piazza del Campo marks the intersection of the three hills on which Siena was established in ancient times. At the edge of the piazza sits the Palazzo Publico or town hall, dating to the thirteenth century. Serving as the cultural centre for the area, its reddish stone Romanesque tower dominates the structure with a height of at least four times the diameter of the Palazzo itself. As we finished our meal along one side of the piazza, the good local wine and surroundings seemed fit for the gods. As Claudia knew the piazza so well she may have seen it in wartime also or perhaps with the love of her life. I had begun to dream of a romantic dinner for two, right here, next year.

After following the narrowest streets I had ever seen en route to the hotel room Claudia had reserved, we were shown up a staircase and into a room made comfortable with fine old furnishings. A delightful surprise awaited me at the window. It was the unexpected view right into the ancient bell tower across the narrow street. During the morning, I went out to buy supplies of ham, cheese and bread for our picnic lunch. Discovering life on the three hills without getting lost or becoming a threat to motorists navigating the narrowest of streets, I soon realized that to allow a Fiat to pass, one must press oneself against the shop walls. Concern arose when an American car attempted to try it. Some years later the Siennese wisely decided to prohibit cars from the area.

Leaving Siena behind we drove south through Toscana, or Tuscany, on small side roads among the fabled vineyards and groves of olive trees. Somewhere we became lost as we climbed and twisted through several miles of what must have been a quarry of some kind. While not apparently marble or alabaster, the light brown stone had been hacked and disfigured on all sides. There was not an olive tree or blade of grass to be seen. As there was no actual road at that point, we stopped to get our bearings.

Suddenly, from nowhere, a small black Fiat drew up beside us. Surely here were the feared *banditti* of Claudia's earlier remonstrances. Flinging open their car door, four unsmiling, swarthy men in gangster-style shiny black suits and white straw hats extricated themselves from the cramped vehicle to surround our car. Convinced that Claudia knew how to prevent any aggressive moves by her own authoritarian manner, and her facility with the language, I decided to maintain a stoic silence in the hope of release. Then, suddenly less assured, as I watched them gradually closing in on us, I wondered if they would take us as well as the car. As the tension built up, minute by minute, bursts of rapidly fired exchanges in Italian went on incessantly.

Erect, severe as a sphinx at the wheel, Claudia was the seasoned commander as usual, imperious, calm, magnificent. Yet they seemed to hum and haw among themselves, not looking at us, smoking nervously, frowning, shifting their feet on the gravel, exchanging guarded glances all around. Were we to stay here all day? The stand-off went on interminably. Finally I saw her push something out the window. It was a very large carton of Camel cigarettes! Vanquished by the Empire, so to speak, the four pathetic, middle-aged *banditti* disappeared as quickly as they had surprised us by their appearance. "Her military background has won the day!" I thought, with amusement and relief. "She wasn't in the *Underground* for nothing."

Just as a commanding officer would refrain from divulging facts to a mere foot-soldier in the ranks, I learned nothing of the altercation with these goons and deeply regret not having known the Italian language. It must have been an exacting and exciting battle of wits for her with those desperate looking characters. "They wanted the car. It was hell," she said, hurriedly, starting the motor, looking more authoritative than ever, her dark eyes ablaze with defiance. She must have threatened them with action from high places in London. I do not recall whatever happened from then on, as we put the miles between us, the four thugs, the strange maze of hills and quarries, then faced into the ever-increasing numbers of election as we joined the autostrada.

Rome

Again becoming anxious about the wisdom of entering Rome in the face of the known prevalence of 'banditti,' Claudia repeated her earlier misgivings about crossing the Tiber on a Sunday evening, the very hour when hordes of people are out strolling on the bridge and the 'banditti' are on the prowl. However, the fact was that before I knew where we were, we were actually entering the outskirts of Rome, about to cross the bridge exactly at the forbidden moment. "What was she thinking of?" I wondered, but of course I said nothing. She had made her decision.

A mellow spring evening had brought out a huge crowd. Courting couples in their best, "the opulent matrons of Rome" as Claudia called them, deploring their colourful summer garb as bad taste: the men, smart in black suits and white starched shirts, children in elaborate Sunday dress, all chattered away in a joyful crescendo.

Was she at this inappropriate moment of arrival simply more defiant than ever, or too tired to care?

No use asking, she would deny it. As she nosed the MG slowly and carefully, through this happy throng, the people surged forward off the sidewalks to crowd around the car, new, shiny, open, and inviting. Suddenly it happened! A motorcycle roared past my window pushing the crowd back momentarily. Pouf! I knew that sound. A puncture! Our tire! The crowd let out a whoop of surprise and concern. A second puncture! Pouf! Another whoop. All was lost! "What would we do now?"

Claudia and I slid from our seats and stationed ourselves at the front and back of the vehicle, purses held tightly under arm. I stood firm guard over the rumble seat-door as did Claudia with the hood. Yet suddenly in this swarming crowd I spotted a handsome, impeccably dressed young man squirming around under the vehicle who appeared to be repairing the tires from a tool-kit. "Where did he come from and why is he so organized? How is it that he was lying on a clean white towel to preserve his fine white shirt and elegant appearance? What is actually going on?" I asked myself in consternation. Pandemonium reigned. The crowd now surged forward in one great wave, pressing around the car, murmuring to each other, excited but subdued, the children chattering no doubt about such an exciting Sunday evening walk.

Another young man of similar appearance writhed around on yet another white towel, mending the other tire. I later learned that this was standard *banditti* practice; the repair job leading to a chance to ransack the vehicle while everyone else is thrown into confusion. They then disappear easily into a crowd, roar off, without anyone being able to confront them, just as in our case.

Nuns and priests were said to be habitual targets of thieves at large gatherings. The operation could be so skillful that flowing robes were sometimes slit and wallets taken without awareness on the part of the victim. Amazingly, we were vigilant and lost nothing. Was it perhaps that these young men had failed to divert our attention from the car itself? This was not at all as I had imagined the historic Roman bridge of my high school Latin class.

So much for an evening on the Tiber or the Arno, both flowing south through Rome into the Tyrrenian Sea. I had actually looked down into the water a moment before, gratified in thinking that it was in fact the Tiber. To this day, the joyful, strolling and sympathetic crowds remain a fond memory of that earlier age, my world of 1951, Italian style, also the world of Federico Fellini, and *Divorce Italian Style, La Dolce Vita,* and many other memorable films.

At that moment, though, the Eternal City lay before me! Triumphant, Claudia drove on calmly, imperiously, through the city, piqued, of course, but victorious. The battle had been won! The *banditti* were the losers. Nothing had been stolen. We had been extremely vigilant during the entire incident. Finally when we arrived at a penthouse apartment in an affluent part of Rome, Claudia's friend, Joan, ushered us onto an enormous flowery roof-top living area for drinks and refreshments. Obviously of similar background and sternness of manner as Claudia, she was soon expounding on the subject of the worrisome election.

Sipping my drink I became aware of the delights of this enormous balcony. The exciting panorama of other outdoor spaces adjoining it led me to savour the Italian taste for walls tinted in sepia, ochre, and terra cotta shades. Embellished with rosy bursts of oleander and bougainvillea, the plants were set in large, impressive pots. Everyone had privacy to enjoy their cooling late-day libations in groups or alone after siesta and before the late evening meal.

As I was to find out during the heat of midsummer, people took to their balconies right away following the afternoon siesta. Here they would enjoy cooling drinks and the caresses of the *Sirocco,* the late-day breeze so magically cooled in transit from North Africa. Others returned to work until mid-evening, sitting down to dinner at an hour when many North Americans retire. Back on the streets again as early as six in the morning; they worked on until noon.

As Noel Coward expressed it in song, "Mad dogs an Englishman, go out in the noonday sun."

Later I did just that and found the sun pressing on the top of my head, forcing me to beat a hasty retreat rather than collapse on the pavement.

Bidding farewell to Claudia and my hostess next morning, I departed with my haversack and suitcase to the youth hostel as planned. It was a wonderfully cavernous old building exuding a warm ambiance with friendly, wel-coming staff. Just as Italians and other Europeans some-times sat with their feet in basin-shaped fountains for cool-ness, so too, we female hostellers enjoyed sponge-bathing around an ancient bronzed fountain. Perhaps a dozen jets of water were available around the large elliptical basin, with taps in the shape of very long swans' necks. With a shelf for soap and towels one took a stand-up bath, using the towel judiciously as modesty demanded. The hub-bub of the bathers, voices like chattering birds, mixed with the sound of the gurgling water seemed to lead to conviviality and new acquaintances.

Agreeing that it would not be wise to go alone, I arranged a trip for a certain day with a girl also longing to Napoli, or Naples. A doubtful travelling companion, it came as no surprise to find that a young Italian with a motor cycle now planned to accompany her. It was just as well, considering my funds and the need for a reliable companion for such an adventure. Young women could not sit down at an outdoor café table without having young Italians roar up to offer a motorcycle ride. If the answer were in the negative, the biker would zoom off to ask someone at another table, and off they would go. Some of them may even have been banditti having their 'break'!

During bathing sessions I had met two girls, one from London, one from South Africa, travelling together. The former, Ida, chic in her straw hat and modest summer dress attracted these cyclists like flies, only to quietly, quickly and courteously decline them.

She did, however, accept the invitation of a Scottish friend from London whom she had expected, that we all visit the Keats and Shelley memorial at the renowned English Cemetery in Rome. We had known about it from school-days poetry classes.

Here in Rome I had seen Keats's name on the house beside the Spanish steps, at Piazza d'Espagna where the young poet died of tuberculosis in 1821. Today thousands of tourists throng the steps to people-watch, to socialize and to rest, some of them en route to stroll further up the hill to the famous gardens of the *Villa Borghese*.

A flourishing flower market was spread out at the base of the always popular concourse. Just below it, the famous seventeenth century baroque fountain sculpted by Bernini, known as La Barcaccia, or the Old Boat, has been enjoyed by the public since 1627, one hundred years before the Spanish Steps were built. Apparently, in the year 1598, the Tiber flooded eighteen feet, causing an old boat to settle at the top of the hill from which the steps now descend. This led to its association with the site. Another century passed before the steps were built, thanks to the French government, rather than an endowment from a Spanish source. Together with Bernini's fountain reflecting the story of the boat, this transformed the former narrow path up to the church, Trinita di Monti, into one of Rome's most-beloved landmarks.

Although Romans customarily drank from fountains, my memory focuses only on relaxed figures and groups sitting on the edge of it, socializing and cooling their feet in the water. Amazingly, in all these celebrated fountains, be it the Trevi, the Triton at Piazzi Barberini, or the many which adorn Rome, the water comes directly from springs and rivers along each separate aqueduct. A system put in place by Pope Nicholas V in 1453 and later Renaissance popes, it is similar to the work of the original engineers at the time of Emperor Augustus Caesar.

Some of the people strolling down the Spanish Steps will also seek out the adjacent Via Condotti or come upon it by chance, enjoying the sight of the chic, the elegantly dressed, and the passing carriages before turning into the Café Greco. Founded in 1760, it offered memorable espresso coffee as well as the sheer joy of taking in the antiquity of the place. From Goethe to Gogol, Wagner, Bizet, Corot, Thackeray and countless others, mementos of their traditional "grand tours" had been retained, to be viewed on the walls.

In 1951 public buildings were usually empty, except for one or two visitors. On one of these occasions I visited the Coliseum in search of a place to sit down and cool off. At the time I knew nothing of the Roman development of the arch, making this once outstanding type of structure possible. Seated half-way up, in a row of seats and looking down to the pit where the lions had roared and salivated for human flesh, I was immediately diverted by an ice-cream vendor pushing a cart. Desperate for American tourists, he cried "Eec, eec, eec!" (for ice-cream), in a long, drawn-out whine. A pale wraith of a middle-aged man,

I could see him as easy prey for the lions of antiquity. He turned out to be a Dane, another race who as sturdy Vikings, like the Romans, marauded and invaded my English ancestors, themselves heroic survivors as well as predators over the centuries.

That ice-cream carts might face routine inspection for sanitation in Rome would seem a ridiculous supposition. I dismissed the thought. "But where was it cleaned or stored at night?" I did not ask! "How inconvenient it is at times to have studied public health!" I scolded myself at entertaining such inappropriate concerns in present circumstances. He disappeared, leaving me alone, content and amused to try to envision the eons of time and the multitudes who had passed through the Coliseum to live or die on the spot.

On another excessively hot day, the old Pope was being carried around in a litter in front of Saint Peter's Basilica among the closely packed crowd of pilgrims. There was the sense of a tired old man forced to endure a primitive conveyance amid the strong, all-pervasive odours of garlic, urine and sweat. It seemed that the clock might well have been turned back five-hundred years or more to medieval times.

However, once inside Saint Peter's, the mind is temporarily overwhelmed by the baroque grandeur of the edifice and its significance rather than the poverty of those pilgrims in the square. That the world remains in need of a plan for humane, benevolent existence above the poverty line as basic morality for all religions, seemed perhaps even more glaringly clear than usual that day. As one hears today, "Poverty is the greatest violence of all," thanks to Gandhi, Mandela and others.

Overcome with the heat, the poverty and the grandeur of the place, I went in search of a café serving fresh lemonade, seasoned with salt. The Italian preference for this thirst-quencher over ice-cream as a cooling remedy for thirst on hot days seemed worth investigating. "When in Rome ... live as Romans do."

Whenever I ventured into poor streets, I saw into kitchens or open areas where the family meal seemed to consist solely of spaghetti with olive oil. Cramped and poor, these neighbourhoods probably stretched for miles. From such places may have come the street singers, the very young girls of ten or twelve years, with a youth, possibly a brother, standing by. Sometimes the young men played a mandolin. Singing their hearts out, the little girls stood at the curb or at our outdoor café table, hands outstretched or holding a tin cup for donations.

These almost emaciatedly thin, yet beautiful youngsters, were so desperate for money that very often the veins in their necks dilated pitifully under the strain of forcing the voice above the traffic sounds. No doubt they loved their Italian street songs as much as we did, but the haunting question remains as to whether they were the victims of a racket at the hands of the mandolin players.

Just as much part of the daily scene, up and down the crowded street, were the open donkey carts and drivers delivering large, classically shaped green glass casks of olive oil or loading the empties. Many such small tradesmen plied their wares, shouting up at the windows to attract attention as they worked their routes.

From time to time one heard discussions about the shocking lack of food transport, up and down the country. What was grown in the south would not be available in the north and vice versa. Agriculture had scarcely been developed in the south. This was completely credible on reading the story of physician and author Carlo Levi, exiled by Mussolini to this uninhabitable region. Trying to survive under such primitive conditions, he wrote about the experience in a work called *Christ Stopped at Eboli*. It is a curious and memorable work, although the title might misleadingly imply concern with religion rather than remote, backward, undeveloped pre-war Italy.

In general, however, I was given to understand that in the late nineteen-thirties Il Duce had at the same time been careful to make notable improvements across the country. Not only had he provided the highways, the autostrada, to allow easy access for troops and war supplies, but he had installed the impressive mosaic-tiled public baths I saw in Rome. The Italians excel in the art of mosaics, being long renowned for this beautiful, ancient art form, especially prominent in Ravenna on the Adriatic coast.

Becoming interested in the story of the *Risorgamento*, the revival or the 'Unification of Italy,' completed in the 1860's, I learned that it had brought an end to the corrupt feudal rule of the various independent states existing throughout the peninsula. Many years in the making, the unified country had been the result of political effort by Garibaldi, Cavour, Massini, Manzoni the author, Verdi the great composer, and many others.

From the time of the French Revolution, the right to personal freedom had become a pressing issue among exploited Italians. Determined to find the life-size sculptures of the first two of these great men, I set out one morning by bus, deciding not to alight until I had passed them twice for a second look. I was in for a surprise.

Totally unaware that this was punishable by a fine, I had just completed the second close view of the two sculptures when I was suddenly almost surrounded by a massive, voluble, and intimidating gold-trimmed inspector with a cohort of excited, young, male fellow-passengers swarming and buzzing around him. I was to pay the fine and leave the bus immediately after he finished sorting his back-pack size satchel full of crumpled paper money and coins to change my bill. In those days paper money of the smallest denomination was in use in Italy and wrinkled and voluminous as it was, it had to be carefully counted. Ejected from the bus by this amusing official, the coterie of young men pushing their way noisily off behind me had apparently hoped to continue the dialogue on the street. Who knows what would have happened next? I might never have left Rome, even spoken fluent Italian, and added a branch of Italian-Canadians to the family tree. Hilarious as it was, we were not making a film.

As I had offered the inspector another ticket the incident could have been easily averted. He had instead turned it into ready-made comedy again in the style of Federico Fellini. Presented in films full of such zany events as this, along with his street music themes, Fellini epitomized what he called the *Circus of Life, Italian Style*, in all its verve and originality under the Mediterranean sun. Forced to ignore my ardent followers as they encircled me, I could only barely suppress the wish to laugh out loud as I waited for the next bus.

Over the years I have learned details of the *Risorgamento*, the struggle in Italy to replace feudalism with a united democratic country. One way to approach the story is to read the novel *I Promessi Sposi*, known under the English title as, *The Betrothed*, written by Alexandro Manzoni in 1825. It is the story of the long, seemingly futile struggles to marry, faced by a young peasant couple over a period of years. They are subject to the rules of the corrupt feudal officials. We can be thankful that Italy finally became the modern nation of today through the efforts of those heroic figures such as Cavour, Garibaldi and the others who responded to the desperate needs of their countrymen.

Although I could not leave Rome without finding the ancient Forum, I was soon aware of the need for a guide in order to make much of this scene of crumbled antiquity around me. Determined as I was to return the following year, I went instead in search of the Pantheon, the first great dome ever constructed. Built in 27 B.C., it illustrates the importance of an understanding of weight-bearing principles in order to construct an arch. The dome consists entirely of arches, unsupported by columns.

People were quick to point out two unforgettable sites, the Michelangelo Gates to the City, still in use in 1951, and the remains of the Roman Wall beside the then new glass railway station. The Sistine Chapel, like most great buildings in 1951, was still almost free of tourists. In two visits to the site I had every chance to observe Michelangelo's great work. Decades would pass before the chapel would be cleaned and restored to the original colours, an enhancement that had not occurred to me.

Obviously, it would require a lifetime's effort to know the great city. Every time I heard that popular street song of the era, *Arrivederci Roma*, or 'Goodbye for Now,' belted out by the street singers it became more unbearably poignant. It would be impossible to leave. The days were running out as if doom hung directly overhead.

Waking me up at six o'clock like the bright spring sunshine, the lively street scene could be heard from my bed at the youth hostel. I wondered how I could live without it. Animated, cheerful as flocks of birds going and coming, people stopped to talk on the way to market or to work, following the daily rhythm of early rising, long siestas and late dinners. One got used to hearing *prego* for please, *basta* for that's enough, or nonsense, *scusi* for excuse me, *ciao* (chow) for hello or so long, *cinque centa lira* for five hundred lira and *grazie* for thanks, on every corner.

The one very serious omission in my Italian interlude had been that the Etruscan Museum was closed for renovations. Although I had read a book on the subject, the actual works of the pre-Roman civilization had eluded me. Art students had recommended it for its joyful, naturalistic sculptures and cave-painting, prints of which continue to inspire me like Italian civilization itself.

It was actually still springtime, with bougainvillea, oleander and wisteria everywhere in bloom around the buildings and the stone walls which line many streets in residential areas. Late one Sunday afternoon I walked through one such pleasant neighbourhood as a guest of an American student also staying at the youth hostel. We were to join her two journalist friends from New York for dinner. Cooling drinks were being served on the living-room sized, flower-draped balcony.

Another guest, a reporter from Boston, was on her way to Lebanon to join her husband on assignment for their respective newspapers. As she explained, Nima was at the height of her career, delighting in the fact that the then peaceful Lebanon was the mutual birthplace of her husband and herself. In her outgoing way she eagerly told us that, like myself, she was educated in a convent, then sent to one of the top Eastern American universities, before being assigned to a press bureau in Rome. She had had the life of which I could only dream. A fascinating, intense and scholarly young woman, she was a pleasure to meet.

As an aside to us, she described one of the plus factors in having been posted to Italy, which gave her such a sense of unheard of luxury. Because great numbers of Italian women had suffered extreme privation during and after the war, they would work for nothing more than the chance to sleep under a kitchen table and to earn three meals a day. In return, such women as Maria would provide all household services, including pressing and repairing clothes. Here was an example of the thousands of Italians who I knew had lived in caves during the war. Naturally, as she proved her helpfulness Nima gave her much more.

We had read of the people's plight, as their hero, Il Duce, or Mussolini, left them to their fate. Earlier he had given them the autostrada and the fine new public baths which had earned their cheers. Some would surely rend the air with derision when he finally faced the especially ignominious disgrace of his execution at the hands of the Italian partisans.

As we sipped our cocktails with these new acquaintances, the Sirocco from Africa, that cooling late-day breeze wafted over us. Earlier I had felt its voluptuous embrace on the balcony of Claudia's friend on my first evening in Rome. At dinner our American hosts told us that they had been thrilled with a recent theatrical presentation at the ancient Baths of Carracalla outside Rome. I knew it only as something to be dreamed of from the advertising posters.

Before we left, our hostess, Julia, introduced their Italian cook, a young Sicilian girl who had produced our marvellous feast of Italian specialties. The apparent reason for her unexpected appearance was to present me with two inscribed pieces of lined paper, remaining in my possession today. It had been mentioned before our arrival that one of the guests was a Canadian girl. Why this news had prompted her to write out one of her recipes in a loose scrawl, in Italian, all over both pages, I still don't know.

When I tried to find out the reason for this kindness, it seemed that having never met a Canadian, she wanted to mark the event with this gesture. What had led to the impulse sadly remains obscure. Was it because Canada fought in Sicily? Was it a mark of gratitude? Or had she once met a Canadian soldier? Perhaps all or none of these reasons. Whatever it was, I remember her affectionate gesture with pleasure. To my own discredit, I have never learned that most enticing language, the folly of which omission is apparent with each day as I continue to find myself attracted by the great music, culture and cuisine of Italy.

And so, before I knew it, it was truly *Arrivederci Roma* as Claudia and I got into the new, smart black MG again. The cloudless, hot, blue sky, heartless in its appeal to the senses, its promise of continued perfection for months yet to come, made mockery of us for heading north. The streets were vibrant, noisy, colourful, scented, pungent by turns, as usual, and throbbing with life, and yet I had to turn back.

By the time we stopped near Basel for a meal, it was suspiciously northern; cool, overcast, and unbearably silent. Where was the funeral? We entered the first restaurant we saw, ordered the available meal of trout and waited interminably in the large, empty, white dining-room, with the waitresses in white, unsmiling, lined up against the walls like sentinels. The trout and boiled potato arrived on white plates, unrelieved by a splash of colour, such as parsley or lemon, save the one hard, bright blue eye of the fish. Mine stared up at me accusingly, while the waitresses all stared solemnly at us as if we were alien creatures. Having never seen a fish served with the head in place, I felt both guilt and dismay, doubly upset at this obvious omen, the folly of leaving the sunny south for the sober northern world. That fish eye declared sternly, "You're a fool to leave!"

The spell of Italy had evaporated without so much as a last slice of pizza or a glass of wine in sight. Over and over again, I said to myself, "why was I not wiser than this! I could find myself back in America too soon!" The thought lurked ominously in the back of my mind, from time to time, as if pulling me home forever!

Encore la France

Although the trauma of leaving Italy was painful, the enforced dash back from our Mediterranean paradise to London by car was relatively free of problems. Claudia had decided to make haste by way of the French Riviera, via Genoa and the Italian section of the Ligurian sea at the beginning of the trip. Just as on the way south, the MG drew many of the same type of people anxious to meet their old wartime allies and to recount the struggle to survive in desperate times. Despite the delights of travelling the by-ways of rural France under such ideal circumstances and devouring their many delicious offerings at market stands along the way, there was no thought of camping out in their fields. Regardless of the shortage of funds, it was clear that one should not trespass on a farmer's property.

At least not that summer of 1951, after Sir Jack Drummond and his entire young family on holiday and equally deprived of British currency did just that. Each and every one of them, to the youngest child, was shot to death by an elderly French farmer who had seen them set up camp on his land, that ideal spot they had noticed from the road. He took action that night. One could almost hear him muttering to himself, *Merde! C'est mon terrain.* "It's my land" as he clutched his gun and stormed out of the house. Screams pierced the night. The papers were full of it. The case dragged on, the death penalty being finally overturned, and the old man being permanently confined to a nearby prison, close to his shocked family and friends. Perhaps he had been hallucinating or imagining himself in a wartime struggle for survival against the Nazis..

Having spent so many years of her life criss-crossing Europe, Claudia knew just where to find a bed on the night in question. Tired from a long day on the road, she remarked that we would soon arrive at our hotel. On the way we passed a long wavering line, a chain of youths in top hats and formal attire, carousing their way along at a slow trot. They seemed to be observing a celebration of some kind. Were they re-enacting some time-honoured ritual of a nearby college? By the time we got to the ancient walled village, we were confronted with another first-time surprise, a kiosk marked 'Board of Trade,' mysteriously requiring that one stop for identification. At the same time, we could see that a lamp-lighter, dressed exactly like the students, was mounting the ornate nineteenth-century gas lamp standards to light them. Had there been no sign, we might have imagined ourselves to be part of earlier times.

Strangely enough, we saw no more of these youths. I felt pleased to think that they were free to behave like young people again, a normal childhood being impossible in wartime. Now was the time to enjoy themselves free of the constraints they must have endured in their growing up years in occupied France.

As we proceeded into the heart of the village, Claudia stopped in front of a modest, unprepossessing looking bistro in need of paint. Hanging out over the street, an old wooden sign read *Le Mounton Blanc* above a roughly painted image of a decidedly woolly sheep. "Is this one of her favourite hotels? Surely, not," I thought, with foreboding, as we proceeded to the door.

After announcing ourselves at the counter we were led courteously up the stairs to our room. It might have been a five-star hotel, given the softness and sleep-inducing charms of the fine feather bed and duvet, the appealing linens, the polished floor of tiny cobblestones, and spotless, unheard of pull-cord toilet in the bathroom. The price was minimal and the hotel was free of distractions such as the possible noise or food odours of a bistro. Accommodations such as this in Canada would have been out of the question. In France only six years after the end of the war, we were treated as well as in a first-class hotel in Canada.

Before we knew it, we had left the continent behind and were in front of Georgie's London flat in Knightsbridge once more. Claudia now had only hours to await the Italian election returns and the announcement of the defeat of the Communist party. It had been 'Arrivederci Roma,' and Italy as well, but it was also

Bonjour Paris as I hurriedly greeted Georgie, picked up my belongings, and returned to France the next day.

On the first weekend in Paris that I was not 'on-call' for operating room duty at the hospital, Max came from Orleans with the motor-bike to take me back to join him and Jessica at the Saturday farm market for breakfast pickings and to tell them about Italy. Breakfasting exotically, or so it seemed to us, accustomed to cereal bowls in Canada, we had our choice of the best from the vast gastronomy of this charmed land. Astonished, I turned away from a row of pigs' heads with bunches of parsley stuck into the bloody sockets. We followed the meal with a ride along the Loire to the peach blossom and chateaux country and to the magnificent cathedral at Chartres.

My eyes fell instead upon the rows of large circular Camembert cheeses just visible on the rough, straw-laden shelves, the rind still showing traces of the barnyard. So much for the difference between them and the packaged, pasteurized and often tasteless cheeses we knew in Canada at that time. If the French could thrive so well on these raw, unpasteurized cheeses, far be it from us not to give them a try. Knowing so little on the subject of French cuisine or cheeses, but assuming that the popular name of Camembert was a great find, I dislodged one from the rough straw between the barnyard planks.

Wrapping came in the form of a useless ten-inch square of newsprint. In their enthusiasm my friends had sent one home to Canada, a most unwelcome, unrefrigerated and foul-smelling gesture. Of course, we soon discovered the very fine assortment of delectable soft cheeses made in France. We were accustomed in Canada to the narrow aisles of small stores full of packaged goods, very little produce and relatively tasteless, boxed processed cheeses. For special occasions, in Canada we might buy a small slice of what was called 'nippy' or aged cheddar cheese cut from a great chunk by the grocer himself, then solemnly and carefully wrapped and tightly sealed in butcher paper as if it were solid gold. Orleans market was the first outdoor market we had ever seen.

On the way home to their apartment in Orleans, with Max and Jessica, we passed by the Cathedral of Sainte Croix with the mounted statue of Joan of Arc, called Maid of Orleans, on her horse in front of the edifice. Both seemed to lean a little, grey with time or neglect. Poor Joan, who was burned at the stake in 1431 for heresy, seemed to sit there still on her steed, forced to endure the stench of sewage pervading the air. Upon questioning, some of the residents claimed quite seriously that the sanitation system had been in need of repair ever since that time.

Later in the day, we visited a young French couple living in the same old greystone row-house building as Max and Jessica. It too had the appearance of extremely run down antiquity. While we were there, Marie Claire and Claude began to talk about the long, proud, yet trying times in the difficult history of their city. My friends had unwisely volunteered to help them change the wall paper. As we tried to pull the faded old paper strips from the walls, confident in Max as a helper, our hosts sat comfortably on the sofa and related the story of survival during World War II.

Although young like ourselves, they seemed small, pale and without much enthusiasm for life. Perhaps it was partly due to past deprivations or their recognition that, given the state of the walls, wall-papering was likely to prove to be an impossible project. As we struggled on, it became apparent that indeed one might as well try to peel an onion. Wet from the continual daubing with sponges, a two-inch deep hole had appeared in the paper on one wall. How many layers had been put on over the centuries? That the damage could be repaired seemed doubtful. Fortunately, it had not been my idea of a way to make friends in another country.

In any event, everyone gave up on the wallpaper for the day. We sat down for coffee to hear more about the city. "Well, you know, we have had our troubles here, long before the war," Marie Claire pointed out. "First of all, it was a Roman settlement, so it is very old. Later, in the medieval period, it was the domain of the warring Dukes of Orleans. There was trouble, always!"

As her voice trailed off, she went in search of the coffee-pot for refills, Claude got to point out the importance of the statue in the churchyard, explaining that according to the story "Joan of Arc repulsed the English who held Orleans in a state of siege. They had already taken all the lands north of the Loire. This, in fact, turned the tide of the Hundred Years War in our favour, you see. We are quite proud of this, after all. But then, you know, I love history," he conceded, as he lit a Gaulois cigarette proffered by Max.

Returning with the hot coffee, Marie Claire lamented the present condition of the town, saying bitterly that "The people of Orleans know all about survival. So did my grandparents, and theirs. Whether we will ever have normal sanitary conditions here is hard to say. But for you it is simple; you will go home to America. You will not need to think of such things, "*no, pas du tout, jamais*, never, not at all," she concluded, half in English, half in French, emphasizing their situation versus ours.

The hole we had made in the wall and its condition being too dilapidated to improve seemed to reflect the place as well. Unfortunately, the great nineteenth century city planner Baron Georges Haussman and others who created present day Paris out of the squalor of the past, did not extend their interests to the nearby provincial town of Orleans, close as it was to Versailles, to the Loire, and to the beautiful peach blossom and chateaux country.

Back in Paris, over lunch at the hospital one day someone mentioned having been to a dance at the Cité Universitaire. Previously ignorant of this remarkable facility at the disposal of the student body, I questioned my colleague Monique the next day to find out more. "Oh yes," she said, "there is always dancing there, a large ballroom, plus French doors leading to the terrace and the lawns. You can dance all the way out!"

She told me which metro line to take, and then put in, "Hurry out to see it. You could live there during the summer vacation period. I knew someone who stayed at La Maison Canadienne and loved it."

"La Maison Canadienne!" I echoed in surprise.

"Why yes! Each country has a house of its own," she explained. "Some great American benefactor set it up, complete with ballrooms, libraries, and a really great cafeteria."

With that incredible information, it was time to get back to the operating-room wing of the hospital and put it out of mind. On my next free day I hurried down the seven flights of stairs to the street, into Metro Port Royal, scanned the illuminated directions indicator, and was soon on my way out of the centre of Paris towards the country. As the greystone buildings gave way to fields, the coach began to fill up with plump farm women getting on with overstuffed bags of cabbages and leeks, hard pressed to find seats among the students.

La Cité turned out to be everything I had imagined from Monique's description. La Maison Canadienne was one of the most attractive buildings of this vast enterprise. I began to go to La Cité for lunch whenever possible in my free time, both for the subsidized price as well as the robust student meals. Included with the main dish one could count on an excellent bowl of thick potato-leek soup or *potage*, with wine or cider, all for a very few francs.

On that first visit I decided to have a look at the ballroom, being anxious to dance the then very popular

Blue Danube Waltz again. I had learned it in Canada from Clive, the RAF cadet, an expert schooled in dancing while taking academic courses in Vienna. Strolling out of the cafeteria and into the adjacent ballroom to the strains of waltz music emanating from the public address system, I saw a vast expanse of polished hardwood flooring. Beyond it were the open French doors, terrace, and lawns.

Barely inside the door I was spotted by a portly, heavily spectacled man of middle-age, perhaps a professor, burdened by an over-stuffed briefcase, frowning deeply as he approached me from the middle of the empty dance-floor. Had he just been spurned by someone refusing to dance with all that freight? In any event there he was.

As I was about to say that I did not dance, out of nowhere strode towards me, a tall, fine-looking young man. Quickly tapping the portly one on the shoulder, he whisked me away in the grand sweep of a perfectly executed waltz. It was, of course, the Blue Danube. Momentarily, I imagined my old ball-gown, left behind in Canada, swirling about me with what felt like an unprecedented and extraordinary elegance as we swept radiantly onto the flagstone terrace.

Being a student on a two-week vacation in Paris from Germany, Wolfgang was also eager to drop in at various student dancing *boites* across the Latin Quarter. Given the traditional German love of music and his regret at having left his violin at home, he liked to stop along the way to play an imaginary sonata or two in the evening. If the café had closed before our arrival, he would take down two of the empty chairs piled up outside the café. Perfectly at home, he would sit down, raise his arms into position and offer imaginary samples of Schubert and Mozart, probably hoping to eventually find another music student able to discuss music more convincingly than I could pretend to do at that time. It was a novel way to enjoy a summer evening's progress home from a dance.

Knowing at least a little about the work of Shakespeare and that German poet and dramatist, Schiller, who was sometimes compared with "the Bard," I dared to ask Wolfgang to give me a sample of the former's poetry in German. As he recited the piece, I was struck by the beauty of the rhythm and the cadence of the lines of the master. Perhaps I should not have been so surprised, had I stopped to consider that when he spoke English it was as eloquently as anyone from a fine English background. However, my first reaction to this short recital was one of shock, imagining that all German was spoken in the guttural, violent tones of the Nazi wartime propaganda films, my only previous exposure to the language.

Although I might almost have taken Wolfgang for a young privileged Englishman or a German born and brought up in England in the best schools, two Dutch engineering students staying at the Cité were not going to let pass the fact that he was actually German. They had spotted us together in the main cafeteria. Germany had not been allowed to have a residence at the Cité during the war or in 1951, and they were determined to get rid of him now. Bluntly announcing this, they upbraided me about my companion. In turn, I knew that I would always be British and loyal to our traditions. There was, however, a tendency of such young men as these youths from Holland, to be attracted to Canadian girls as a means of immigration.

I knew quite well that resentment still ran deeply and would continue to do so. Their anger precluded any further dialogue to explain that common cultural interests, such as the joint visits to galleries, museums, love of classical music, literature, or dancing, need have no political or ideological basis to make for understanding. Wolfgang had been eleven in 1939 and had no part in the war, nor any antagonism towards the Allies. After several days of trying in vain to coerce me into long walks across Paris at top speed, the two Dutchmen realized the futility of their entreaties and disappeared.

Later, as we stood at Place de la Concorde with its splendid view of the Champs d'Elysée from l'Arc de Triumphe or l'Étoile, at our feet, on the fourteenth of July, le Quatorze Juillet, 1951, we were thrilled and exhilarated to welcome the parade of the French military proceeding towards us down the Champs d'Elysées from l'Étoile for the celebration of freedom and the hopes for a new world order.

I had come to Europe expressly to look closely at what it meant to survive those terrible years. I had no difficulty in identifying with the two Dutchmen and all those who would continue to find life painful or heart-breaking for years to come. Likewise, I knew that during this short-lived post-war period of hope for a brighter future my companion was equally pleased to celebrate the French and the Allies. For young people there was a sense of jubilation in the air, as if a new day had dawned. Everyone tried to anticipate the future with cautious optimism, and that thrilling new slogan, once so unusual, was being uttered, here and there, "I am a citizen of the world." Borders would change; not then, but later.

Quite recently I was reminded that in 1945, Hitler ordered his staff to raze Paris to the ground, an incredible thought for all those who consider themselves to be part of humanity and western culture. Standing there at Place de la Concorde I was not conscious that it was on this very spot in 1793 that King Louis XVI of France, Queen Marie Antoinette and the nobility faced the guillotine.

Had the significance of the square in this regard been pointed out to us, we might have been somewhat less thrilled with our chosen location. I knew, however, that La Place de la Concorde was part of the magnificent cultural achievement of Baron Haussman and his architects. Together they transformed medieval Paris into a European capital worthy of the new phenomenon of liberalism, subsequently embraced across nineteenth century Europe.

A less enjoyable look at Paris came as the result of a request from strangers. For the sake of courtesy, I felt obliged to deliver apartment rent money for an

American couple whom I had met through Max and Jessica. It was to be dropped off at a busy commercial area on the Boulevard des Italians. As I had apparently mentioned that I would be going in that direction, Sandra had felt no hesitation in pushing a fat wad of bills across the coffee table to me, insisting "Drop this off on the third floor, won't you, honey?"

Instead of claiming other commitments in response to a such condescending request, I thought, "After all, I am not yet at all familiar with the layout of the city!" While wondering what I would do in case of a purse-snatcher as I departed along the hallways, I realized, "There's just no way I can replace this amount of cash." Located in the affluent Trocadero district of central Paris, near the Eiffel Tower, Sandra and Bill's address was a costly one. I regretted being involved in any way.

Alighting from the Metro station I wondered how I would find the building and the office in question. Perhaps as an unconscious stalling technique, I made the mistake of stopping at a Metro kiosk for a newspaper. Struck by the headlines I had perused, I paid for it, nodded to the elderly female cashier, mumbled "Merci Madam," and moved out into the swirling traffic to hunt for the building. Breathing a sigh of relief once inside the foyer, I decided to check my wallet, count out the bills again, and find the floor in question. In an instant I knew that I had left it on the counter of the kiosk in front of the old lady who had served me. As she reminded me vaguely of my grandmother, I could pick her out of a crowd easily, but would she and the wallet still be there? I had never before done anything so careless.

Almost panic-stricken over my own important identification papers and cash as well as the large sum of entrusted rent money, I was at the same time agonized to think that although I had gotten myself across the Atlantic, this mistake could turn out to be my complete undoing. Where would I be without my *permis de séjour*, or visitor's permit? I tore out to the Boulevard des Italiens only to discover impenetrable, fast-moving traffic in all directions. If I had to get to the Metro on foot, it could mean that the wallet had long since disappeared. If I found a taxi now, there might be time! "What to do?" I wondered. As I teetered on the curb, hailing cabs with outstretched arm, the drivers shrugged as they skimmed by. "Were they going off duty? How can I know if one will ever stop? Anyway, I have no money! Had I better give up and go there on foot?"

Just then a cab stopped quietly beside me. The youthful driver remained calm and non-committal even when I admitted that at present I did not have so much as a 'sous' to offer. Without so much as a Gallic shrug he delivered me to the Metro station in seconds. We agreed that he would slip into the adjacent bistro while I searched the kiosk. Turning up in a suppressed state of breathlessness in front of the same pleasant old woman, I could tell immediately by her expression that all was well. She reached a hand under the counter and brought forth my shabby old wallet.

Speechless with shock, I picked it up, wondering if it were still intact, yet too embarrassed, being young and poor, to look inside or to offer a really heartfelt reward. I thanked her as well as I could in my agitated state, my mind swirling with astonishment to think that here in *the nombril du monde*, literally the navel of the world, everything was quite alright.

The old lady seemed genuinely pleased, through misty blue eyes, as if she quite understood the enormity of the situation. I passed her a small reward, wanting to give her ten times as much, yet too overcome with emotion to explain the circumstances. Even though I wore my Canada badge, I could possibly be mistaken for an American, as I was obviously not French, and therefore someone with more wealth than the French working-class of the early fifties.

In my agitated state it was useless to try to explain that I was carrying money for a friend. She stood there, pale, poor and old-looking, in the blue denim smock. After the suffering and poverty of wartime, she could easily have claimed ignorance of the *la fortune* in paper rent money left with her and put it to good use.

On the other hand, she may have seen my Canada badge and wanted to express the sort of feeling I had heard from so many people, Dutch and French in particular, toward Canadians for having assisted in the Liberation of 1945. Likewise, had the taxi-driver also seen my insignia? Otherwise, why had he so quietly agreed to help·me with no apparent reward in sight on a busy afternoon when he might have done well with normal passengers?

I found him waiting in the bistro, as agreed, paid for his beer and the fare. Although he deserved a generous tip, I parted from him without feeling the slightest sense of condescension on his part. Again I was at a loss to adequately express the depth of my thanks for his chivalrous though fortunately impersonal attitude. Whenever people who have visited France choose to enlarge on stories of the rudeness of the French or of theft of their wallets, I have always stood up in defence of Parisians. They have treated me so well in time of need, leaving me to regard them with warmth and admiration.

Renée, Herta and Other Brave Women

By now I was getting to know my way around the hospital and to be acquainted in the cafeteria with a few of my colleagues, from parts of the globe. The very first of these was with Renée Chomed and her sister Herta. Considering the tragedy of their lives, they might well have become two embittered young women. Natives of Salzburg, Jewish and cultured they were the most calm, warm-hearted of caring individuals who treated me as if we were long-time friends. Their parents had put them on one of the children's trains, or *Kindertransport*, from Vienna for the safety of Britain in 1938, to face Auschwitz and death themselves.

As mentioned before, I recall so vividly the photographs of the event in the papers and newsreels that year just before the war began. As a thirteen year-old I had stared in disbelief with my parents that such a thing could happen. Whether or not that train for Britain left before or after the notoriously destructive event of Kristallnacht, on November 8 or 9, I am not sure.

Hitler had annexed Austria to Germany in May, the event known as the *Anschluss*. Recently, a friend told me of her own confusion and fear as an eight-year old in Germany, on finding her parents listening to the radio, distraught upon hearing the announcement of *Kristallnacht*, the burning, looting, window-breaking of all Jewish property. For me, safe at home here in Canada as a child, the news had been horrifying, yet non-threatening.

Renée and Herta recalled their father saying that "Nothing will happen here, not in Vienna; we will just make sure that you are out of harm's way, and send for you later." He apparently believed the widespread rumour that transport and resettlement to another area would be provided. They had also heard him say that they should have all gone to America earlier along with so many other Jewish people, but he felt responsible for his parents. For how many years did Renée and Herta wait for a letter, crying themselves to sleep among strangers in a foreign country before they were finally informed of the horror of their parents' deaths in Auschwitz?

As it had all come flooding back into my mind, I could scarcely believe that I was now acquainted with two of these transported survivors. Drawn as I was to their warmth, sense of humour and intelligence, we became close friends, with similar dreams of broadening our education. Brought up in an institution in

Scotland for young refugees, they were given training as hospital workers along with their schooling and language courses and then subsequently directed into the state registered nursing diploma program.

Having always intended a university education like myself, before the death of my own father, they too hoped to find a way ahead. Renée was quick to take advantage of my offer to help them learn the typing which they would need as students. Then we moved on to the rudimentary shorthand which I had also learned in the Canadian Army. We were all aware that the physical and financial strain of a nursing career could not be sustained indefinitely, without private funds and the hardy physique which none of us possessed.

Together we attended many of the great cultural events, including concerts, opera, ballet and theatre, thanks to *Jeunesse Musicales.* Such was the good fortune of being young, having friends and being in Paris in 1951, with a government disposed to fund the arts in a way unknown in Canada. On payment of the equivalent of roughly twenty-five cents a year, one became a member, wore a small gilt pin, and walked freely into a variety of performances, some matinées, some evening performances. It was an unbelievable and unforgettable experience and was open to all young people up to the age of thirty. Just to have seen the interior of the Opéra de Paris would have been a thrill, let alone fearlessly proceeding up the grand staircase in casual attire, sitting down to enjoy one performance after another, month after month. It was amazing! It was "la vie en rose!"

As Christmas 1951 approached, Renée surprised me one day by telling me of the contents of a letter from her aunt in Salzburg. How fortunate, I thought, "She does have a living relative to whom she can relate." Smiling and thrilled at returning to Austria again, she said, "My aunt would like us all to join her for the Christmas break. She lives very close to the cathedral and we will be able to take in plenty of Mozart." "Fantastic, Renee!" I answered, "thank you so much!"

We were delighted, and in my case quite flattered to be included. Even more amazing was the fact that we managed to get time off on the same sequence of days. I made plans to get a visa, while they looked into their own travel regulations. By the time we were counting the hours to our departure, news came that Jewish travellers would be stopped by the forces then controlling Vienna. It lay in the Russian sector. This being 1951, Europe was still under the jurisdiction of the four powers: America, Britain, Russia and France.

Although I had found such good friends in Renée and Herta, there was one colleague who posed a daily challenge in the operating room. Henriette was a moody, tempestuous woman in thick spectacles who continually shouted routine orders, grating on my nerves, as if she were a Nazi officer from a wartime propaganda film. One evening my colleague Ursula and I found ourselves having coffee with Henriette in a bistro. That was when we learned that she had been taken so roughly from her classroom in rural France to a munitions works in Germany and kept there for the entire five years of the war.

She described herself as having been a very cocky young teenager who always wanted to rebel against authority. Although the camp was the wrong place to risk attracting notice, she had decided not to sing but to simply *mouth* the compulsory German patriotic songs. Before long she was apprehended and summoned to appear alone in front of an officer the following week. She spent the waiting time in terror of being shot on the appointed day of the interview. Coming away from the interview with no more than a reprimand and a fixed date to begin a course in singing lessons, Henriette belted out those odious patriotic Nazi songs forever after, all thought of protest abandoned in favor of survival.

As with millions of others, survival was all that mattered to Henriette for a long time. At the end of the war it remained for women to make their way across Europe without food, money or transport, often travelling under the cover of darkness and stumbling over bodies to avoid rape by soldiers also in transit. Although in her case it was a relatively short distance from Germany to France, the group she fell in with was in such an advanced state of starvation that they were slumped along the roadside with, as she said, "Nothing to eat except our fingernails."

Forced by starvation to raid the pockets of the dead on the battlefield for food, she was too weak to stand any longer when she found a decaying sandwich in a soldier's pocket. With all the debris around her, she had no choice but to sit on the headless body, eat the revolting food and gather strength and courage to press on. Otherwise she too would die.

Much later, on a main road, the first American vehicle they had ever seen stopped beside them. Everyone shouted at once, "Food!" They were wrong. "No," she said, "They were dumping cases of Dole pineapple juice. We devoured it all at once, couldn't help it, starving, crazed, rather than sipping it a little at a time. Everyone was painfully ill at the side of the road, waiting hours for more American troops to bring food. We were all too weak to move."

When Henriette finally arrived home to France after five years detention at the Nazi munitions factory still cherishing the dream of reunion with her parents, she found other people in the house. On locating her father, she found that he was living with another woman and had different people in his life. Her mother had left no message for her and her whereabouts were never identified. Finally, she found a means of entering a training school for registered nurses with the hope of trying to rebuild her life as best she could.

After the graduation Henriette had accepted a position in Geneva. It was a private Swiss hospital whose chief surgeon was possessed of a very foul temper, attributed to the rumour that he had once studied and worked in a Soviet Communist military hospital in Russia. She apparently had no idea that she too shouted at us having picked up the habit in the operating room in Geneva. One day she heard the surgeon shouting furiously at a cardiac patient. The man turned pale and died within half an hour. She decided to submit her resignation. "This hospital is a wonderful trade-off for that madhouse in Geneva," she said, looking very different from our whip-cracking sergeant of the operating-room staff. After that, Henriette kept a reasonably low profile at work, having formed a bond with us.

On the other hand, from the start, Ursula was one of the very best colleagues one could encounter. She was already more experienced in emergency situations than any of us could ever have imagined. During the three-month Russian siege of the German Silesian city of Breslau, in 1944, now known as Wroclaw, Poland, her family home was taken over by the Russian Army. Her family scattered to find beds wherever they could. Ursula was taken out of school and put to work picking up the dead and wounded and removing furniture from buildings ahead of the Russians who were intent on setting fires.

One day a phone rang repeatedly in a building she had been assigned to help clear. Afraid to answer it, in case it was a Russian officer, Ursula was startled and surprised to hear an Italian accent on the line. Wounded and trying to extricate himself from some extremely hazardous location, Mario explained to her in German that he was an Italian working in Breslau. Telling him that rescue was at hand, she summoned aid with great difficulty and in the dark, finally reached him while dodging an officer bent on assault.

As the siege of the city went on she found herself late one night unable to get to wherever her family had found temporary haven. Her only recourse to safety was to swim the river, managing to keep her wristwatch dry, while cloaked in pitch black and dangerous conditions. Later, a bomb fell on a basement room in which she and her grandmother sheltered. The old lady died instantly. Ursula was pulled out of the wreckage unhurt.

By the last year of the war, food shortages were so severe that the city faced starvation. The family made their way to Holzminden, in West Germany, escaping in a wagon with straw piled on top of them. With them was an aunt who kept insisting that she was sure that she would at last have a real bedroom again after so many years of misery. When they arrived safely and were ushered into a crowded attic she burst into tears at having entertained so fanciful a dream. Although the family finally became established in West Germany, with high schools and amenities, starvation remained a nightmare in their lives.

Eventually in 1946 Ursula learned from a German newspaper that Britain was offering a registered nurse training program in London. "I knew that there would be more food for the others in our family if I went to London," she told us. As it was open to English-speaking high school graduates, and offered food, lodging and a small stipend, she sent in her application. "Now," she added, "Hitler having ruined our lives thus far, I am studying languages in my spare time as a beginning. I wouldn't have left home at all, except that it meant more food for the others in our family."

As Ursula spoke of those days, I recalled that back in Canada I had watched an emaciated refugee silently placing pats of butter on plates in a hospital dining-room. She did it as if in a state of wonder, as though handling gold itself. Another such person from rural Holland who knew enough English to tell me about himself while being treated in that hospital told us that as well as starvation, the severe cold was extremely difficult to bear, especially after one's shoes wore out. It meant that finding fresh cow dung was the only way to warm the feet.

While enjoying a day off, I liked to stroll along the Seine, by the *bouquinistes,* or the book sellers stalls. I had picked up an old book, a Pulitzer Prize winner of 1933, about life in Paris, called *The Street of the Fishing Cat,* by Jolan Foldes. The central characters were not French, but immigrants from Central Europe, struggling to adapt to a new life. One could see that for labourers and semi-skilled workers trying to stay afloat economically in 1930's France, it would be a difficult struggle outside the mainstream life in Paris. Clearly, in real life, for nationals across Europe, living outside their own country, September the third, 1939 must have been even more frightening.

Drawn to their neighbourhood not far from mine in the student quarter, I went in search of clues, despite the fact that the street of the Fishing Cat no longer existed. It had perhaps been eliminated by Haussman's massive slum clearance and major renovations of the city during the eighteen-hundreds to bring Paris into

325

the modern world. Located in the neighbourhood of rue de la Huchette, a *huche* being a storage box, perhaps a shed for freight brought by boat. The street had been near the Quai Saint Michel where fishermen had sat along the Seine. Supposedly a cat had once caught a fish on that spot, long before the modernization of the poor streets of the city by the famous architect and planner.

What I did find on the day that I searched out the area was a very small shop, selling odds and ends of mainly food supplies. High on a shelf I saw a row of very old-looking, small, stoneware jars filled with what I knew to be a liqueur derived from apples. Sealed with wax, the labels were marked 'Calvados' and in smaller print the word, 'Normandie'. The moment my eye fell on them I thought of the Calvados drinker, the hero of my teenage years, the central character in a story of the French Resistance movement in the war. I knew that I must sample it. Since then I have heard it said, although I never knew for sure, that it had helped to fuel American Jeeps in France in desperate moments during the war. Was it a joke? Or very strong?

Dislodging the cork with extreme difficulty when I tried to open it, I was startled by a roar of escaping vapour. Putting it to my lips, knocked off my feet, I landed with a thud on the floor. I could well believe the story of the Jeeps. So that was Calvados! Waiting for hardier souls to finish it, I kept the rustic old stone bottle for several years. I have been told recently that the method of preparation must have been considerably refined since then as it is now a liqueur like any other.

L'ecole des Beaux Arts, Fellow Artists and Survivors

A s I had never felt that life was complete without a pencil and a block of drawing paper, it was quite predictable that I would one day enroll as a casual spare-time Saturday student at l'École des Beaux Arts, that most venerable of French schools dating back to 1648. Rusty as I was, I had never tired of the challenge. Surprisingly, the day arrived when the instructor remarked that he would now regarded me as a serious student, worthy of instruction. We had been working on the figure of a seated female nude.

Standing near my easel as she worked on her own assignment was an older woman. Una put down her charcoal and came over to have a look at my work. By the end of the session we had decided to adjourn to a nearby café to continue our acquaintance. I became immediately interested on hearing that she had not only studied oriental art but had joined a colleague to put together a gallery collection of it in Boston following his researches in Japan.

Just back to Paris from her chalet at Glion, a village above Lac Leman, or Lake Geneva, near Montreux, Switzerland, Una was pleased to relax over coffee for an hour or so. We soon became firm friends. A widow, now settled in Switzerland where they had been forced to stay for the duration of the war, she had never returned to Boston.

As a result she now felt more Swiss than anything else, yet confessed a natural curiosity about life "over there in the new world." Not surprisingly, she admitted being drawn to newcomers like myself in hope of forming a better picture of life in America today.

Not wishing to make the trip without her husband, Una had looked for someone with whom to share the adventure, but with no meaningful personal contacts remaining "across the pond" to welcome her, she had at last simply remained in Switzerland, the imaginary country as it is sometimes described, high in the mountains, safe from the war, in a perfect climate. For Una, an avid reader, a published author who loved classical music as well as the world of art, she was in the end, comfortable enough just to sit on the balcony overlooking Lac Leman, the sailboats and yachts below, with a glass of fine Swiss champagne and a friend or two.

Life at Glion had no connection with the everyday international hustle and bustle of Geneva at the other end of the lake, much less a concern about the congestion and traffic jams to be faced in New York or Boston. One could always put on another recording of Dvorak's New World Symphony or listen to the French classical music of the Orchestre Suisse Romande conducted by renowned Swiss conductor Earnest Ensermé and forget the world of today.

For that matter, cars and traffic hardly existed in Glion, while the funicular, the cable car which ran on pulleys took one to Montreux in minutes. Glion remained a place of privilege, scarcely disturbed by modernity, dreaming beside Lac Leman, as it had been since the days of its popularity with the *literati*, that latest wave in the 1920's of British writers and travellers to sojourn at Menton, near the Mediterranean on the French-Italian border.

However, Una was determined to make Paris her own again after the war. With frequent visits, she finally settled for a small flat to use whenever she wished. I became a regular dinner guest along with a group of interesting types she had met over the years. One evening I met Michel, instructor in sculpture at L'École des Beaux Arts. Good-naturedly she regarded him as a colleague, having also taught fine arts in Boston in her youth. With those large dark eyes under the bushy eyebrows he leaned across the table to ask me, "Do you know what is a *Sprainch*? No, well it means that I am of mixed French and Spanish ancestry. So is Picasso." He said it as if pretending great pride, the expressive, laughing, yet sometimes melancholy eyes seeming to reflect his considerable life experiences. Later admitting a French-Swiss connection, I liked him all the more.

Apart from sculpture, it seemed that cooking was another of the passions he had used as a way to make friends. In gaining access to their kitchens he would prepare a feast and become a friend. It was Michel rather than Una who had prepared the delectable food and drink set down in front of us. He liked to say that he never went anywhere without a pocket full of *les épices*, or spices. To prove it, he pulled a whole nutmeg and a grater from his jacket pocket. For one thing, he went on, "Spinach simply isn't fit to eat without nutmeg and cream." Convinced that no social gathering was tolerable without *a bibble*, he saw to it that a bottle of wine was always within reach.

Michel had no real kitchen of his own. Having become used to such extreme hardship during the war, he preferred the well-stocked supply of pots and pans of his friends. His Gallic charm, teasing, good-natured guise appeared to hide a certain mysterious air of regret. At ease anywhere, he was among the ranks of Citizens of the World as people called themselves and were beginning to look outward at other cultures and political groups.

During the introductions around the table Una had announced, "Michel is a Canadian too, from Québec." I learned that he had won a scholarship in sculpture to Paris in the late thirties. Somehow, like others who felt that they could not leave the city, could not tear themselves away in 1939, he had turned up at the Canadian Embassy too late to get out of the country before that fatal day, September the third, the beginning of World War II. Thus began his desperate five-year struggle to stay alive.

Rather mysteriously, vaguely, he implied that his passport and documents had disappeared mysteriously. Or perhaps the truth was that he had actually offered his identification to one of the many desperate French Jews trying to escape. It was a period of desperate effort filled with cold, hunger and fear to keep out of the sight of the authorities. Given his very generous nature, and vagueness as to details, one could easily imagine such a scenario.

Premier Petain of the Vichy Regime, had been forced to turn Jews over to the Nazis while at the same time the French Resistance movement worked ceaselessly to save many of them. I believe Michel who cared deeply about others had also been involved in this work, but would not elaborate. At war's end, too weak to walk, he was returned to Canada on a stretcher. After treatment to cure the tuberculosis which had ravaged him, he finally returned to France.

In his book "Just Raoul," author James Bacque discusses the bravery of the French Resistance Movement worker, Raoul Laporterie, mayor of a small town in Vichy, France, who risked his life to save sixteen hundred Jews from deportation to the Nazi death camps. Could he have known of another of his heroic colleagues, a Portuguese consul, a diplomat in Bordeaux, France, who provided ten thousand visas to desperate Jews to escape through Spain? Memorials in his name, Aristides de Sousa Mendes, exist in many countries, from the US to Israel, including a forest of ten thousand trees in that country.

At his factory in Krakow, Poland, the German businessman, Oskar Schindler concealed the identity of twelve hundred Jewish workers, classified as slaves at his enamel works production plant considered essential for the Nazi war effort. Also on the grand scale, we still recall from time to time, the Swedish diplomat Raoul Wallenburg who saved one-hundred-thousand Hungarian Jews, before disappearing from sight permanently when the Russians marched into Budapest. Among monuments to his memory is one thoughtfully placed in a miniscule park in the heart of downtown Montreal. Seated in front of it, one can hope that many others have paid homage here to his courage and at other sites around the world and will continue to do so forever.

Michel had found no reason to stay at home in Canada. He had lost contact with life in Québec and in Paris, as his old friends had moved on to greater success in their field. Before 1939 there had been the camaraderie with all his fellow sculpture students and some of the great names in art and literature in the cafes and bistros of the Latin Quarter. Now he hid his angst behind his colourful *Sprainch* personality. Thankful to be alive and an art instructor at least, he had of course lost his youthful ambition to be the sculptor of note, another Picasso or a Henry Moore.

Michel was witty, generous and thoroughly likeable human being, wise enough not to court bitterness. All his energy had been required to keep out of sight of the Gestapo. He had been starving, cold and always forced to move on. Becoming markedly Parisian, Michel sometimes reminded me of Georges Brassens, a well-known musician of the era in Paris, whose then popular songs can still be heard on CBC French radio from time to time.

Una often mentioned her fond memories of Lake Constance, along the Swiss, German and Austrian borders, and Munich, a little further east and north. Eventually she persuaded Michel to drive us along the lake when he and I had free time on our hands. We drove from Paris south to Basle into the Black Forest and along the shores of idyllic Lake Constance, through the spectacular mountain area of Hitler's hide-away at Garmisch-Partenkirchen. At Mittenwald, a village close to Munich, we stopped long enough to stroll along the main street. Spotting a violin-maker's shop, we stepped inside to admire the enterprise underway at the moment. Although not customers, we seemed to be quite welcome to gaze upon an ancient art being carried on again now, amidst all the enthusiasm of the post-war years.

Once out on the street again, we saw that the village baker had just arrived with baskets full of fresh-baked rolls. He was greeted by a boisterously eager crowd. Sampling them out of our curiosity about the rumoured superiority of the nutritional content of German 'black bread,' we decided unanimously that it must be the *ersatz* or sawdust adulterated flour we had read of during the war. To us it seemed to be barely edible, yet to them it may have become normal. We were shocked to think that it was still in use.

As they strode vigorously through this incredibly scenic mountain country, men and women wore the attractive and practical traditional Tyrolean grey and loden-green woolen hats, jackets, coats, boots and heavy knee socks. This clothing enhanced them with a sturdier appearance than one would see anywhere else, as for example, England or France, or for that matter in rural Canada where it could be useful in our cold climate.

In Munich, I saw piles of rubble from World War II bombing raids for the first time. In central London everything had been restored by the time I visited it in 1951. However, despite the nearly impassable streets of Munich, the thoroughfare was full of office workers managing to make their way homeward for the evening. As we passed by, one robust group of singers could be heard as loud song wafted down from an apartment complex. Naturally beer was being quaffed enthusiastically around an outdoor table by eager young stalwarts in lederhosen.

On the return trip to Paris we noticed that several small bridges on the French-German border had not yet been rebuilt. As young friends of mine liked to say, "The Germans have rebuilt more quickly. They come out to do road work at six in the morning. We French take our time; in Germany *arbeit* or work is the most important issue in life, you know." I had heard it said that it is the

German "black" bread and beer that give one strength to fight as well as to work, rather than French baguettes and wine. On seeing Octoberfest in full swing in Munich, I was easily convinced but prefer French cuisine.

Back in Paris, after short acquaintance, I let myself be persuaded to join three young people from the hospital for a student-priced theatre production in an unknown, distant part of the city at night. I expected that we would stay together long enough afterwards to make sure that each of us knew how to get home, counting on a little chivalry from the two young men.

Afterwards, excited by a great performance, we flooded out into the darkness, totally unaware of our surroundings. With no pre-arranged plans to help each other, everyone panicked and rushed off to find separate metro trains. Shaken by sudden isolation and necessary haste, I disregarded the lighted Metro wall indicator as to the right line to Port Royal Station. At such an hour, I was afraid to linger long enough to get my bearings. Consequently, rather than risk any doubtful types haunting the disturbing blackness of the unlighted streets, I took a wild guess and jumped into the coach arriving that particular second.

A few moments later, I had decided to be rational and to alight at the next stop to correct my error sooner than later. The platform, devoid of a direction indicator, emptied rapidly at this time of night, with everyone anxious to reach their own doorways. Suddenly I was completely alone. It was not only fear of the possibility of an assailant, but now the shock of observing that millions of lights seemed to be trained down on me from a short distance.

I was horrified by the darkness of the platform. My peripheral vision caught a sky full of a thousand lighted apartment windows, like brilliant stars, as if *le tous Paris*, all of Paris, stared down at me, indignantly demanding an answer to, "Why are you there? Get away with you. It is the middle of the night. This is no place for you. *Va!* Go away, go away, go away!"

"But if only someone could see me and come to my rescue," I implored the gods insanely, my mind grasping at a fleeting straw. At the same time, dumbfounded by the lights, as if they were again, the Milky Way, in the Caribbean, I was seized for a fleeting, disturbing moment with the sense of being still part of the storm at sea, less than a cork afloat on a dark and hostile ocean. The image faded in and out in less than a second as the instinctive need to escape, to find a taxi, immediately took precedence over all else.

Making things more difficult was the fact that in 1951 not only were the streets poorly lit but quite unbelievably, Parisian taxis were identifiable only by colour and make. These ancient dark or maroon-red coloured Renaults were easier to see on a half-lit street than in some others. One of them crawled past me. Like a mirage to a desperate traveller in the desert, it disappeared silently into the murk again with only a barely visible Gallic shrug of the driver's shoulders.

When finally one stopped, I was forced to slide into a back seat shrouded in total obscurity, not knowing whether someone there might be poised to strike me over the head before snatching my purse. Nor could I get the driver, whose face was totally shrouded in the darkness, to reply when asked if he knew my address. Was this eerie silence a tactic left over from the war, and now a habit, a form of self-protection they had used against contact with abusive German soldiers in occupied Paris?

Cringing in the back seat in total ignorance and disbelief, the murky, half-lit, silent streets revealed no clues as to our whereabouts. The stony silence of the driver increased my desperation as the minutes dragged on like hours. Would I have sufficient francs to pay for the trip, and if not, what then? Finally, without comment of any sort, he very slowly and silently brought the car to a stop at 12, rue de l'Observatoire.

While I passed the mumbled fare to him, he did not so much as turn his head before disappearing like a phantom back into the night. Summoning the courage to climb the half-lit seven-floor wooden staircase to my student quarters, I met no one to give me a sense of reality. Had cell-phones existed in 1951, there would have been no friends to call for help, a factor which adds to the sense of isolation. Once safe on my cot, it occurred to me that in all likelihood I would come to feel quite secure in this amazing metropolis, silent and distant as some of its drivers might be. "Whatever happened to Gallic charm?" I wondered as I drifted off to sleep, excusing them and at the same time recalling other positive scenarios.

As planned, I enrolled at l'Alliance Francaise to improve my knowledge of the French language. It was there that I happened to meet Irena, a tall, ash-blonde Polish woman with piercing blue eyes and an intense, intelligent manner. She looked both elegant and sophisticated as she offered me a cigarette, explaining in faltering English her need to learn the language to emigrate to Canada, a final escape from a Europe still causing her to wake with devastating nightmares. Smoking nervously, she told me that it had been such a great relief to land a job in a Polish bookshop in Paris. In the meantime, she hoped to learn to speak both French and English convincingly.

I found myself called upon to help her with pronunciation, made difficult by her assumption that English should be pronounced exactly as it is written. Despite her difficulties, I could see the intelligence in her expression and knew that she would very soon master her problem. Having spoken French at home in Poland with her parents, as was the custom for educated Russians, she had made a good start already at l'Alliance Francaise.

Irena had treasured childhood memories of a hospitable home in Warsaw before the war. I began to look forward to the evenings I spent as a guest in the cramped apartment over wine, coffee, cheeses and Polish desserts. On the first visit I was to meet Leo, of whom she had spoken. He was a tall, dark, very foreign-looking, French-speaking but with a suggestion of Slavic background. Smoking a Gaulois cigarette in an easy-going, good-natured manner, he seemed to be sociability itself.

They had met shortly after the war in a seemingly mysterious political organization somewhere in Europe which she hinted darkly at as having been a dangerous youthful adventure. I assumed that they had been caught up in Soviet Communism. Finally they had both come to his parents in Paris, made amends and tried to plan their lives.

This allowed Leo to learn his father's bookseller's business which he described as being the right future for him. With an expressively elegant Gallic shrug of his long, outstretched arms, the Gaulois burning from an expensive-looking, elongated ivory cigarette holder held in the right hand, he explained, *moin d'effort, moin d'effort*, by which he meant that it would take less effort than a university career would demand of him. I could not of course, imagine anyone trying to avoid the benefits of attending the Sorbonne University, free of charge as it was.

Apart from their strange meeting in the confused aftermath of the war, Irena and Leo had recognized in each other a similar background, each being the children of privileged White Russian parents who had fled the Bolshevik Revolution in 1917 for Paris and Danzig. Despite their seemingly very different attitudes to life, their beginnings seemed to have given them a sufficient bond to join forces. Although opposites are said to attract, I could not help wondering how such a marriage would succeed, one partner being so ambitious,

339

so nervous and lacking in the other's ready sense of humour and easy-going attitude.

Enabling them both to practice their English, we would sip red wine together , listening to Leo's remarks on the best films and books. He often referred to Dickens as his key to understanding the strangeness of *les Anglais*, and their language. In the end he learned to speak quite naturally and to be a friend, probably in part due to his relaxed attitude.

As time went on I learned that on September 3, 1939, Irena's father, a Polish officer, was shot to death by a Nazi official on a station platform in Warsaw. Irena, then a twelve year-old school girl, was taken with many others to spend the entire period of the war at a German weapons factory, leaving her grieving mother all alone. In 1945, with no news of her, Irena and thousands of lost girls had to make their way back to Poland and elsewhere, not only on foot but without food, money, or a map to guide them.

With all the women who had been caught up in the vortex of war, rape was a constant fear. Obliged to head for empty buildings of any kind to hide in during daylight hours, Irena tried to make progress on foot under the cover of darkness. Bodies were everywhere, piled up in the woods, floating on the lakes. Unnerved, highly strung, intelligent, starving and alone, Irena finally set foot in Warsaw only to learn that her lonely mother had hung herself. If she had been told what else could have befallen this poor woman before her death, she of course kept it to herself. It was probably torture and rape, as a preliminary show of hatred for the Poles. Irena would always swear never to set foot in Europe again if only they could get to Canada. Leo would give another shrug, another flourish of the cigarette holder. He wasn't so sure.

Little by little I found that despite the horror she had so recently come through Irena too was after all actually possessed of a robust sense of humour as well as intelligence. Whether or not she ever escaped her demons, her nightmares, her fear of being in unlocked rooms and cars, is difficult to conjecture. The war was still very much with her in the early 1950's, much as she tried bravely to be part of the new era. Naturally torn apart with grief, she could still very readily dissolve into tears, moods and desperation.

After an elaborate candle-lit church service, Irena observed a Polish Easter custom in the tiny Paris apartment, serving the delectable, tall, light-textured ceremonial cake, with wine, goodwill and probably deep gratitude for her survival. At such relaxed occasions, I got to know her better and to find that she wanted to introduce me to the delights of several Russian authors, Gogol and Pushkin among them. Without her would I have stumbled on Gogol's *Deal Souls* or his charming rural tale of *Mirgorod* or laughed over Goncharov's lamentable character *Oblamov* in a work of the same name.

Irena liked to tell me that I was *waiting for a knight on a white horse.* Not having been challenged by war, I felt free to hold out for a soul mate rather than seek someone to save me from disaster. I could see that as a teenager caught up alone in a war, lost in forests

341

and fields, strewn with corpses and always imminent danger, she might easily have fantasized about a
magical rescue. Being more fortunate, I would meet my
equal when the time was right and not before. It was
that magical scenario as dreamed of long ago in ado-
lescence, which came to mind, of hiking a grassy slope,
preferably the Swiss Alps, and meeting a professor, a
scholar, someone possessed of interesting ideas.

As I was to witness myself, the impossibly romantic did happen now and then, a most memorable case
being that of Madeleine and Pierre. During the life
drawing classes as L'Ecole des Beaux Arts, a certain
tall, attractive student named Madeleine had sat near
Una and me. It was there that I learned of the recent
extraordinary events of her young life. 'Missing and pre-
sumed dead,' as listed in the official report in 1945, her
fiancée Pierre, a tall, gaunt, six-foot tall hero, had suddenly walked back into her life from a Siberian prison
camp a few months earlier, in 1950, after having been
held by the Germans. One day Una and I came upon
them in a nearby café, still quite obviously enchanted
that the impossible had happened. From time to time
we would meet Madeleine blissfully wheeling her infant
son in the Luxembourg Gardens.

Pierre was adapting well to his new life and had
a teaching post at the university. One evening when he
was giving a class, she invited us for a meal. It seemed
that her family had given them financial support to provide household help. Just as they worked in the shops,
seniors were also employed in private homes. Madeleine

was apparently quite fond of these old women, one of whom would arrive in time to prepare the vegetables, another to cook them, while yet another would serve and put everything away.

In a country where the pleasures of the table were taken seriously, it appeared to be a friendly arrangement. That the plates and cutlery were changed several times during the meal, the green beans being served as a separate first course to enhance enjoyment of the very fresh flavour of *les haricôts verts,* illustrates the French capacity for attention to detail in fine cuisine.

After we listened to Madeleine's excited account of the forthcoming baptism of the baby, she again chose a day when Pierre was absent to show us her mother's preparations for the family event. There were the elaborate ancestral linens and the antique wrought-iron cradle used for generations past. Later we saw the photos of the very dignified grandparents looking solemnly down at the miraculous child, swathed in ancestral white lace. His cradle hung from an ornate, *art-nouveau* type of wrought iron armature suspending it so that he could be rocked to sleep.

These proud grandparents must have looked on in wonder, having assumed after six long years that their son had perished in World War II. They had also survived the First World War and probably heard the stories of the hardships of the Franco-Prussian conflict of 1870 from grandparents. Here was an occasion for them to indulge in personal hope, as well as to dare to dream of long-term peace for Europe at last.

Rue Monsieur Prince et La Suisse

Meandering through the Left Bank in a mixed group of young people from La Cité one Saturday evening, we turned onto rue Monsieur Prince. I began to keep my eyes open for a certain street number memorized all those years ago back in Canada. My love affair with student life in Paris had begun at thirteen years of age, while perusing that important British weekly, the *Picture Post*, with my parents. As well as large photographs of enemy action on London and elsewhere, the paper contained articles of general interest.

I had been utterly amazed, of course, to come upon full-page footage and photos of student life around tables in a Left Bank café or *boite*. It was situated on a certain rue Monsieur Prince near the Sorbonne University, now known as *l'Universite de Paris*. It interested me as I thought classrooms were the exciting places to be. On the opposite page appeared a scene from the film of Somerset Maughn's tale, *The Razor's*

Edge, at that time popular on both sides of the Atlantic. This was, to me also, as today's teenagers say, definitely "cool," to become aware of adult literary and film discussion around me.

Of Canadian universities I had had no impression whatever, at thirteen years of age, having heard only of teacher training diplomas earned in prairie colleges. Yet suddenly I had caught a glimpse of academic life in the centre of the world itself. The photographic article of the student scene on rue Monsieur Prince as it was identified below the picture, had stayed in my mind through all the intervening years of struggle until then, the summer of 1951.

Now, quite incredibly, here in Paris, while searching the streets of my own neighbourhood, near Boulevard St. Jacques, I came upon rue Monsieur Prince and recalled the exact address as well. One evening I persuaded my companions to follow me through the doorway to enjoy the dancing. "Who would believe me had I told the story?" I asked myself before we went in. They would think I had made it up. The place was now entirely devoted to dancing. Although we had arrived early, a few couples had already taken to the floor in response to the strains of *April in Portugal*, then very popular, and while not knowing Portugal, I always translated in my mind to 'April in the paradise of Paris.' We hastened to the floor.

While the players sat along the back of the room with the bar at the right, a tall and personable young man slouched over one of the bar stools, close enough to the door to welcome the public. Sitting cross-legged to support his guitar, he sang plaintively, arrestingly, strumming the instrument. From time to time we skimmed past him and saw that his shirt sleeves were rolled up to the elbows, revealing the incredibly enlarged blue veins of his hands and forearms. At his elbow, on the polished counter was a small glass. Glinting in the bottom I noticed a pale, clear liquid from which he occasionally took a sip.

Very sure of himself, he would smile and sing quite passionately. Perhaps this was what he did to stay alive in Paris. He looked as if he might be a GI who had stayed behind in France at the end of the war. Mentioning it to my Swiss student friend Georges as we sailed by, I remarked, "He's got a lot in common with Degas's absinthe drinking street people, don't you think?" I was referring of course to the painting, *The Absinthe Drinker.* In this century everyone knows that Pernod should be taken sparingly and diluted with water. I knew enough of its properties, despite my attraction to it, to order it only as a rare treat. It was a convivial place. Eventually we fell into conversation with him between dances. Carl told us that he was in fact an ex-GI who had stayed on in Paris for the most plausible of reasons, "I couldn't bring myself to leave."

"Of course not," I thought, as we danced to the music of Edith Piaf, Juliet Greco, George Brassens and many others. It made good sense. We finally left with him and the good-natured Pedro, a Caribbean fiddler turned Frenchman in a black beret. *Ciel de Paris* was still swirling delightfully around in my head as we stepped into the cool, inviting, semi-dark of an early summer morning in the Latin Quarter. That seductive closing number permeated the charm of the now empty, silent cobbled street, simultaneously, momentarily, evoking the bewitching aura of the brilliant, starlit night-time sky in Vincent van Gogh's *Midnight at Arles*. To him the scene is said to have connotations of unhappiness related to his long association with prostitutes. Since I was ignorant at that time of his unfortunate life story, both Arles and this night in Paris had coalesced in my mind into a single image of youthful delight.

The players had suggested that we might like to follow them through the historic 'Les Halles' produce market to a favourite breakfast spot where revellers customarily finished off their celebrations. We decided to go along in order to see this popular market because of hearsay that students passing by in the small hours had always gotten away with raiding the stands of produce.

Determined to be part of this traditional clandestine amusement, we picked off the odd apple and banana, waving at the burly workers as they either smiled, winked, or turned a blind eye while piling cabbages and crates, creating a certain bond among strangers in the night. "What a great day it must have been for Parisians when Les Halles re-opened at the end of the war," Carl called out as we bit into our prizes, edging our way through the market in single file between

347

the piled up crates, proudly acting out the time-honoured ritual accorded to youth. While life in Paris had already enhanced and enriched my life miraculously, and permanently, I knew it for a certainty at Les Halles as I have known it ever since.

Finally arriving at the restaurant, probably much as travelling players carrying instruments have done through the centuries, I noticed a cluster of labourers lined up at the outdoor counter, drinking their customary draft of *Byrrh* before sunrise. Inside as wine flowed and glasses clinked, we were pleased to be directed to tables apart from the serious crowd of older, well-to-do patrons in evening dress.

I settled for a plate of garlic snails and a glass of wine. The fiddlers finished their plates of oysters and kept us awake with rounds of first-class jazz. Eventually we dispersed and caught the Metro, ready to sleep until noon. It was almost as if our fiddlers had known for how many years I had anticipated a visit to rue Monsieur Prince. Would that I were now free to study nearby at La Sorbonne University, I thought, and become a journalist in this magical place. *La vie en rose, tousjours, mes amis,* always, I said to myself, as I fell asleep.

In any event, the evening had allowed me to relax and to store up physical strength for my next week of operating-room duty. While the exacting nature of this discipline takes its toll on everyone involved, the fact that the nurses and doctors on staff spoke French with accents of various national backgrounds made the necessary split-second responses even more difficult to grasp in emergency situations. Being repeatedly called to work for emergency surgery at three in the morning tested not only physical stamina but also ready comprehension of the language. Surprised to find that I had begun to think in French, instead of translating, while answering the phone at such an hour, it was clear that difficult as it might be, I had gained strength in that domain.

It was therefore with obvious delight that I welcomed the relaxing forays with Una to the Swiss Alps. Free of all cares and tensions, I wrote short articles about the neighbourhood and sketched the natives and the scenery. Whenever a work break occurred, a drive to her Swiss chalet was in order. We were to spend a day with her amazing friend, Mrs. Pym a local character. A ninety-one year old, she was a revered mountain climber, community worker, and an Honorary Citizen of the Canton of Vaud, site of both Montreux and the nearby village of Glion.

Choosing a lightly wooded Alpine slope, Mrs. Pym led us to a large drift of perce-neiges, or snowdrops, carpeting the hillside all around us. As she happily picked blossoms, we followed her, tying each small bundle with a rubber band just as she did, then dropping them onto the surface of the nearby cattle-trough of water to avoid wilting.

"I always pick as many as I can to give to the charity sale, you know," she said enthusiastically. Sinking down under a tree every hour or two for a dram of whisky this tiny, agile, English woman would be on her feet again shortly to repeat the process, not once complaining about her small, cold-looking hands. Naturally she claimed that the doctor had recommended the whisky!

After the day of gathering snowdrops, she later phoned from her villa to express delight saying, "I am sitting on a small Persian rug in my bathtub, gazing out the window at a fine sunset hitting the tops of Les Rochers de Naye." "Here is a woman with a flare for life," laughed Una, who knew of her youthful horseback adventure around the Grand Canyon, financially rescuing an orange plantation owner along the way, the brother of the maid accompanying her on the trip. Both Mrs. Pym and her friend Miss Stewart seemed to be late-day versions of the tide of British gentry who had been known to come to Glion for centuries on their grand tours, sometimes to remain close to the Mediterranean in Montreux, Vevey and Lausanne on Lac Leman.

Presumably she would enjoy many more fine expeditions for the successive crops of wild blossoms, narcissi and daffodils fighting for supremacy of every square inch of alpine turf, the sheets of color under a canopy of pink and white trees in bloom. Later, during the haying season, much of this was cut and lost until replaced with blue gentians, buttercups, *trollis* or golden globe flower, pink or white cyclamen, daisies and many other species growing in the grass. The memory of French Switzerland, its pastures, its peaks, its people, its customs and festivals, make it swirl in my head as even today I see it as that imaginary country, almost too beautiful to be real.

When it was time for *the récolte*, or harvesting of the grapes on the slopes above Montreux, overlooking Lac Leman, Una sent me off to a neighbouring vineyard. I was handed a pair of shears, assigned to an area and shown how to carry a large straw basket strapped to my back to fill up with the glistening bunches of crisp and juicy green grapes. Far below was the Château de Chillon at the water's edge and Lac Leman dotted with sailboats and yachts. Every once in a while someone would pass by with a cart to empty my basket.

At the end of the day all the pickers were to head for the vineyard owner's quarters to share *le mou*, the juice extracted that day from the press. It was a convivial drink among strangers on a very special day ending with a short friendly talk by the owner about his hopes for his business. With that we all raised glasses over a sample of last year's wine poured directly from the spout of one of the great wooden casks.

Having been singled out for questioning about the Canadian wine industry, I was at a loss at the time to name any vineyards outside Ontario. Fortunately, wine production in Canada has expanded vastly since the 1950's. The next day I made sure to return to the area with my water-colour paints, the results of which impressions still hang on my walls.

On another occasion, insisting that I must see the sunrise from the top of the cliffs, according to the custom of sipping coffee as the sun appeared, Una sent a young friend of hers along as a companion. We rose just before dawn, then followed a narrow trail up through the wooded hillside until we emerged at the top. There, spread out before us was a meadow, a few cows grazing and a cowherd's rustic cabin visible in the soft early light. Following the well-worn path to the place, we took two or three steps up to the deck or stoop in front of the narrow entrance and knocked.

We heard him hit the floor, perhaps awakened by that sound. A surprised and tousled young man flung open the door. To the left was the double-decker bunk from which he had jumped on hearing us. Along the opposite wall facing us was a long rustic wooden table and above it shelves of food supplies. Beyond that a door stood open as a typically picturesque brown cow mooed and gazed curiously in at us. Urgently pulling down a large, crusty home-made loaf and a wheel of cheese from the shelf, the cowherd took our order and ushered us out to wait for breakfast and watch for the sunrise.

In minutes it arrived properly served on a tray. Just in time to see the sun make its appearance over the Alps we sat on his porch, enjoying café au lait, baguettes and cheese. Would that life was this easy in Canada with livable, cultivated and productive green mountain sides! On the way down the rugged slope we picked armfuls of *trollus*, or huge, cup-shaped "golden globes," as they were also known, gathering more than enough for friends, without in any way depleting the supply for others. It seemed that the bounty of the Canton of Vaud was limitless at that time. It is to be hoped that nothing has changed in this regard.

On each visit to Una's villa at Glion, Una and I took a walk, stopping at last for coffee at the tables outside the pension frequented by the weekend visitors. On one such day we met Hughette and Georges for the first time. Both were students at the Sorbonne, Hughette had probably come with Georges on his visit to his parents who lived in the area. I was to get to know her better in Paris where her mother ran a bookstore in the Quartier Latin.

It seemed strange that I should meet Georges, the architectural student, in Switzerland, at the delightful location of Glion, above Montreux. Naturally, I recalled the romantic image I had always cherished of the actor, Robert Donat, playing the professor in *Good-Bye Mr. Chips,* as he met his future mate, Greer Garson, on an alpine hike, and of Leslie Howard and Wendy Hiller in the same roles.

There at Glion and in Paris, Georges made several attempts to visit me, having never met a Canadian, so much so that Una teasingly hummed Hammerstein's popular song of the day, "Some enchanted evening, if across a crowded room you see..." hoping that I would hint at romance. I thought that he was quite perfect, tall, dark, intelligent, with a gentlemanly manner. I suspected, of course, that he might have one or more serious liaisons going on at the Sorbonne, if not with Hughette. She was always refreshing and friendly, telling me about the struggle for survival of herself and her mother in the war. Left alone in Paris after her father had been imprisoned, they had been reduced to surviving the winters on raw potatoes, with no heat and with nothing for warmth but their blankets and the endless frightening military presence.

Safe in Switzerland, Georges had never known the meaning of suffering. He felt quite sure of himself, perhaps too much so, in "a very Swiss way," as he often remarked about himself. In any discussion among students in Paris he would say, "No, no, I don't agree, not at all. Why? Well, because I am Swiss. That is just the way we are!" They were fascinating people and perhaps more. Would he turn out to be the professor on the alpine path?

The last thing I heard from Renée and Herta was from London the following year, where they had been courageous enough to pursue the option of trying their typing and shorthand skills. It was a change of pace and would help them look into the possibilities for combining work and university studies. Renée had asked me to join them for a holiday in the Channel Islands, pointing out that she considered me to be her true lifetime friend. Possibly the benevolent aunt in Salzburg had sent money to make up for our missed holiday in Vienna at Christmas.

I had already been obliged to make plans to return hurriedly to Canada due to inaccurate reports that my mother was seriously ill and that I was badly needed. Had I joined Renée and Herta instead, especially as we shared a common purpose, my life might have been altered radically for the better. The freedom I felt in Europe was a new and exhilarating experience. Anything seemed possible, especially with friends like Renée, Herta, Una, Michel and all the others as well.

At this point I had no idea of the challenges which lay ahead or that Renée, Herta and I would each move and lose addresses over such a distance. Because I was unable to find Renée through the offices of the International Jewish Congress or the International Nursing Commission in London, the parting gift of a book on Paris with her name inscribed is the only remembrance that I have. We were firm friends, sure to care about each other always.

Despite modern communications I know of no way to locate them, or any family either of the two sisters may have acquired. It is a sorrow, this profound, irreparable loss borne by thousands whose lives were overturned by the war. I carry it with me perhaps due only to the relative postal inefficiency of the pre-technological age of the early 1950's. It is a misfortune that probably could not happen today. All over the world people continue to search for loved ones, some with great success. It was not to be my luck, or will it yet be so by some extraordinary circumstance?

Backtrack

After a brief idyllic sojourn with English relatives near the south coast, I boarded a crowded ship full of immigrants at Southampton. As I stumbled up the gang plank, it seemed impossible that I was already destined for small-town central Canada. Situated just north of the prairies, where fields give way to woods and lakes, it is beautiful country, yet remote from Europe and everything then meaningful to me. It was a cold, grey late November day in 1952 as we headed into the forbidding, stormy North Atlantic bound for Halifax, Nova Scotia. The sea heaved about us, a sullen gun-metal grey, to use the term of the day, looking like something to avoid at all costs.

This trip bore no resemblance whatsoever to the voyage of a lifetime, which had brought me to Europe. Yet grim and determined to show family responsibility, I tried to make believe that I would see Europe again next year. Even though the "Returning Canadians" group was separated from the immigrants in the dining and entertainment area of the ship, I shared a cabin with two very dejected young German girls, unable to exchange a word in English.

At the table, the meals were as totally uninspired as the conversation, dependant on a monologue from one of its residents on the life of a small southern Ontario town. Although a native of Stephen Leacock country she had neither the gift of storytelling nor the humour with which to spice to the tasteless meals.

However, one evening a new face appeared at the dinner table, having heretofore been mistakenly assigned to immigrant rather than visitor status for dining-room service. He was a slightly built young American from the south of France, unremarkable in appearance or manner, but with a memorable tale to tell. Brought up in Pittsburgh, he had worked for years, like his father before him, in what he described as the worst of the industrial sweatshops.

But his war service had changed all that. Afterwards he had stayed in France, having found his way most remarkably to make a successful life in agriculture. Not only had he prospered on the land and married a French girl from the area, but he had been accepted in a closely-knit community of French farmers. Unfortunately his wife now felt entitled to be part of the American way of life, a luxury she thought he could provide. Sadly, and very soberly, as he now admitted, he was on his way back to America to see what could be done about it. Perhaps the beleaguered husband was equally as desperate as myself to change ships in mid-Atlantic. As the saying goes, "One falls in love with France, just as one falls in love with a woman."

The returning Canadians, being an elderly circle, had not seemed to listen to the stranger's tale too closely and so to say the least, their comments were negligible. I do not recall my own response, nor did I explain my presence. The sullen, grey cold hung over the Atlantic as we spent day after day indoors in a floating hotel with no reason to stroll on the frigid deck. The sense of loss increased with every hour.

Arriving in Halifax a few days later, I was directed into a wharf-side shed to send a telegram as to my date of arrival in Prince Albert. As there was a crowded atmosphere and little supervision for boarding the train, I then found myself in the immigrant coaches rather than in those reserved for 'Returning Canadians.' Fortunately I was able to share a seat with Greta, the woman who had been beside me at the telegram counter. She spoke English and was pleased to have the company of a Canadian to provide reassurance en route to the unknown. I, in turn, felt comforted and less alone in this separation from my European friends. By strange coincidence she had sent a message to her family in Holzminden, home of Wolfgang, my dancing partner and friend of Paris days. That at least cheered me up for the day without affording an actual ray of hope.

Naively supposing that Canada could do better, I was shocked to find that the immigrant section was fitted with wooden seats rather than the standard padded furnishings. Opposite Greta and I were two pale, apprehensive-looking individuals, a couple who like all the others, sat with an opened packet of sliced white bread beside them on the windowsill. Surprised, I wondered aloud to her, "Greta is this all they have to eat, these strange machine-made soft slices, while missing their crusty European loaves?" It remained a mystery. Like all the others, they sat staring wistfully ahead, forced to sit very upright on those hard seats, wondering what was in store for them.

Glancing at the endless uninhabited, empty landscapes of the lakes and woods across Nova Scotia, New Brunswick and Quebec the immigrants surely longed for a landmark of some kind. With no map or information posted on the coach or along the track about the area through which we passed, they must have wondered where they were, how much longer it would be before reaching a city or a centre of some kind. The image of these apprehensive post-war immigrants has stuck in my mind as clearly as those of Depression era Canada of the 1940s' epitomizes economic deprivation. These faces were also scarred by war.

Unlike the others, I could jump out at a hamlet or fuelling stop, as was the custom for young Canadians at the time, to pick up coffee and a hamburger for Greta and myself. I had always been accustomed to dining-car and snack-bar service on Canadian trains anywhere across the country.

Yet suddenly one forenoon, we found ourselves piling out of the train and onto an escalator up into

Montreal's then magnificent new station, La Gare Centrale, or Central Station, full of life and cheerfulness, but without the tempting gourmet choice of food and drink offered today. At liberty for two hours to explore the neighbourhood, Greta and I made a dash for rue Ste. Catherine, which was quite obviously a main downtown thoroughfare and into a café, but not before glancing across the side street at the remarkable Cathedral St. Jacques, a replica in miniature of St. Peter's at the Vatican in Rome. Ahead of us, glowing in the sunshine on the rise of land called *la montagne*, or the mountain, was a resplendent display of imposing nineteenth-century residential architecture against a background of trees and Montreal's landmark cross.

That Canada could boast such a city had completely escaped me until this priceless moment. A chicken sandwich and coffee seemed transformed to caviar and champagne. Although Greta had seen Rome itself, but not Paris, she appeared to be lost in her own thoughts, unaware of our great city. I had already gathered that a return to Paris via Montreal was a must on my list.

Saint Catherine Street was not in any way similar to our other great city street. Toronto's then dreary Yonge Street, a main artery through miles of the unremarkable grey buildings of 'Toronto the Good,' as it was called in those days, it was nothing like this. As a late teenager in the Canadian Women's Army Corps, passing through Toronto in the forties, I had looked down from my window at the YWCA to see that three of the four corners were marked by gothic style stone or brick churches. On the fourth corner was a funeral home sporting a large clock over the entrance, presumably ticking off one's remaining hours in this "vale of tears." I had actually shed one or two at the very sight. As people loved to say in those days, "The best thing about Toronto is the night train to Montreal." Fortunately, times changed radically with post-war immigration so that Toronto became our largest and perhaps most diverse and exciting city.

Taking yet another glance at the Montreal street life as we left the café, Greta and I were forced to leave it all behind for the western leg of the rail journey across Canada. With a great sense of relief I sank into the plush seats of the normal passenger coaches, rather than facing the wooden benches again. Dining and sleeping-car service was ours at last.

Yet, three days later, bidding goodbye to Greta, bound for Calgary, I was forced to disembark at Prince Albert in the black of the November night. No eastbound train approached from the opposite direction. This was surely the worst mistake in my life. Shuddering as the frozen and shrivelled leaves scudded across the ice on the arctic wind, I felt my own destiny mirrored before my eyes as I hailed a cab.

The Cree

Reception to my homecoming was sombre, unwelcoming and heart-breaking. The past two years of my life had not been commonplace. I had anticipated some show of interest on the part of my mother and sister in addition to what they had learned from my letters. Working and travelling as I had done was still unusual for poor young westerners. Now on my return from Europe my mother seemed to have become a martyr, frozen in silence by the agony of her life as a widow. In that I had never been permitted to ask her anything about herself or talk about my father, there seemed very little that I could accomplish after having come all this distance.

I felt even more cut off from my very real connections in Europe than I might have done on returning home, had I found family life as it was in my father's lifetime. I would exert myself to try to improve my mother's wellbeing in so far as possible.

However, now that I had returned to provide financial help and a hoped for family closeness, the professionally rewarding work of a public health worker on the Cree Indian reserves would divert my mind from Europe as well as serve a good purpose. Assigned to the outlying lake country north of town, with its lakes and forests, I was reminded of the nearby summer holiday country of our childhood. I had always felt affection and sympathy for these easy-going soft-spoken people with the often markedly self-deprecating sense of humour.

With each assignment from the medical officer, I would pack up the medical supplies for the trip from the local headquarters, and then depending on the destination, head for my van or for the bush pilot in the waiting Cessna aircraft. The pleasure of walking off the end of the pontoon into a few inches of sun-streaked water near the sandy shore, or of landing in a muskeg, with a native volunteer at the ready to row me to the campsite was a fine start to a day's work. A large slab of Canadian shield rock-face protruding at the shore usually served both as a ledge for the syringes and medical supplies to inoculate the pre-schoolers as well as for the large, battered tin mugs of tea offered by the Cree women.

During the winter there were many such trips into areas with deep snowfall. Bringing the Cessna down near a village nearly buried under an overnight fall of soft fluffy snow made for a magical sight. The glistening bark of the silver birches stood out among the heavy-laden spruce branches all around the shore of this bucolic place. The wind rose, whipping snow off the branches. Displacing more of the fluff, the whiskey jacks stirred into action for the day, then flapped their way through the spruce needles, streaking off along the shore. It seemed however that the Cree were not yet awake. No dogs barked or came out to meet us, nor did doors open or anyone appear as we landed, or even when we crunched our way over the snow to their cabins.

We knocked, and waited. Fortunately, all was normal, the youngest children still curled up uncomplaining in their hammocks while the adults sat about chatting. Where was their breakfast? Perhaps they ate it hours ago. One always wondered why there was so little sign of food in their dwellings and what could be done about it. Now and then a grandfather rocked the hammock to keep a child happy, perhaps because as we had heard, the child's mother might be preparing a pad of moss from under the snow in place of diapers. Slowly and pleasantly enough, we got them organized for the clinic of the day. Were we more content with our warm urban environment than these First Nations people seemed to be with theirs?

Despite the apparent level of well-being observed at this otherwise uninhabited, small, lakeside encampment of one of the many bands of natives in the Federal reservation system, there were others, as there are today, where extreme privation, overcrowding, inadequate shelters, disease, alcohol, and bitterness were the norm. Without amenities of any kind except for a small stove in the center of the drafty, one-room shanty, survival was more than problematic. Furnishings consisting of a few rough planks of wood and one ragged old army-style blanket lined up on some sort of rough foundation of tree stumps to get it off the freezing floor seemed to represent the sleeping quarters for several occupants!

The sole wooden shelf in such a place was usually bare. At best it might support only a bag of white flour, sugar, and tea. On the stove might be found a piece of *bannock,* the homemade white flour, baking powder and water biscuit propped up beside a battered aluminum pan of strong tea. Or occasionally one might have to put up with the stench of muskrat or of other small animals not favoured by most of us, boiling on the stove in the centre of the room.

Yet even in the comfortable village described earlier, had we been intent on looking for *moonshine,* we might have found a barrel with a piece of "gunny sacking" thrown over it. Usually hidden as much as possible, it was said that the childrens' allowance money from the government went into this brew. As reported to me by the Indian Agents and Mounties, it contained such ingredients as alcohol, sugar, fruits, nuts and potatoes. During the fermentation process going on quietly in the corner, one might lift the sacking and observe the rich, brown, inviting-looking mixture partially obscured by the white froth riding on the surface. What a shame to spoil the party! And so nutritious! Living under such circumstances, who would not dream of *moonshine* too?

In such appalling conditions, any sign of food was reassurance that the people were not completely starving. Occasionally, we would see fish drying on poles erected in tepee formation. The presence of a small slaughtered deer could bring on the pathetic elation one might associate rather with winning millions in a lottery. It was sometimes quietly suggested by superiors that the government had not taken measures to ensure sufficient fish and game available on the reserves for their hunting and fishing needs.

I was inclined to believe this might be the case in one particular area when I saw the euphoria caused by one young, lean deer lying there on its side. Amid the inebriated rejoicing around it, the blood dripped off the corner of a rickety old enamel table to form a pool on the floor. When had they last had a piece of meat? Curiously, there was never a sign of alternate protein such as beans, nuts, cheese or eggs among their meager provisions, nor was there, as far as we knew, any type of storage provision such as a root-cellar.

The placid children were left in their home-made hanging cradles or hammocks until they were a couple of years old. Having been nourished solely on breast-milk, their soft, fat flesh brimmed over the sides of the cradles swung by the doting grandparents. The children were amiable but weak and undernourished; there were the obvious overtones in regard to their future development. Before long though, when they started to crawl and to walk, they would discover that a piece of bannock and a tin cup of sugared tea might sometimes be found on top of the heater. It was said that the practice of long-term breast-feeding was thought to be a method of birth control.

This alone put these fat toddlers at considerable mental and physical developmental disadvantage with other children, graduating from their liquid diet long after most Canadians who began to eat solid food at six months of age. In the 1950's one still heard the old story from the Indian Agents that the government had originally assessed the First Nations to be in steady decline in Western Canada. This was supposedly due to the then high incidence of tuberculosis and malnutrition. With the advent of penicillin by the mid-forties, together with the fine system of Saskatchewan sanatoria administered by the renowned Dr. George Ferguson, the disease was finally eradicated in ensuing decades.

Today, it seems that most First Nations people are not really aware of it or the endemic disease which had decimated their numbers. Unfortunately, we know that even at present many of them lack adequate nutrition, housing, or education. As sometimes mentioned by the media, Canada would benefit by their increased input as a labour force and as administrators of their own social structures. This eventuality would, of course, require a normal standard of living and education, the continuing absence of which in certain areas continues to be pondered inconclusively by the federal government, despite other progressive efforts.

Any attempt at generalization as to living conditions, then or now, is pointless. One half-blind, disconsolate and irate old chief, faced with the Indian Agent who had unaccountably brought cans of outdoor house paint to him for his overcrowded one-room shanty loudly declared, "If you want it painted, you'll git some-un else to do it!" Naturally, at this absurd offer, the chief sat scowling up at us from a tree-stump in front of the place. By and large none of their dwellings were painted or cared for in any way and needed replacement with adequately serviced and weather-proof housing, painted or not.

However, on a flight to a distant reserve, I was surprised to see something very different. Despite their isolated location, I gathered that this band was one of the most advanced. As in any average Canadian village their homes were close together. They were largely two-story, each one painted in quite delightful and intriguing patterns of mostly red and green, forming a sort of mosaic. Once inside, I was directed to the young mother I had been sent to investigate, by several of the older women, perhaps the village elders, down a hallway to her room. There I found women holding up colourful homemade green-red tartan quilts, as if for privacy, in a circle around the patient's bed. The babe itself was swaddled in matching tartan. It was all very clean, calm and welcoming. One could stay overnight without concern for comfort or cleanliness.

It seems reasonable to think that some of the residents of the painted village had attended the right kind of residential schools, where I knew that in some instances they had actually been well-treated and subsequently created the kind of village described above. This fact was sometimes indicated to me by the women themselves. The more usual comments as to the desolation of life on the reserves could lead to the assertion that after attending a well-run residential school and then being forced to return to life on a reservation, death itself would have been welcome. They talked of despair and degradation; we lamented their degeneracy. Obviously in this case these conditions had been avoided by creating an acceptable lifestyle.

If instead, in the 1950's, some opted for red ticket status allowing them to live among white people, or off reserve, such an adventure meant paying one's own way for the very first time. "How was this possible without education and job training?" I would ask young girls. Hence the suffering of First Nations people experimenting with life in such cities as Winnipeg, Edmonton and Vancouver's notorious East Side.

Although much has changed in the more than half-century since then, many of the problems remain. Most encouragingly, a growing number of First Nations people have risen to important professional positions in law, medicine, health care and other fields, putting their skills and knowledge to use for the benefit of their own people. Yet many, once educated, permanently abandon the reservation which actually needs their help to improve the quality of life.

I recall a memorable instance of meeting a Cree woman whose grandson I had returned to her after treatment. I suspect that she had been in a school where she had been loved. As I stood in the doorway of her immaculate small cabin, my eye was drawn to a plaster image of the Virgin Mary on a shelf. Decorated with small pink paper roses, as in the convent school I had once attended, I could sense a certain background in her life. Beside it was a fine looking example of an antique porcelain and gold-trimmed coffee urn. Startled as I was, when she went to the shelf and then handed it to me, I was even more amazed to see that it was genuine porcelain, bearing the mark 'Royal Bayreuth, Bavaria, established 1759.'

While I protested repeatedly, she would not let me leave without it, insisting that she knew of my work and her friends in the sanatorium appreciated my mother as a staff nurse. Apparently the daughter for whom she had bought it from a second-hand store on a trip to the city, had died in the sanatorium. I have cherished it to this day as one of my most valued possessions.

There were times when a tour of treatment on a reservation could take a week, and in such cases rural hotels, rare and doubtful wayside cafés, and a diet of salt pork and northern game made for a most unfortunate onslaught on the digestive system. On these visits I would run an immunization clinic, remove fish hooks embedded in and infecting fishermen's hands, several at once, suture the wounds, and treat the black sores around the mouths of the native children who would greet me tearfully, chewing still on the problem, unwashed wild turnips freshly pulled from the soil.

Neither the hands nor the sores could be dealt with in less than a week of constant attention. The fishermen were of course unhappy and resentful at being immobilized. Tears would splash down the childrens' ruddy faces at the indignity of being cleaned up, rubbed with smelly ointment around their mouths and precluded from eating unwashed wild roots for a week.

It evokes the memory of the comical predicament of a small boy in an old 1950's French film by Jacques Tati called *Mon Oncle*, or My Uncle. The indulgent relative rescues his overprotected nephew from meal-time discipline and takes him to their favourite vacant lot to join his chums, to eat food in the rough, they way they liked it, dirt and all!

There were also the routine searches to find not only new cases of tuberculosis but also to apprehend those patients who habitually discharged themselves from the sanatoria in the night to seek out the *shaman*, or medicine man for an alternate cure. One day the RCMP and I found the runaway grandfather in question sitting in the shaman's hut in front of a fire with the smoke rising up to a hole in the centre of the roof. The older female band members held blankets up in a circle around him, keeping silence during the hallowed procedure, as the shaman lay warm bricks on the patient's chest and back in the ritual to fight the demonic disease.

In between applications of heat, a large towel would be slung over his shoulders to hold in the warmth. From time to time one of his grandchildren would wander in suddenly and unexpectedly, come close to him before we could intervene, only to have the old man spit a foamy, bright red stream of blood from his lungs onto the dirt, then pick up the child in his arms and embrace him.

One reason why we had been so anxious to find the latest runaway that day was that on the scale of measurement of the disease, he had the dubious distinction of registering the highest possible level of tubercular infection from the bacillus. Obviously they would think that we were the "spoil sports" of the afternoon. One sole reason to be there was to once again isolate this poor man to save his grand children. He was known to have an extraordinary number of grandchildren, all of whom he may have hugged, coughed at and infected.

On another occasion we were told to find and transport to the sanatorium a small group of displaced Chipewayan natives from Northern Alberta. The women, known to us for their small, fine-boned beauty were said to be in dire need of medical aid. Our directions led to a cluster of tents crowded with people in a shocking state of deterioration. In one we found half a dozen extremely old and emaciated women sitting cross-legged on the ground, rooted to the spot and unable to move. When did they last eat? Their water supply? There was an all-pervading odour of urine, illness and neglect while their expressions defined both the agony of their condition as well as their fear of incarceration at the hands of the government. They were so weak, so stiff with arthritis that they could not rise from the forest floor. It took considerable time and effort to help them into the van.

One of these aged Chipewayan beauties with the almond-shaped eyes and the delicate features was sadly disfigured with something more than the pall of extreme need. Lacking the flesh of her nose as she did, I knew that the medical report would list yet another of the dire diseases as old as time apart from the tuberculosis brought to them by European explorers. How we got them settled or whether I had to call another Mountie for transport and assistance, I do not recall.

My mother would certainly take an interest in their very fine, quite delicate appearance when she came to care for them later in the day. The recent publication of the tale of *Kontiki* by Thor Hyerdahl had stirred interest in the long ago migrations across the Bering Strait from Asia when a land bridge joined the continents.

There were so many needs to be met, all requiring individual house calls. Carrying my bag of medical supplies a long distance in from the road to the house, I was often sorely challenged by the Indians' lean, hungry looking dogs. In the case of huskies, the cry would remind me that a chain is as good as its weakest link. It seemed to take forever to reach the door.

On one such occasion, just after dark and eager to get home in extreme winter cold, I made a wrong turn, tried to correct it too quickly and struck a snow bank, involving a run half a mile back to the nearest farm to seek help rather than freeze to death overnight. The closer I got, crunching along the hard-packed snowy road, the louder the cries of the huskies. Once I reached the yard the next challenge was to mount the back stoop and knock on the door with the dogs howling menacingly just below my feet.

When the gruff European farmer opened the door an inch or two to hear my plea for help, he shut it quickly, leaving me to freeze alone while he put on his heaviest clothing. The minutes seemed like an hour as the howling increased to a new crescendo of horror on my part. This was nothing like the time I had spent on that other door stoop with breakfast and the sunrise in the Swiss Alps!

To endure a tractor ride on that shared, icy-cold metal seat was one thing, but the savage cry of the huskies was quite another. I realized how fortunate I had been that the Indians' mongrel dogs, despite their menacing, starved appearance and habit of trailing me from the car to the doorstep, were really as benign as their masters who greeted me with laughter, swearing that their dogs were tame. Rumour had it that they were hungry and therefore sometimes vicious. The added punishment of writing a cheque with freezing hands when the engine started again was enough to guarantee that I would never again be caught in a snow-drift.

Some of the RCMP as well as the few MD's and nurses in the field may have derived as jut as much satisfaction from their efforts to help the natives as I did despite the restricted nature of the system. Of the two I worked with, each revealed to me privately over coffee that he would like to change places with the other. Why an MD and a Mountie were attracted and envious of each other's career fascinated me. Did they sense inadequacies in themselves, the government systems, or both? With them I did not mention my own intended goal of study and a return to Europe, but I knew very well that as there was no plan to improve living conditions across the board for the native population, none of us would aspire to remain in the Federal Service.

Probably the efficient operation of the Saskatchewan Sanatoria League by Dr. Ferguson had made the most necessary and practical contribution to native welfare by stamping out the scourge of endemic tuberculosis, together with the introduction of penicillin and other antibiotics in the 1940's and 1950's. Had the federal government of the day, then or later, been equally efficient in meeting the challenge to provide acceptable overall housing, nutrition and education, the First Nations people across Canada might now meet a standard of health, fitness and education closer to the national average, rather than the unacceptable discrepancy frequently reported in the press and continuing to exist in certain areas in the Canada of the twenty-first century.

Never Give Up

Rewarding as it had been to work with the largely Cree population scattered through the nearby woods and the lakeshores of the boreal forest, that privilege was short-lived. The native population of five thousand were spread out over a large area. A superior had told me the work could occupy a public health nurse twenty-four hours a day, seven days a week, for an entire lifetime. Few who had tried it had been able to maintain the pace for long.

All this had crossed my mind as I began to feel a great fascination for the beauty of the landscape as well as the good-natured, colourful native people, generally appreciative of the assistance of the nursing service. In view of my fixed goal of obtaining a university degree and returning to Europe rather than living in northern isolation, I took care not to become entirely mesmerized by the richness of my surroundings, attractive as they were.

On one of the most colourful of autumn days, I was to pick up an elderly Cree chief and take him to hospital as I returned to town from work at the end of the week. A very straight-backed, dignified, yet amiable old man sitting beside me in the van, he told me that he could remember being at the scene of the Riel Rebellion a few miles away at Batoche in 1885. He was both cheerful and personable as a character. His aged, long, bony face and high, prominent cheek bones made me long to capture a likeness in a sketch.

However, from the point of view of a health worker, as this thought often crossed my mind with such people, his most noticeable aspect was the almost burnt-orange tone of his skin. Autumn was the season in which the highly infectious disease known as hepatitis most often occurred. The back of the van being full of medical supplies, there was nowhere for him to sit except on the front seat.

By the time he died twenty-four hours later, I was being admitted to the same building with severe epigastric pain and high fever. I had infectious hepatitis. Beginning with the morphine injections during the first week, I had shown sensitivity to drugs that very first day by hurling myself from the elevated hospital bed to the floor.

"Might they have used more care in administering this heavy sedation?" I had thought before I fell asleep. After all, I understood that bed rest was required to prevent damage to the liver.

In the strange and lonely world of an isolation ward, I was occasionally aware that on that small bed, all alone in that desolate white enclosure, my life seemed to be ebbing away. Existence had suddenly become a complete 'tabula rasa,' a cold and empty stage of nothingness against which I was too stupefied by medication to react. It was as if I were part of the disastrous brainwashing experiments carried out at the Allen Memorial Institute in Montreal in that same period, between 1950 and 1965.

As if to no purpose I was floating around above vaguely familiar countryside. "What is going on?" I wondered, as I faded in and out of fleeting dreams of favourite Swiss mountain paths. Where on earth am I, and how did I get to this bed?" What had happened? This muddled state was utterly overwhelming and incomprehensible.

Finally, after an extended period of treatment I recovered and learned that for the next year I was to refrain from anything but sedentary public health work. Taking on the demands of a program of studies must be postponed. This made sense on the basis of my weight loss and my gaunt frame. With a handshake, a smile and a wish for future success from the doctors, I emerged shakily into a crisp, delightful, sunny winter day with dazzling snow. It seemed like a promise of great things to come.

Carrying out the suggestion of the agreeable medical man who had discharged me, I spent the year in the public health sector in the city liaising with medical, surgical, and psychiatric specialists to identify and address the problems of rural adolescents new registered in the city high school system. Consequently, heretofore serious unnoticed problems such as cleft palate, congenital hip and mental illness received appropriate care from one specialist or another. Much as I cared for these youngsters and the need to resolve their health issues, I could not consider permanency. Something in me kept saying, "Don't give up. Don't give up," as my brave father had always emphasized by his attitude to life. I longed to settle down seriously at last to work for an education of my own choice

At the same time I had had a proposal of marriage from a young physician. What had I been thinking of? Classical music and warm fireplaces were all we had in common. So preposterous a situation had arisen from the appalling loneliness of existence since returning to Canada. Instinctively one seeks the company of other human beings, especially in small communities given the restrictions of long, cold winters. One cannot forever dream of meeting one's true love on a mountain path, yet this was not for me. I was not about to give up.

The confusion of this phase of life finally resolved itself in the mother of all nightmares. I awoke in terror to see that in pitch-black night I was pulling a slimy wooden coffin, over-grown with moss on the end of a rope in blinding rain while slithering down an unknown muddy road full of ruts. Stumbling about, desperate to escape, and badly shaken, I knew that my road led elsewhere.

A short time later, returning from a film, I trudged along on a frigid forty degrees below zero night in January. I shuddered with the sense of being utterly and completely alone in the universe. In such biting, cold temperatures with no wind, no sound, there was only the eeriness of nothing between myself and that piercing silver globe. Riding high across the firmament, in mid-winter, cruel, sinister and all-knowing, the moon's rays glared down on the sheets of ice and snow ahead of me. Chilled to the marrow, ears and toes freezing in the lonely void, I made my way across the open prairie town, marked off without differentiation on the grid plan of soulless, identical streets, homes and unsightly telephone poles. It seemed as if everything that had ever mattered to me had now been taken away as I trudged on over the icy streets.

My father, my home, and a life that had seemed so promising in Europe had evaporated. I saw no way to return to France. Courage to face the future eluded me at this point. Obviously, I had lost sight of my father's enormous courage, his ability to pursue creative ambitions in the face of adversity. I felt like "one of the damned," doomed and stricken.

Yet before I arrived home I thought of Michael in Montreal. In these pre-television days, CBC radio kept me in touch with Eastern Canada and the world. Strangely enough, it was a young Hungarian free-lance journalist from London University, living in Montreal and reading his own series called *Footloose in Japan* on CBC, who later became my model and friend. With his infectious *joie de vivre* and literary background, Michael gave me important book titles, and courage. Occasionally he asked for suggestions on subject matter for broadcast talks. Forced by his father to study engineering, sheer determination led him to eventually break free to succeed remarkably well in journalism.

Fortunately, Montreal still attracted me as the perfect place to live in Canada as well as to speak French again. After all, I had just heard the incredible news that it was the one city in the country that offered degree granting university courses at night. The image of that beautiful city had stayed in my mind since the day I had passed through it on the way back from Europe. In Montreal, I would be much closer to Paris, although another visit to "the city of light," would probably have to wait at least until the day after graduation.

With that I posted a note to CBC offices in Montreal and on arrival had a date for coffee. Michael and I were to meet at the Ritz-Carlton hotel. As we quickly adjourned to a less expensive, though appealing European coffee house on neighbouring Stanley Street, the stage was set for my own metamorphosis, one which my father would have rejoiced in, heartily, so close to the McGill University gates where he began his eventful life in Canada.

Montreal je t'Aime!

There it was in July 1955, the day after my arrival in Montreal, as Michael and I looked down the mountain or *la montagne,* from the Westmount and Beaver Lake lookouts on either side of Cote de Neiges Road. Laid out below was the city with the St. Lawrence River itself slightly visible in the far distance, southward, beyond the downtown, and this great hill. At night the magnificent view of the metropolis, highlighted by the myriad of glittering and shimmering lights, stretches like a string of diamonds as far as the eye can see from east to west along the river to the docks themselves and to those very historic old streets from whence the city grew and spread for miles.

One day in my tiny midtown quarters, while perusing a copy of the classified advertisements in the anglo-Montrealers daily, the Montreal Star, now called The Gazette, my eye fell upon a request for a proofreader. The brief two-line ad read "No experience necessary," amusingly bringing to mind the colourful tales of success in earlier times of reporters, editors

382

and writers who began their careers from such meagre status. "Living on sardines," as he called it, my journalist friend Michael had also made his first modest start in journalism in freelance assignments. That is how I heard his series from Japan, the airfare funded by his parents. Yet despite his display of independence, he was at the same time able to enjoy the comfortable fact that his family abroad enjoyed deep pockets.

A few days later I found myself pouring over endless strips of print for a professional journal in a busy, crowded office, full of workers from Egypt, France, Britain and Australia, trying to meet the deadline for the next month's issue. The secretary, a vivacious Egyptian-Jewish girl, would stand beside her desk to indulge us momentarily with her favourite middle-eastern dance. Hips and arms gyrating to the rhythm of her tuneful voice she instantly diffused the stress of her working day. It was an unlikely collection of characters working to produce each edition, tenuously held together by the unlikely skill of the editor, known to like "the bottle," naïve in that he supposed no one knew his secret. A professionally meticulous academic, he had at the same time an air of one still living another life, that of the RAF man of action that he had been.

Somehow, with tact and perseverance, one could learn the trade from Moira, his hard-working, chain-smoking assistant editor. A resolute woman, and a would-be author, proud of her Irish literary heritage, she had worked her way through McGill University, and claimed descent from the mid-nineteenth-century

Irish potato famine immigrants to Montreal. Indeed, her painfully thin appearance brought to mind that tragic influx of oppressed humanity, known to have arrived half-dead or worse at the dock. Queen Victoria was said to have *turned the other cheek*, ignoring their plight.

Not without justification, Moira worried that I too would have a difficult time of it, a hard road to hoe, as the saying went, working day and night, at the office and the university, as she had done, losing her youth in the process. On Fridays, Moira and I and all the women on staff escaped the usual hurried bag lunch routine to crowd into the small European cafes adjacent to neighbouring McGill and Concordia universities.

Montreal had yet to see any sort of new, overall downtown building development. Much of the city was probably unchanged since the end of the Great Depression. This meant that newly arrived immigrant booksellers, set up in old basement store fronts and outdoor stalls nearby, offered rare or unusual used books for a pittance. While not Paris itself, it was reminiscent of the *bouquinistes* or booksellers along the Seine.

Small cafés served the best French regional country cooking, and equally fine, inexpensive wine. The newly immigrated proprietors squeezed us into their intimate little lunch rooms, some above and some below ground level. At a miniscule one-woman operation, *Le Colibri*, the hummingbird, the atmosphere was sometimes enchantingly like Paris, attracting a clientele of Europeans.

As 1955 turned into 1956, Montreal was suddenly teeming with new immigrants from the Hungarian revolution. From the back exit of Concordia University one could slip directly out of a lecture into a popular Hungarian café, le Pam Pam, named after another in Paris. With a menu listing fourteen types of coffee, chopped liver on rye bread, thick hearty meat soup or large, steaming plates of Hungarian goulash, with chunks of tender beef amid the vegetables, these were the perfect and economical meals for immigrants and students alike. After adding cheap red wine to the order, one could face the sunny yet biting mid-winter cold.

These colourful, industrious and obviously life-loving newcomers also offered Montréalers an alternative to the ridiculously light weight winter clothing to which we were all accustomed. As mentioned before, most Canadians in the 1950's, wore rubber and cloth footwear, hats exposing ears to frostbite and interlined wool coats. The era of synthetic outerwear was still a decade away. Hungarian immigrants having arrived from Hungary bounding around in warm, attractive gear, soon set up shops to provide knee-high sheep-skin-lined leather boots, jackets, mitts and ear-flapped hats, all made the same way.

On the front of one small shop near the café, an amusing homemade butcher's sign on a furrier's shop announced "Mutton for Sale," meaning *mouton*, French for sheepskin. Everyone realized the dilemma of adapting to English and French from the Magyar spoken by Hungarians. Definitely, a new level of comfort was at hand in which to enjoy the sparkling sunshine and heavy snowfall of a cold Quebec winter.

In marked contrast to the long, wearisome east-end bus route, soon to become familiar, I walked home along historic, appealing and upscale Sherbrooke Street West, through the centre of the city from both my workplace and the university. Each window of such prominent art galleries as Dr. Max Stern's renowned Dominion Gallery allowed me to consider the relevance to my fine arts classes of these important new Canadian and European works being displayed. Throughout the post-war art boom of the 1950's, from the McGill University gates to Guy Street it was one long six-block storefront exhibition, including the Montreal Museum of Fine Arts and other side street venues of importance at the hub of downtown Montreal.

Yet, with all the attractions of life in Montreal, the meager stipend of a proof-reader called for another source of income. Facing the challenge, I replied to an advertisement for a registered nurse to do part-time work in a special mental health unit at the Royal Victoria hospital. I was to help cover the weekends for extra support for occasions such as the sudden arrival of young, strong, male schizophrenics feeling the first violently expressed symptoms of their tragic disorder. Sometimes brought in by distraught family members, these patients required three or four strong men to wrestle them to the ground, restraining the unfortunate youth, enabling me to inject sedation.

However, my main service was to assist in the administration of continuous "sleep therapy." These patients, of all ages, were purposely dehumanized by drug therapy for experimental purposes. During sleep they were to hear a repetitive message from under the pillow. Before long patients who had appeared to be normal or only slightly depressed could neither stand, control bodily functions, speak coherently or respond to their own names. None of this was explained to the staff, expecting a cure to follow the treatment.

Naturally, leaving each night in a state of mind close to tears, I came to realize that this work was for me actually a violation of the traditional Florence Nightingale Pledge. Taken upon entering any school of nursing study program, it was a solemn promise never in any way to cause harm to a patient. Refusing to give notice or accept a pay cheque, I left immediately.

Finally, what I had heard rumoured by one of the temporary medical men on the team before I resigned, became hot news in the press in Canada and the US in later years. I had been part of a brainwashing experiment in force between 1950 and 1965 between the Canadian government and the CIA. After that date many legal cases were pursued as a result of the permanent damage inflicted on patients whose families had been given no intimation of the true nature of the procedures. Under the guise of help for depression and other disorders, irrevocable harm had been inflicted. I was horrified to have been drawn into it for even a few weeks.

However, I then found weekend work *to keep the wolf from the door*, in a small medical and surgical unit treating tuberculosis of the lungs and other forms of the disease. This was a reminder of the year spent on the highly successful surgical team of such a unit before sailing to Europe. Here one encountered the type of patient not generally to be found in larger institutions. These were the misfits of society, many of whom were impoverished long term patients living on welfare and smoking themselves to death despite rules to the contrary.

One day a vivacious, stunningly attractive black dancer was admitted to the institution. Intent however on escape to find her lover, assumed to be on the run from police, she did not readily accept hospitalization. Before long her bed was empty. She was gone. Someone had obviously slipped in with clothes to replace the ones taken from her on admission.

On a free evening a friend of mine and I went looking for her in old Montreal. We hoped to find her at the bar she had talked of working at as a dancer. As we dallied in hopes of catching a glimpse of her, the management began to cast searching glances at us. Certainly no one could be indifferent to so magnificent, so gifted a creature, especially a tubercular beauty, so at risk to herself and the public. Had we found her then, or later, she would, of course, have smiled broadly, made some ravishing twirl, a spectacular apparition disappearing behind a screen.

At other times, the trip home on the midnight bus from this remotely located hospital highlighted life in Montreal's then poverty-stricken east-end. One hot summer night a gun-fight stalled the bus itself. Rigid with apprehension, all of us, the driver included, were forced onto the very edge of our seats, half-amused at the movie-like setting, half in fear.

Another exercise in persistence and apprehension of the outcome happened at "the car barns," the street car and bus terminus, in complete darkness after midnight on a snowy New Year's Eve, as I finished my evening duty at the hospital. Quite unbelievably, after milling about hopelessly, and with growing apprehension at the power failure, I eventually came upon a taxi and sped home to friends awaiting me with a glass of red wine to celebrate the new year.

Sometimes it seemed as if my need for this part-time work would never end, yet the day finally arrived when my university studies, and further training in editorial work elsewhere had provided me with an adequate salary to decline further forays into this colourful working-class neighbourhood.

When young Quebecers later developed a taste for slang or *joual*, I felt little interest in the craze, on stage or anywhere else. It had been enough for me to contend with the jargon used by the patients, peppered with *icit*, (ici), meaning here, *char* for car and punctuating nearly every remark with *astar*, and many other terms unknown to me and not listed in the Larrouse French dictionary, then or now. Purposely careless speech, heavily slurred into a rapid jargon for their private world made for difficulties of comprehension, sometimes probably with the intent of subterfuge, of cannily avoiding the treatment at hand. Living on their wits could only ultimately circumvent their own well-being. They knew by and large that they would end their days comfortably enough, right where they were, with occasional skirmishes at escape to break the monotony of their lives ruined by tuberculosis.

Meanwhile, with the postwar blossoming of the arts, a market for art as valuable real estate had begun to flourish, in part because Quebec painting had entered a new era of extreme importance to Quebec and all of Canada. A surprise to me and to most people from outside the province was the fact that in 1948 Quebec artist Emile Borduas and colleagues had embraced the postwar, post-Depression era with their proclamation of *Le Refus Global*. This document renounced the all-pervasive restrictions heretofore imposed by the Roman Catholic Church on the creative spirit since the arrival of Samuel Champlain in 1608.

The winds of change had begun to blow! Quebec painting took off in new and exciting directions, acknowledging the pre-eminence of European and North American art of the twentieth century over the religious art sanctioned by the clergy. The *Refus Global* led to La *Revolution Tranquille*, or the Quiet Revolution, the birth of modern secular Quebec following the demise of Premier Duplessis in 1959 and the subsequent election of Liberal Prime Minister Jean Lesage.

At the same time, many of the European careers interrupted by the war had miraculously taken root in

Canada, including that of Dr. Max Stern, an esteemed art dealer from Germany who was credited with promoting the important works of unsung west coast artists Emily Carr and E.J. Hughes, putting them front and centre in the imposing bow window of Dominion Gallery directly across from the Montreal Museum of Fine Arts in the heart of downtown Montreal. A rich cultural lode of European talent flooded into Canada, including that of Viennese conductor and musical authority, Dr. Nicki Goldschmidt, in Toronto. He and others were surely responsible for the spread of interest in classical music performances as well as the beginning of the choice of international musical events we now take for granted across the country, and from which we first began to feel the exhilaration in 1950's Montreal and Toronto.

Before great halls like Place des Arts were built to house such events or conductor Charles Dutoit was appointed by mayor Jean Drapeau as its conductor of the Orchestre Symphonique de Montreal, we crowded into smaller, less suitable locations in churches and cinemas.

At Her Majesty's Movie Theatre and the old Monument National Theatre we had always previously fought for seats to hear such renowned personages as Spanish guitarist Andre Segovia, soprano Joan Sutherland, pianist Glenn Gould, and others. In the case of the latter, we were sometimes forced to crowd onto the stage for a rush seat, an embarrassing occasion. While Gould's extreme discomfiture at having the audience on the stage with him was more than lamentable, one could see why he later escaped to the recording studios to bring his works to the public without the physical presence of an audience to disturb him.

From the rafters of Notre Dame Basilica and elsewhere we were equally thrilled by the operatic outpourings of our own Montrealer, contralto Maureen Forrester, then just starting her stellar international career. Maria Callas and the young Pavarotti also first made their appearance to eager crowds and adoring fans in these places.

With the new freedom and ferment of the nineteen fifties, French Quebecers were also eager to launch a number of theatres, chief among them being Le Theatre du Nouveau Monde, replacing the smaller venue at Salle Gesu. Actor Jean-Louis Roux left his medical studies to enjoy fame in classical and modern theatre. Instrumental in the creation of the Théatre du Nouveau Monde, he was also involved in founding the bilingual National Theatre School. The popular team of esteemed Quebec actor Jean Gascon and Frenchman Guy Hoffman from Paris, consistently worked through the great repertoire of French and classical European plays as well as playwright Bertolt Brecht's then widely popular epic Mother Courage. We French-speaking Montrealers were more than privileged.

The Rideau Vert, directed by Yvette Brindamour, expanding also from small quarters, became the source of a wide range of important theatrical presentations. Free from the strictures previously imposed by the

Quebec's Catholic clergy, veteran actor Gratien Gelinas opened the very popular Comedie Canadienne, offering plays based on working-class life. Not to be outdone, Yiddish-speaking theatre-goers were able to benefit from the growth of the Jewish theatre, directed by Dora Wasserman, at the Sadie Bronfman Centre into one which also tackled works in English from New York and London stages. Within a few years, performances of English language theatre were underway at Centaur Theatre.

Meanwhile as I had finished university studies in English literature and European history, I had succeeded in quickly moving on to a position as editorial assistant for the publications of a medical research group. For the first time my income allowed me to live normally and to make frequent visits to my family now resident in Vancouver. I knew, of course, that this was only the beginning of the realization of my intended creative career and possible return to Europe, perhaps even to my old neighbourhood in Paris. Life had begun to move in the right direction. It would be a life concerned with writing, with the additional enjoyment of creating art for the pleasure of it. The result of my efforts has led to the life I had in mind from the outset, both interesting and satisfying. Ironically, sometime later, nurses like teachers before them, campaigned for professional salary scales and won the right to professional recognition.

However, one day in Montreal I met a tall, slim professor called Eric. It happened that friends of mine had invited me to a reception at the university. They had devised a plan to introduce us at this gala, surmising that we would have a number of ideas and interests in common. Although the university sits atop Montreal's mountain, I did not until later connect the incident with my adolescent dream of an eventual momentous meeting of minds on a mountain path, albeit in Switzerland.

These friends were right. We were both leading lives intent on enjoying great music, concerts, especially with violin and cello occurring all around Montreal as well as the French and English theatre. Over the dinner table we might discuss literature, or history or politics, both local and international and decidedly left-wing in concept.

Yet both of us being devoted to hiking since childhood, Eric and I had begun to use weekend afternoons to explore the Laurentian mountain trails and villages located within easy reach of Montreal. Since that first spring day we never ceased to be fascinated and to rejoice in the lush and varied country around Montreal, or of our lakeside home, an hour's drive from our work places. It is a delightful parkland in which to enjoy the scenic areas lying between the mighty St. Lawrence and Ottawa rivers, the Lake of Two Mountains and the Laurentian mountains. The lake is said to have a breadth of three kilometers in certain places.

One could surmise that there is some truth in our village wisdom to the effect that we live in a special micro-climate of our own, protected from winds by the dense stands of conifers and nourished by the many streams that water the earth. Enormous weeping willows, wild grape vines and blossoms proliferate along the banks. Among the wild strawberries and marguerite daisies in the field across from our home, I have found the deeply tinted 'blue gentian' bellflower last seen in French Switzerland, that other almost imaginary country of delights.

Be it a stream, a historic village, a ruin from the eighteenth or nineteenth century, a country market-place or a welcome café, one soon discovers an inviting view along each bend in old well-worn secondary roads used by the farmers, ranchers and retirees. In the distance, here and there, as if in France, stately Lombardy poplars mark a rise of land. Perhaps a dozen or more types and shades of deciduous and evergreen trees, including vivid and towering growths of mature cedar draw the eye. Ditches fill up with red sumac, pampas grass and wild flower colours, spectacular at any time of year. As summer fades to autumn, the goldenrod appears just as it does across much of Canada.

By Thanksgiving week in October, it is a time to take to the woods to find a spray of *bittersweet* for the dining-table presentation of the festive meal. With its clusters of tiny, round orange-red pods, the long delicate vines cling to tree-trunks, often just out of reach. In these parts bittersweet is considered 'a must' for an autumn celebration and sure to increase one's zest for another glass of red wine. Around the room, tall vases stuffed with Quebec sugar maple branches are ablaze with scarlet, crimson, and orange leaves. At this still warm time of year these colours radiate against the cloudless deep blue sky of autumn for miles around, as if the spell will never end.

This mild and protracted autumn festival of colour allows us to crunch through the bright leaf-fall for further exploration of the countryside. Included is a day at Lachute market. It is a huge acreage near Hawkesbury, Ontario in which to find everything from beer to fine old books, furniture, rugs, antiques, horses and much else. Honey comb, apples from Oka, and tables of farm preserved pickles, jams and jellies are proudly sold by the farm women themselves.

We are entirely captivated by the vivid, modern-looking geometrics of a Moroccan rug in red, gold, white and black. We load it in the car with everything else, thrilled with our bargain, while the vendor shrugs, telling us cheerfully that it was just a detail in a large transaction he made. The finances of it are "Greek to us" as they say, but we love it anyway, especially in front of the hearth.

Another day we visit Oka to purchase and to enjoy the sight of the ripe apples, both on the trees and in cone-shaped piles around the orchard. Meanwhile, the classical songs of our great Canadian contralto Maureen Forrester, then at the height of her great career, pouring out of the CBC car-radio lend a gala atmosphere to the outing as we find our way through this delightful yet uneven, hilly terrain.

As pesticides were, for the first time recognized in the press for what they are, I foolishly asked the vendor about his crop of applies while paying for a box of them. *"Oui, madame, il y'en a douze!"* he bellowed. I couldn't believe my ears. "There are twelve of them." In future outings we search for the new organic apple orchards and the delectably tangy wild apples in ancient open farm fields whose owners asked us, in worried tones, "Please pick them, otherwise the horses will eat them all and be seriously ill." With autumn fading it was time to remember to plant the spring bulbs and make sure that the skis are in good order.

The deep, powdery snow of early or sometimes late December allow us to ski out the driveway, across the road and directly into the fields, now transformed with great white puffs and poufs on every branch. It is one of nature's extravaganzas. When we return from our trial run it is to find that we are not alone. The winter bird population has taken over the front garden. A scarlet-coated cardinal and his mate have moved into the high cedar hedge across the front of the property. One of them is sitting on the fluffy ledge of snow along the top of it, the other one inspecting their hideaway quarters nearer the ground.

As echoed heartily by then popular Quebec singer, Gilles Vigneault, *"Mon pays, ce n'est pas un pays, c'est l'hiver"*, celebrating that "My country, it's not a country, it's winter!" While the eloquent bard wrote of the more austere climate north and east of us along the St. Lawrence River, our winters are temperate, benign, sunny, yet full of character, full of welcome.

We realize that our new home is in a virtual bird sanctuary. Glancing out the window we may see a fat grouse sitting in the apple tree, with cardinals, blue jays, red-headed woodpeckers and a myriad of others on the wing, all vying for space at the feeder trays hanging in front of the windows. After the frigid weeks of January and February, yellow grosbeaks, the gorgeously multi-coloured cedar wax wings, and the mourning doves each arrive in sizeable flocks to bask in milder days.

Fortunately, there is other food available, of course, which brings them to these woods for such treats as the velvety crimson cones of the red sumac bushes and the glistening black fruit of the brambleberry tree hanging in clusters by the kitchen window. Later on, avid 'birders' erected houses on high poles to attract the mosquito-eating purple martens to return to the area, and others at fence-top levels for a certain type of elusive blue bird.

Spring comes relatively early in this protected location. One is surprised to see that one day in March, the weeping willows in the field are in that transitional stage between dormant and green as the bark becomes almost a blur of light apricot. It is a promise of things to come. The stems of the common underbrush at the roadside have reddish streaks and the pussy willows are puffed up. The snow, now crystalline, begins to sink into the warming soil. "Goodbye to a magnificent winter," we say to each other rather sadly as we pass by.

We are about to put our skis away when Christophe, our friendly European neighbour, a naturalist and ecologist by inclination, invites us into the woods after a last fresh snow-fall to look for the rare snowy owl. If he can locate mouse bones in the snow at the base of certain trees, he will know that they are still here. Suddenly he comes across a small pile of them, the remains of the owl's dinner, lying on the snow crust. Smiling broadly, he says "Thanks God, thanks God, we must not lose our beautiful birds, no?" No, indeed, we agree.

He also wants to find some moosewood. This turns out to be the second great find of the day as he spots the antler-like branches at the end of which are buds sticking up through the snow. Transferred to a vase of water, one soon has apple-blossom look-alikes. An amazingly resourceful, vigorous immigrant, Christophe found enough of them one year to decorate the arch he had made with bent tree branches for his daughter's wedding. We understand his aversion to commercial blooms. He says, "This is better, no? You do not think so?" We agree most enthusiastically. I have always known him to be a true and discerning artist, eager to work hard for his beautiful creations, whatever they may be.

On the way home along the ski trail, we take a last look at the dried, frozen beech leaves glistening in the late afternoon sun, lighting up the evergreen woods. Strangely enough, they do not fall in autumn. As the sun hits the dead, translucent leaves, warm golden irides-cent lights glow in the woods. At close range, one sees thousands of tiny lights sparkling in the sun against the conifers.

One soon learns that the Quebec red maple sap is dripping into pails now, down the road at Rigaud on the maple sugar tree plantations. The owner invites visitors to Sunday's festivities at the sugar shack. Especially given the modest price of purchase by the litre at the site in those days, we hasten to procure a year's supply for pancakes and desserts.

Others greet the new season with a mania to win the bet on when the ice on the Lake of Two Mountains will break up this year. The ice road across the lake to Oka has been declared unsafe. Until such time as the ferries re-open at the Hudson-Oka and Carillon, Ontario sites, drivers must cross the bridge over the Ottawa River at Hawkesbury. The lake is a wide bulge in the Ottawa River which finally joins the St. Lawrence River at Montreal enroute to the Atlantic Ocean.

The fishing camps that have littered the ice with cabins and old cars have been ordered off its thinning surface. We see their numbers dwindle each time we pass by on the way back and forth from work. We hope no one will drown this year.

In early April we attend the boat races on the Raisin River, a stream named for the wild grapes, or in French, *raisins* on its banks, which runs into the St. Lawrence River across the Ontario border. This event gives adventurous young men a chance to show their skill at white-water canoeing over the sharp rocks in the torrents of water unleashed between the charmingly unspoiled historic settlements of Martintown and Williamstown.

For us it is a chance for a vigorous day of hiking as we take the path along the treed edge with

400

the enthusiastic crowd following the many mishaps. Suddenly, a canoe careens out of control in the churning water, leaving the owner to swim for it. It all ends at the historic Mill restaurant. This establishment was originally built to grind the grain for the early settlers of the fertile territory known as Green Valley.

In time, the torrents of water attracting young boaters to such adventures have shrunk to a trickle over rocks and pebbles to become the lazy streams of summer. One weekend we pack the picnic basket, the books, the sketch pad and the paint box in the car and take off. Not for us today, as spectators, are the yachting and sailing races enjoyed by many on the *Lac des Deux Montagnes*. Instead, we drive a few miles west to an area marked by small family farms along a quiet stream.

These ancient barns are so old that some of them appear to be about to slide down the shallow bank into the Rigaud River. This is not too surprising since the area was originally named for the seigneur, le duc de Rigaud, pronounced *Rigo*, as was our area, Hudson, once called Choisy, for the duc de Choicy, pronounced *Shwasy*, both officials sent out by the King of France in the days of New France, before Canada came into being. At that time seigneuries controlled lands all along the St. Lawrence River.

Munching our sandwiches in an ideally attractive spot under a small, derelict wooden bridge used for goat-crossings, we dangle our feet in the water, well out of site of any farm buildings. Momentarily surprised at what seems to be an amusing combination of natural sounds close at hand, we realize that we are hearing the afternoon song of the frogs and other subterranean creatures who inhabit it. Suddenly, short sepulchral and bassoon-like sounds punctuate the calm of the summer afternoon. Now and then, other voices of the deep pipe up with their own sometimes squeaky or bluntly assertive comments. Perhaps as old as time, this dialogue is hilarious and not unlike certain pieces of modern music. The scent of fresh hay wafts around us. Reaching for the coffee thermos and the books, we are in no hurry to depart.

Autumn returns before we know it. Suddenly, thousands of migrating geese fly noisily over our home as they did last spring, heading for the lake, so I am told, for rest and food, their deafening and frenzied cries announcing the beginning of another season. The intensity of the sound of the flight piercing the very roof of the house seems to bring with it a sense of jubilation. I rush to the door to watch them.

Next spring, we too will take to the air most eagerly for a sabbatical leave to Europe. We will visit the old haunts we both knew at different times, in different ways. While there, I will try to discover the whereabouts of my friends Renée and Herta, to see if these two holocaust survivors also found a way to attend university and reach their own goals.

This time I will return to Canada with no regrets, but with *joie de vivre* at being part of Montreal, its environs and countryside. As bilingual Canadians, we feel particularly at home in this city, this friendly cosmopolitan and historic metropolis in our own country. Such a delightful sense of belonging was a need that tragically eluded my immigrant ancestors and thousands of other urban misfits like them. Fortunately we were not to hear the FLQ, *le Front de Liberation Quebecois*, and the *War Measures Act* put in place by Prime Minister Pierre Trudeau for more than a decade.

With our return to Canada there will be for the first time the pleasure of returning to a permanent home, with the sense of belonging. "No use mentioning it to Eric of course," I said to myself, eagerly packing, "as he knows nothing of the pioneer experience, good, bad or indifferent." Lazy, perhaps, but I had never told him the appalling story of 1908. He would not understand. His family had been clever enough to come straight to Vancouver. Their own bankruptcy had not, as the saying goes, prevented them from landing on their feet.

The only time it came up in the conversation was years ago, when I said jokingly, "Such clever people; perhaps that's why you have a PhD today and I don't." I had long since gathered that they were business people who know what they were doing. Then he admitted, "Well, Uncle Bob did come out ahead of the others, looked at prairie life, decided against it, and moved to the coast." That made sense. They had had a good life instead of one of desperate homesickness and poverty. All my early life I had felt the reverberations of the trauma in my immigrant family pressing down on me, grinding my hopes into the dust, echoing despair and futility.

Yet now I knew for certain that I would no longer yearn for Europe or western Canada as the best place to call home. Actually, I had discovered the change in my heart even before meeting Eric, marrying, or buying the house. As a new arrival in Quebec, I had been walking home from work on a suffocatingly, hot, humid, early September day, wondering at the delayed arrival of any sense of autumn.

The dilemma was resolved at the next corner as I paused for the traffic lights to change. Suddenly, while I was crossing the intersection onto a residential boulevard, a high, swirling wind rattled through the the tall trees before me. Sweeping cool air into my lungs for the first time in weeks, it tossed my hair around as if to pull it by the roots. Excitedly I voiced my thoughts to the now fast, scudding grey clouds of the suddenly overcast sky. "I'll stay! I'll stay! I'll stay!" My cry released forever two months of emotionally pent-up declarations "that I cannot possibly endure this unbearably hot eastern climate. There are no intermittent cool temperatures to make it livable."

I was suddenly charged with fresh resolve, new energy. Now I knew that I could, in fact put up with it permanently. Almost on cue, autumn had arrived, grandly, irrevocably, reinforcing my faith in the desirability of the place and the four distinct seasonal changes, normally part of the bracing Canadian climate east of the Rocky Mountains. In spirit, that moment, I became a Quebecer, assured that Quebec and eastern Canada in general were heart's desire. Following in Ali Baba's wake had brought me home at last.

A Backward Glance

In those now long ago days of the mid-century, I was surrounded by others who had found new homes in Quebec. On any given day in Montreal one noticed new arrivals on the streets, at the markets, and in the parks. Among these clearly war-weary countenances, many were Jewish. In a glance one saw in their faces possibly five or more years of struggle in occupied Europe. Obviously, their need to relocate could not be compared to my own relatively insignificant quest to belong, important as it was to me.

Whereas I no longer found myself in the midst of the colourless, haunted faces of the elderly western Canadian survivors of the Great Depression, I was now shocked by the facial expressions of the battered looking Europeans, here and there among the French and English Canadians on the streets of Montreal. They would bear the scars of war long after leaving the scene. At certain times I felt confused. Were we in Quebec? In Montreal? Or in Paris, where I had seen so many of them?

Even among the non-Jewish victims I had met in Europe, many wished to move to Canada not for the adventure but as a final precaution against getting caught up again, ever, in further hostilities. War had flattened France twice in their grandparent's lifetime. They would not be caught again. Happily for the European immigrants arriving by the boat-load at Halifax and Montreal in 1945 and later, relatively few would find themselves arbitrarily confined to pioneer life or if so, not permanently as in the case of earlier arrivals.

Many of them moved into the crowded older apartments and rooms on the edge of Montreal's east-end, the traditional home of the immigrant Jewish population and the other great waves of oppressed humanity from Greece, Portugal, Italy and elsewhere, closer to the city centre. Although the next generation would spread out into the general population at will, these people had to face a new beginning, usually in poverty. Some had lost all family members and were without financial means, or language capability. Even in the safety of Canada, life in lonely, cramped rooms would present a challenge to the overcoming of the lingering nightmares of the war like those related to me over and over by the still tearful women in Europe. Amazingly, however, in the intervening generations many of them have built meaningful lives and families in this country.

How can we, the privileged people of the western world possibly imagine survival in the face of dehumanization? Accustomed as we are, in critical moments, to the expression of a certain degree of compassion from others, we cannot deal with its total absence. It is considered normal to civilized life. It is, after all, only through a well-developed sense of humanity in those around us that we are able to endure or recover from our personal tragedies.

The loss of a loved one is acknowledged to be the most painful experience of our lives. To be capable of enduring the emotional strain, the sufferer requires a sympathetic, compassionate response. It is the essence of the *Golden Rule*, reaching back to antiquity, to treat others as you would have them treat you. Civilization does not thrive without it.

Soon the monster bares its fangs ... *nature red in tooth and claw*, as the saying comes to mind again and millions die. As Karl Kraus, Viennese satirist, poet and Jew wrote on the rise of Hitler, *"the word went under when that world awoke"*. Not only was the press paralyzed but millions died without one word of normal empathy from a loved one. The loved ones were often already murdered.

Yet, now and again even in our own surroundings here in peaceful Canada, we may be at a loss to understand hostile behaviour suddenly thrust in our wake. In recent times, I faced the death of my husband, Eric. We found ourselves in a city hospital far from home and garden, an appalling ending for both of us. Now, at life's worst moment, while I murmured my last fond thoughts to my just departed life companion, the door suddenly burst open. In stamped a foreign physician in a white coat. Great black eyes ablaze, he glowered at my sister Janet and myself, bellowing "Get out!" "Get out!" He had come to confirm the death. No nursing staff were present to take charge of the situation, to allow us the customary few moments of privacy, of leave-taking. Seemingly in his country death was not necessarily considered as a time to show special respect to family members.

Faint with shock as if thrown by force, we found ourselves in the hallway, barely able to stand on our feet. In what seemed an instant, we faced an empty room, the bed stripped down to the mattress. Half an hour before as I was bending over Eric, the superb sunset at the window had seemed to sum up our days together. The sun once vanished, then only a heartless expanse of plate glass and a leaden sky remained. That morning Eric had welcomed all comers with a smile. He had never borne malice against anyone in his life.

Before being driven home to the country, we were to be picked up at the front door to spend the night with an acquaintance. Without a nurse in sight or present at the nursing desk to offer a word of comfort or a smile, we somehow propelled ourselves through the empty halls, down the elevator, and out the front door. Our escort had arrived and stood stiffly there at a loss for words. Beside her was an unkempt elderly Jewish woman of considerable girth, flailing her arms from side to side, wailing loudly, inconsolably, "Mama, Mama, take me home!" in a colourfully inflected Yiddish accent.

To us, it was as if we had become the most casual of taxi passengers shoved into a car rather than treated kindly as the newly bereaved. I was in desperate need of at least a momentary suggestion of compassion, a smile, a drink, a hug, some tangible expression of understanding; it seemed impossible to face life for another second.

With no means for us to escape from the cruel, unfriendly prison of the moving vehicle in swirling traffic, I wept desperately into Eric's flowers in my lap. Shaking and barely able to keep silent, I wanted to throw myself violently out of the car and onto the street corner at the first turn. In present circumstances, the old lady's high pitched wailing, the stench from her clothes, the traffic lights and the noise as we whirled around the Jewish quarter reduced me to a feeling of near hysteria. From the back seat beside the troubled senior, from time to time, I heard a small, carefully restrained moan from my sister as if from a small wounded creature. She had no idea why she had such a passenger beside her, given her own illness and our enormous grief.

As the autumn darkness gathered quickly and the traffic swelled, the endless search for someone to take the old lady to her own people meant continually facing into the oncoming headlights, each more menacing than the last. Emeshed in it all, the bedside images of the piercing dark eyes and the hostile face of the doctor stared at me through the darkness and the bright glaring lights. In the seemingly brutal onslaught of traffic, from time to time he appeared something like the image of a Nazi officer in pursuit.

Finally, our escort turned the old lady over to a group of people standing on a corner. Half an hour later we pulled into the driveway for the night. No mention was made then or later of the incident or of our loss. Obviously, we were expected to behave as if nothing had happened. I was soon to realize that only on suffering one's own bereavement is it possible to respond meaningfully to others in that situation. Next to our own demise, loss of loved ones is our deepest fear. Although a part of the human condition, it is a subject to be avoided. Silence ensues.

Yet I recall at the time speaking with a young married Dutch woman, whose family endured the Nazi atrocities in Holland. She had just lost her mother, a survivor and friend of mine. She said, "It is one thing to lose one's mother; it is bad enough; yet it is quite another to lose one's husband." As I left her I felt comforted. She was not a widow and had not experienced Nazism, and yet I sensed that she had thought about grief, that she showed understanding, possibly by the fact that she had lived among the Nazi victims.

Perhaps she would also have understood why I was horrified rather then normally elated to see shrubs beginning to form buds at our kitchen window as I looked out in March of the following year. It surely meant that there was no magic at play. Time had moved on, much as I could not bear it. Eric would not return no matter how long I waited. In fact, the fantasy stage of bereavement had expired.

I had, at last, to face it head on. I had to learn to enjoy the spring again rather than trying to deny the passage of time by telling myself that he would return before the new season arrived. This was not at all like the death of a mother in old age. One understands that nature takes her course and learns to accept it more easily, if sadly, than the death of one's contemporary, one's best friend and husband.

Presumably, these two women with whom I had been forced to endure extreme distress had felt the full brunt of totalitarianism on a large scale. It is bizarre that my own brief moment of utterly bewildering desolation should happen in their presence. The tables had been turned. In their place, I now suffered. Quite obviously then, given my own vulnerability to even this minimal exposure to indifference, to lack of compassion, one could say that the average person cannot withstand it any more than actual violence. We have been brought up on the wisdom of the ages, the *Golden Rule*, a life of shared compassion. That is what we understand. It shapes our lives, so that we even take it for granted.

From all the millions who perished along the way, only a very few could withstand the complete absence of compassion to be endured under totalitarianism. Old people, unable to face box-car transport to the concentration camps, either committed suicide by means of a cyanide pill or faced instant violence, imprisonment or death. The young were forced to leave their own families to this fate or to stay behind and also perish without the chance to save themselves or anyone else.

411

Surely then, the men of the *Resistance*, or the *Underground* and such organizations were possessed of very special qualities? Recording his thoughts to a compatriot, a hardy young Polish-Jewish man with previous military training put it down to the fact that despite complete exhaustion in the extremity of the crisis for survival, such self-discipline enables one momentarily to harness increased will-power, even calling forth new reserves of strength. As he explained, the expected moment of total collapse unleashes another throb of energy. One surges forward, determined as ever, never to give in. When asked why he responded in this way rather than in hopelessness to nearly certain imminent annihilation in a concentration camp, he said, "I had to stay alive long enough to see the death of Hitler."

To all those who so courageously endured World War II long enough to make it to our shores we surely owe the deepest respect. After all, sixty million of their peers did not survive. Some of these remarkable and rare personages, now in their eighties and nineties are with us yet. They are probably among the hardiest, most determined people the world has ever known. There have been individuals who clawed their way out of it all, one escaping from Hitler, the other from Stalin, searching for and finding their long since promised marriage partner, finally able to enjoy family life in Canada or elsewhere.

And now, seven decades later, time and time again, the obituary reports in the national newspapers carry either a full-page or a single column tribute to their now remarkably long and courageous lives. We are thankfully, joyously brought up to date with at least a small sampling of the survival stories of those courageous victims and the gratification they have had in family and careers. They deserve our cries of "Bravo!"

It is my fervent hope that all of the women whose stories I recorded in earlier chapters have somehow found rewarding lives and compassionate friends and family. Unfortunately most of us never meet these extraordinary, intrepid victors against savagery. Should Canada not assign a day each year to honour those residents among us?

In the summer of 1952, when I was in Europe, an international conference on *world-changing* by peaceful means was in session close to my friend Una's home at Glion, Switzerland. We got tickets for one session and walked over to it. At a glittering affair on that afternoon, the young African speakers chosen for the event held the floor. Magnificent orators, gorgeous in long colourful robes, fresh from such great halls of learning as Oxford and Cambridge, they spoke a vibrant English with such command, such eloquence as to evoke envy on my part. Could the young Mandela or a friend have been among them?

Decades have passed. We now see the true gift Africa has made to us in the name of decency, peace and democracy. Exemplified by Mandela's life, his great sacrifice, his death underlines an important guide to the future of the civilized world in the tradition of Gandhi and his ancient predecessors, spokesmen for non-violent policies in settling political disputes, down the ages.

The former Governor-General of Canada, Michaël Jean wrote of her attendance at Mandela's funeral saying that in addition, we might do well to also appreciate the work of Mr. de Klerk, president of South Africa at the time, for his support of Mandela, actually putting into effect the necessary legislation to end apartheid and to create a democratic South Africa. She points out that Canada needs a de Klerk to do the same for an aboriginal Mandela, waiting to join him and in making a final parliamentary transition to full equality for the First Nations people of Canada.

Extraordinary! All of us who have lived through the era of Hitler, Stalin and finally of Gandhi and Nelson Mandela will have cried out *Bravo*, again and again, over the years, on appreciating the life of this great African, this *Man for the Ages*, as he has been described.

Fortunately, world statistics now indicate that due to education, urbanization and prosperity, engagement in war has hit its lowest level in recorded history, with rates of absolute poverty having declined by half in the past twenty years. "Extraordinary times!" you say as you read these figures, globally localized, despite Middle East conflagrations.

Perhaps, therefore tragic events like those of the twentieth century will not be revisited upon their descendants. "Extraordinary possibilities." A lesson learned at last?

End

CPSIA information can be obtained at www.ICGtesting.com
Printed in the USA
LVOW12s1702280714

396371LV00002B/383/P